The 4-Hour Workweek

"It's about time this book was written. It is a long-overdue manifesto for the mobile lifestyle, and Tim Ferriss is the ideal ambassador. This will be huge." —**JACK CANFIELD**, cocreator of *Chicken Soup for the Soul*®, 100+ million copies sold

"Stunning and amazing. From mini-retirements to outsourcing your life, it's all here. Whether you're a wage slave or a Fortune 500 CEO, this book will change your life!" —**PHIL TOWN**, *New York Times* bestselling author of *Rule #1*

"*The 4-Hour Workweek* is a new way of solving a very old problem: just how can we work to live and prevent our lives from being all about work? A world of infinite options awaits those who would read this book and be inspired by it!" —**MICHAEL E. GERBER**, founder and chairman of E-Myth Worldwide and the world's #1 small business guru

"This is a whole new ball game. Highly recommended." —**DR. STEWART D. FRIEDMAN**, adviser to Jack Welch and former Vice President Al Gore on work/family issues and director of the Work/Life Integration Program at the Wharton School, University of Pennsylvania

"Timothy has packed more lives into his 29 years than Steve Jobs has in his 51." —**TOM FOREMSKI**, journalist and publisher of SiliconValleyWatcher.com

"If you want to live life on your own terms, this is your blueprint." —**MIKE MAPLES**, cofounder of Motive Communications (IPO to $260M market cap) and founding executive of Tivoli (sold to IBM for $750M)

"Thanks to Tim Ferriss, I have more time in my life to travel, spend time with family, and write book blurbs. This is a dazzling and highly useful work." —**A. J. JACOBS**, editor-at-large of *Esquire* magazine and author of *The Know-It-All*

"Tim is Indiana Jones for the digital age. I've already used his advice to go spearfishing on remote islands and ski the best hidden slopes of Argentina. Simply put, do what he says and you can live like a millionaire." —**ALBERT POPE**, derivatives specialist at UBS World Headquarters

"Reading this book is like putting a few zeros on your income. Tim brings lifestyle to a new level—listen to him!" —MICHAEL D. KERLIN, McKinsey & Company consultant to Bush-Clinton Katrina Fund and a J. William Fulbright Scholar

"Part scientist and part adventure hunter, Tim Ferriss has created a road map for an entirely new world. I devoured this book in one sitting—I have seen nothing like it." —CHARLES L. BROCK, chairman and CEO of Brock Capital Group; former CFO, COO, and general counsel of Scholastic, Inc.; and former president of the Harvard Law School Association

"Outsourcing is no longer just for Fortune 500 companies. Small and mid-sized firms, as well as busy professionals, can outsource their work to increase their productivity and free time for more important commitments. It's time for the world to take advantage of this revolution." —VIVEK KULKARNI, CEO of Brickwork India and former IT secretary of Bangalore; credited as the "techno-bureaucrat" who helped make Bangalore an IT destination in India

"Tim is the master! I should know. I followed his rags to riches path and watched him transform himself from competitive fighter to entrepreneur. He tears apart conventional assumptions until he finds a better way." —DAN PARTLAND, Emmy Award—winning producer of *American High* and *Welcome to the Dollhouse*

"*The 4-Hour Workweek* is an absolute necessity for those adventurous souls who want to live life to its fullest. Buy it and read it before you sacrifice any more!" —JOHN LUSK, group product manager at Microsoft World Headquarters

"If you want to live your dreams now, and not in 20 or 30 years, buy this book!" —LAURA RODEN, chairman of the Silicon Valley Association of Startup Entrepreneurs and a lecturer in Corporate Finance at San Jose State University

"With this kind of time management and focus on the important things in life, people should be able to get 15 times as much done in a normal workweek." —TIM DRAPER, founder of Draper Fisher Jurvetson, financiers to innovators including Hotmail, Skype, and Overture.com

"Tim has done what most people only dream of doing. I can't believe he is going to let his secrets out of the bag. This book is a must read!" —STEPHEN KEY, top inventor and team designer of Teddy Ruxpin and Lazer Tag and a consultant to the television show *American Inventor*

The 4-Hour Workweek

The 4-Hour Workweek

►ESCAPE 9–5, LIVE ANYWHERE,
AND JOIN THE NEW RICH

Expanded and Updated

TIMOTHY FERRISS

Vermilion
LONDON

20 19

First published in the United States by Crown Publishers in 2007

Published in 2008 by Vermilion imprint of Ebury Publishing
A Random House Group company

This edition published in 2011

The Random House Group Limited Reg. No. 954009

Addresses for companies within the Random House Group can be found at
www.randomhouse.co.uk

A CIP catalogue record for this book is available from the British Library

ISBN 9780091929114

Copies are available at special rates for bulk orders. Contact the sales development team on
020 7840 8487 for more information.

To buy books by your favourite authors and register for offers, visit
www.randomhouse.co.uk

The Random House Group Limited supports The Forest Stewardship
Council® (FSC®), the leading international forest-certification organisation.
Our books carrying the FSC label are printed on FSC®-certified paper.
FSC is the only forest-certification scheme supported by the leading
environmental organisations, including Greenpeace. Our
paper procurement policy can be found at
www.randomhouse.co.uk/environment

Printed and bound in Great Britain by Clays Ltd, St Ives plc

For my parents,

DONALD AND FRANCES FERRISS,

who taught a little hellion that marching to a different drummer

was a good thing. I love you both and owe you everything.

SUPPORT YOUR LOCAL TEACHER—

10% of all author royalties are donated to educational

not-for-profits, including Donorschoose.org.

►CONTENTS

Step IV: L is for Liberation

Last but Not Least

THE BEST OF THE BLOG

The *4-Hour Workweek* was turned down by 26 out of 27 publishers.

After it was sold, the president of one potential marketing partner, a large bookseller, e-mailed me historical bestseller statistics to make it clear—this wouldn't be a mainstream success.

So I did all I knew how to do. I wrote it with two of my closest friends in mind, speaking directly to them and their problems—problems I long had—and I focused on the unusual options that had worked for me around the world.

I certainly tried to set conditions for making a sleeper hit possible, but I knew it wasn't likely. I hoped for the best and planned for the worst.

May 2, 2007, I receive a call on my cell phone from my editor.

"Tim, you hit the list."

It was just past 5 P.M. in New York City, and I was exhausted. The book had launched five days before, and I had just finished a series of more than twenty radio interviews in succession, beginning at 6 A.M. that morning. I never planned a book tour, preferring instead to "batch" radio satellite tours into 48 hours.

"Heather, I love you, but please don't $#%* with me."

"No, you really hit the list. Congratulations, Mr. *New York Times* bestselling author!"

I leaned against the wall and slid down until I was sitting on the floor. I closed my eyes, smiled, and took a deep breath. Things were about to change.

Everything was about to change.

Lifestyle Design from Dubai to Berlin

T*he 4-Hour Workweek* has now been sold into 35 languages. It's been on the bestseller lists for more than two years, and every month brings a new story and a new discovery.

From the *Economist* to the cover of the *New York Times Style* section, from the streets of Dubai to the cafes of Berlin, lifestyle design has cut across cultures to become a worldwide movement. The original ideas of the book have been broken apart, improved, and tested in environments and ways I never could have imagined.

So why the new edition if things are working so well? Because I knew it could be better, and there was a missing ingredient: you.

This expanded and updated edition contains more than 100 pages of new content, including the latest cutting-edge technologies, field-tested resources, and—most important—real-world success stories chosen from more than 400 pages of case studies submitted by readers.

Families and students? CEOs and professional vagabonds? Take your pick. There should be someone whose results you can duplicate. Need a template to negotiate remote work, a paid year in Argentina, perhaps? This time, it's in here.

The Experiments in Lifestyle Design blog (www.fourhourblog .com) was launched alongside the book, and within six months, it became one of the top 1,000 blogs in the world, out of more than 120 million. Thousands of readers have shared their own amazing tools and tricks, producing phenomenal and unexpected results. The blog became the laboratory I'd always wanted, and I encourage you to join us there.

The new "Best of the Blog" section includes several of the most popular posts from the Experiments in Lifestyle Design blog. On the blog itself, you can also find recommendations from everyone from Warren Buffett (seriously, I tracked him down and show you how I did it) to chess prodigy Josh Waitzkin. It's an experimental playground for those who want better results in less time.

Not "Revised"

This is not a "revised" edition in the sense that the original no longer works. The typos and small mistakes have been fixed over more than 40 printings in the U.S. This is the first major overhaul, but not for the reason you'd expect.

Things have changed dramatically since April 2007. Banks are failing, retirement and pension funds are evaporating, and jobs are being lost at record rates. Readers and skeptics alike have asked: Can the principles and techniques in the book really still work in an economic recession or depression?

Yes and yes.

In fact, questions I posed during pre-crash lectures, including "How would your priorities and decisions change if you could never retire?" are no longer hypothetical. Millions of people have seen their savings portfolios fall 40% or more in value and are now looking for options C and D. Can they redistribute retirement throughout life to make it more affordable? Can they relocate a few months per year to a place like Costa Rica or Thailand to multiply the lifestyle output of their decreased savings? Sell their services to companies in the UK to earn in a stronger currency? The answer to all of them is, more than ever, yes.

The concept of lifestyle design as a replacement for multi-staged career planning is sound. It's more flexible and allows you to test different lifestyles without committing to a 10- or 20-year retirement plan that can fail due to market fluctuations outside of your control. People are open to exploring alternatives (and more forgiving of others who do the same), as many of the other options—the once "safe" options—have failed.

When everything and everyone is failing, what is the cost of a little experimentation outside of the norm? Most often, nothing. Flash forward to 2011; is a job interviewer asking about that unusual gap year?

"Everyone was getting laid off and I had a once-in-a-lifetime chance to travel around the world. It was incredible."

If anything, they'll ask you how to do the same. The scripts in this book still work.

Facebook and LinkedIn launched in the post-2000 dot-com "depression." Other recession-born babies include Monopoly, Apple, Clif Bar, Scrabble, KFC, Domino's Pizza, FedEx, and Microsoft. This is no coincidence, as economic downturns produce discounted infrastructure, outstanding freelancers at bargain prices, and rock-bottom advertising deals—all impossible when everyone is optimistic.

Whether a yearlong sabbatical, a new business idea, reengineering your life within the corporate beast, or dreams you've postponed for "some day," there has never been a better time for testing the uncommon.

What's the worst that could happen?

I encourage you to remember this often-neglected question as you begin to see the infinite possibilities outside of your current comfort zone. This period of collective panic is your big chance to dabble.

It's been an honor to share the last two years with incredible readers around the world, and I hope you enjoy this new edition as much as I enjoyed putting it together.

I am, and will continue to be, a humble student of you all.

Un abrazo fuerte,

TIM FERRISS

San Franciso, California
April 21, 2009

First and Foremost

Is lifestyle design for you? Chances are good that it is. Here are some of the most common doubts and fears that people have before taking the leap and joining the New Rich:

Do I have to quit or hate my job? Do I have to be a risk-taker?

No on all three counts. From using Jedi mind tricks to disappear from the office to designing businesses that finance your lifestyle, there are paths for every comfort level. How does a Fortune 500 employee explore the hidden jewels of China for a month and use technology to cover his tracks? How do you create a hands-off business that generates $80K per month with no management? It's all here.

Do I have to be a single twenty-something?

Not at all. This book is for anyone who is sick of the deferred-life plan and wants to live life large instead of postpone it. Case studies range from a Lamborghini-driving 21-year-old to a single mother who traveled the world for five months with her two children. If you're sick of the standard menu of options and prepared to enter a world of infinite options, this book is for you.

Do I have to travel? I just want more time.

No. It's just one option. The objective is to create freedom of time and place and use both however *you* want.

Do I need to be born rich?

No. My parents have never made more than $50,000 per year combined, and I've worked since age 14. I'm no Rockefeller and you needn't be either.

Do I need to be an Ivy League graduate?

Nope. Most of the role models in this book didn't go to the Harvards of the world, and some are dropouts. Top academic institutions are wonderful, but there are unrecognized benefits to not coming out of one. Grads from top schools are funneled into high-income 80-hour-per-week jobs, and 15–30 years of soul-crushing work has been accepted as the default path. How do I know? I've been there and seen the destruction. This book reverses it.

> Whenever you find yourself on the side of the majority, it is time to pause and reflect.   —MARK TWAIN

> Anyone who lives within their means suffers from a lack of imagination.
> —OSCAR WILDE, Irish dramatist and novelist

My hands were sweating again.

Staring down at the floor to avoid the blinding ceiling lights, I was supposedly one of the best in the world, but it just didn't register. My partner Alicia shifted from foot to foot as we stood in line with nine other couples, all chosen from over 1,000 competitors from 29 countries and four continents. It was the last day of the Tango World Championship semifinals, and this was our final run in front of the judges, television cameras, and cheering crowds. The other couples had an average of 15 years together. For us, it was the culmination of 5 months of nonstop 6-hour practices, and finally, it was showtime.

"How are you doing?" Alicia, a seasoned professional dancer, asked me in her distinctly Argentine Spanish.

"Fantastic. Awesome. Let's just enjoy the music. Forget the crowd—they're not even here."

That wasn't entirely true. It was hard to even fathom 50,000 spectators and coordinators in La Rural, even if it was the biggest exhibition hall in Buenos Aires. Through the thick haze of cigarette smoke, you could barely make out the huge undulating mass in the stands, and everywhere there was exposed floor, except the sacred

30' × 40' space in the middle of it all. I adjusted my pin-striped suit and fussed with my blue silk handkerchief until it was obvious that I was just fidgeting.

"Are you nervous?"

"I'm not nervous. I'm excited. I'm just going to have fun and let the rest follow."

"Number 152, you're up." Our chaperone had done his job, and now it was our turn. I whispered an inside joke to Alicia as we stepped on the hardwood platform: *"Tranquilo"*—Take it easy. She laughed, and at just that moment, I thought to myself, "What on earth would I be doing right now, if I hadn't left my job and the U.S. over a year ago?"

The thought vanished as quickly as it had appeared when the announcer came over the loudspeaker and the crowd erupted to match him: "Pareja numero 152, Timothy Ferriss y Alicia Monti, Ciudad de Buenos Aires!!!"

We were on, and I was beaming.

THE MOST FUNDAMENTAL of American questions is hard for me to answer these days, and luckily so. If it weren't, you wouldn't be holding this book in your hands.

"So, what do you do?"

Assuming you can find me (hard to do), and depending on when you ask me (I'd prefer you didn't), I could be racing motorcycles in Europe, scuba diving off a private island in Panama, resting under a palm tree between kickboxing sessions in Thailand, or dancing tango in Buenos Aires. The beauty is, I'm not a multimillionaire, nor do I particularly care to be.

I never enjoyed answering this cocktail question because it reflects an epidemic I was long part of: job descriptions as self-descriptions. If someone asks me now and is anything but absolutely sincere, I explain my lifestyle of mysterious means simply.

"I'm a drug dealer."

Pretty much a conversation ender. It's only half true, besides. The whole truth would take too long. How can I possibly explain that what I do with my time and what I do for money are completely different things? That I work less than four hours per week and make more per month than I used to make in a year?

For the first time, I'm going to tell you the real story. It involves a quiet subculture of people called the "New Rich."

What does an igloo-dwelling millionaire do that a cubicle-dweller doesn't? Follow an uncommon set of rules.

How does a lifelong blue-chip employee escape to travel the world for a month without his boss even noticing? He uses technology to hide the fact.

Gold is getting old. The New Rich (**NR**) are those who abandon the deferred-life plan and create luxury lifestyles in the present using the currency of the New Rich: time and mobility. This is an art and a science we will refer to as Lifestyle Design (**LD**).

I've spent the last three years traveling among those who live in worlds currently beyond your imagination. Rather than hating reality, I'll show you how to bend it to your will. It's easier than it sounds. My journey from grossly overworked and severely underpaid office worker to member of the **NR** is at once stranger than fiction and— now that I've deciphered the code—simple to duplicate. There is a recipe.

Life doesn't have to be so damn hard. It really doesn't. Most people, my past self included, have spent too much time convincing themselves that life has to be hard, a resignation to 9-to-5 drudgery in exchange for (sometimes) relaxing weekends and the occasional keep-it-short-or-get-fired vacation.

The truth, at least the truth I live and will share in this book, is quite different. From leveraging currency differences to outsourcing your life and disappearing, I'll show you how a small underground uses economic sleight-of-hand to do what most consider impossible.

If you've picked up this book, chances are that you don't want to sit behind a desk until you are 62. Whether your dream is escaping the rat race, real-life fantasy travel, long-term wandering, setting world records, or simply a dramatic career change, this book will give you all the tools you need to make it a reality in the here-and-now instead of in the often elusive "retirement." There is a way to get the rewards for a life of hard work without waiting until the end.

How? It begins with a simple distinction most people miss—one I missed for 25 years.

People don't want to *be* millionaires—they want to experience what they believe only millions can buy. Ski chalets, butlers, and exotic travel often enter the picture. Perhaps rubbing cocoa butter on your belly in a hammock while you listen to waves rhythmically lapping against the deck of your thatched-roof bungalow? Sounds nice.

$1,000,000 in the bank isn't the fantasy. The fantasy is the lifestyle of complete freedom it supposedly allows. The question is then, *How can one achieve the millionaire lifestyle of complete freedom without first having $1,000,000?*

In the last five years, I have answered this question for myself, and this book will answer it for you. I will show you exactly how I have separated income from time and created my ideal lifestyle in the process, traveling the world and enjoying the best this planet has to offer. How on earth did I go from 14-hour days and $40,000 per year to 4-hour weeks and $40,000-plus per month?

It helps to know where it all started. Strangely enough, it was in a class of soon-to-be investment bankers.

In 2002, I was asked by Ed Zschau, übermentor and my former professor of High-tech Entrepreneurship at Princeton University, to come back and speak to the same class about my business adventures in the real world. I was stuck. There were already decamillionaires speaking to the same class, and even though I had built a highly profitable sports supplement company, I marched to a distinctly different drummer.

Over the ensuing days, however, I realized that everyone seemed to be discussing how to build large and successful companies, sell out, and live the good life. Fair enough. The question no one really seemed to be asking or answering was, Why do it all in the first place? What is the pot of gold that justifies spending the best years of your life hoping for happiness in the last?

The lectures I ultimately developed, titled "Drug Dealing for Fun and Profit," began with a simple premise: Test the most basic assumptions of the work-life equation.

- ►How do your decisions change if retirement isn't an option?
- ►What if you could use a mini-retirement to sample your deferred-life plan reward before working 40 years for it?
- ►Is it really necessary to work like a slave to live like a millionaire?

Little did I know where questions like these would take me.

The uncommon conclusion? The commonsense rules of the "real world" are a fragile collection of socially reinforced illusions. This book will teach you how to see and seize the options others do not.

What makes this book different?

First, I'm not going to spend much time on the problem. I'm going to assume you are suffering from time famine, creeping dread, or—worst case—a tolerable and comfortable existence doing something unfulfilling. The last is most common and most insidious.

Second, this book is not about saving and will not recommend you abandon your daily glass of red wine for a million dollars 50 years from now. I'd rather have the wine. I won't ask you to choose between enjoyment today or money later. I believe you can have both now. The goal is fun *and* profit.

Third, this book is not about finding your "dream job." I will take as a given that, for most people, somewhere between six and seven billion of them, the perfect job is the one that takes the least time. The vast majority of people will never find a job that can be an unending source of fulfillment, so that is not the goal here; to free time and automate income is.

I OPEN EACH class with an explanation of the singular importance of being a "dealmaker." The manifesto of the dealmaker is simple: Reality is negotiable. Outside of science and law, all rules can be bent or broken, and it doesn't require being unethical.

The **DEAL** of deal making is also an acronym for the process of becoming a member of the New Rich.

The steps and strategies can be used with incredible results— whether you are an employee or an entrepreneur. Can you do everything I've done with a boss? No. Can you use the same principles to double your income, cut your hours in half, or at least double the usual vacation time? Most definitely.

Here is the step-by-step process you'll use to reinvent yourself:

D **for Definition** turns misguided common sense upside down and introduces the rules and objectives of the new game. It replaces self-defeating assumptions and explains concepts such as relative wealth and eustress.[1] Who are the **NR** and how do they operate? This section explains the overall lifestyle design recipe—the fundamentals—before we add the three ingredients.

E **for Elimination** kills the obsolete notion of time management once and for all. It shows exactly how I used the words of an often-forgotten Italian economist to turn 12-hour days into two-hour days . . . in 48 hours. Increase your per-hour results ten times or more with counterintuitive **NR** techniques for cultivating selective ignorance, developing a low-information diet, and otherwise ignoring the unimportant. This section provides the first of the three luxury lifestyle design ingredients: time.

---

1. Uncommon terms are defined throughout this book as concepts are introduced. If something is unclear or you need a quick reference, please visit www.fourhourblog.com for an extensive glossary and other resources.

A for Automation puts cash flow on autopilot using geographic arbitrage, outsourcing, and rules of nondecision. From bracketing to the routines of ultrasuccessful **NR**, it's all here. This section provides the second ingredient of luxury lifestyle design: income.

L for Liberation is the mobile manifesto for the globally inclined. The concept of mini-retirements is introduced, as are the means for flawless remote control and escaping the boss. Liberation is not about cheap travel; it is about forever breaking the bonds that confine you to a single location. This section delivers the third and final ingredient for luxury lifestyle design: mobility.

I should note that most bosses are less than pleased if you spend one hour in the office each day, and employees should therefore read the steps in the entrepreneurially minded **DEAL** order but implement them as **DELA**. If you decide to remain in your current job, it is necessary to create freedom of location before you cut your work hours by 80%. Even if you have never considered becoming an entrepreneur in the modern sense, the **DEAL** process will turn you into an entrepreneur in the purer sense as first coined by French economist J. B. Say in 1800—one who shifts economic resources out of an area of lower and into an area of higher yield.

Last but not least, much of what I recommend will seem impossible and even offensive to basic common sense—I expect that. Resolve now to test the concepts as an exercise in lateral thinking. If you try it, you'll see just how deep the rabbit hole goes, and you won't ever go back.

Take a deep breath and let me show you my world. And remember—*tranquilo.* It's time to have fun and let the rest follow.

Tim Ferriss

Tokyo, Japan
September 29, 2006

An expert is a person who has made all the mistakes that can be made in a very narrow field.
—NIELS BOHR, Danish physicist and Nobel Prize winner

Ordinarily he was insane, but he had lucid moments when he was merely stupid.
—HEINRICH HEINE, German critic and poet

This book will teach you the precise principles I have used to become the following:

- ►Princeton University guest lecturer in high-tech entrepreneurship
- ►First American in history to hold a Guinness World Record in tango
- ►Advisor to more than 30 world-record holders in professional and Olympic sports
- ►*Wired* magazine's "Greatest Self-Promoter of 2008"
- ►National Chinese kickboxing champion
- ►Horseback archer *(yabusame)* in Nikko, Japan
- ►Political asylum researcher and activist
- ►MTV breakdancer in Taiwan
- ►Hurling competitor in Ireland
- ►Actor on hit TV series in mainland China and Hong Kong *(Human Cargo)*

How I got to this point is a tad less glamorous:

1977 Born 6 weeks premature and given a 10% chance of living. I survive instead and grow so fat that I can't roll onto my stomach. A muscular imbalance of the eyes makes me look in opposite directions, and my mother refers to me affectionately as "tuna fish." So far so good.

1983   Nearly fail kindergarten because I refuse to learn the alphabet. My teacher refuses to explain why I should learn it, opting instead for "I'm the teacher—that's why." I tell her that's stupid and ask her to leave me alone so I can focus on drawing sharks. She sends me to the "bad table" instead and makes me eat a bar of soap. Disdain for authority begins.

1991   My first job. Ah, the memories. I'm hired for minimum wage as the cleaner at an ice cream parlor and quickly realize that the big boss's methods duplicate effort. I do it my way, finish in one hour instead of eight, and spend the rest of the time reading kung-fu magazines and practicing karate kicks outside. I am fired in a record three days, left with the parting comment, "Maybe someday you'll understand the value of hard work." It seems I still don't.

1993   I volunteer for a one-year exchange program in Japan, where people work themselves to death—a phenomenon called *karooshi*—and are said to want to be Shinto when born, Christian when married, and Buddhist when they die. I conclude that most people are really confused about life. One evening, intending to ask my host mother to wake me the next morning *(okosu),* I ask her to violently rape me *(okasu).* She is very confused.

1996   I manage to slip undetected into Princeton, despite SAT scores 40% lower than the average and my high school admissions counselor telling me to be more "realistic." I conclude I'm just not good at reality. I major in neuroscience and then switch to East Asian studies to avoid putting printer jacks on cat heads.

1997   Millionaire time! I create an audiobook called *How I Beat the Ivy League,* use all my money from three summer jobs to manufacture 500 tapes, and proceed to sell exactly none. I will allow my mother to throw them out only in 2006, just nine years of denial later. Such is the joy of baseless overconfidence.

1998   After four shot-putters kick a friend's head in, I quit bouncing, the highest-paying job on campus, and develop a speed-reading seminar. I plaster campus with hundreds of god-awful neon green flyers that read, "TRIPLE YOUR READING SPEED IN 3 HOURS!" and prototypical Princeton students proceed to write "bullsh*t" on every single one. I sell 32 spots at $50 each for the 3-hour event, and $533 per hour convinces me that finding a market before designing a product is smarter than the reverse. Two months later, I'm bored to tears of speed-reading and close up shop. I hate services and need a product to ship.

Fall 1998   A huge thesis dispute and the acute fear of becoming an investment banker drive me to commit academic suicide and inform the registrar that I am quitting school until further notice. My dad is convinced that I'll never go back, and I'm convinced that my life is over. My mom thinks it's no big deal and that there is no need to be a drama queen.

Spring 1999   In three months, I accept and quit jobs as a curriculum designer at Berlitz, the world's largest publisher of foreign-language materials, and as an analyst at a three-person political asylum research firm. Naturally, I then fly to Taiwan to create a gym chain out of thin air and get shut down by Triads, Chinese mafia. I return to the U.S. defeated and decide to learn kickboxing, winning the national championship four weeks later with the ugliest and most unorthodox style ever witnessed.

Fall 2000   Confidence restored and thesis completely undone, I return to Princeton. My life does not end, and it seems the year-long delay has worked out in my favor. Twenty-somethings now have David Koresh–like abilities. My friend sells a company for $450 million, and I decide to head west to sunny California to make my billions. Despite the hottest job market in the history of the world, I manage to go jobless until three months after graduation, when I pull out my trump card and send one start-up CEO 32 consecutive e-mails. He finally gives in and puts me in sales.

Spring 2001   TrueSAN Networks has gone from a 15-person nobody to the "number one privately held data storage company" (how is that measured?) with 150 employees (what are they all doing?). I am ordered by a newly appointed sales director to "start with A" in the phone book and dial for dollars. I ask him in the most tactful way possible why we are doing it like retards. He says, "Because I say so." Not a good start.

Fall 2001   After a year of 12-hour days, I find out that I'm the second-lowest-paid person in the company aside from the receptionist. I resort to aggressively surfing the web full-time. One afternoon, having run out of obscene video clips to forward, I investigate how hard it would be to start a sports nutrition company. Turns out that you can outsource everything from manufacturing to ad design. Two weeks and $5,000 of credit card debt later, I have my first batch in production and a live website. Good thing, too, as I'm fired exactly one week later.

2002–2003   BrainQUICKEN LLC has taken off, and I'm now making more than $40K per month instead of $40K per year. The only problem is that I hate life and now work 12-hour-plus days 7 days a week. Kinda painted myself into a corner. I take a one-week "vacation" to Florence, Italy, with my family and spend 10 hours a day in an Internet café freaking out. Sh*t balls. I begin teaching Princeton students how to build "successful" (i.e., profitable) companies.

Winter 2004   The impossible happens and I'm approached by an infomercial production company and an Israeli conglomerate (huh?) interested in buying my baby BrainQUICKEN. I simplify, eliminate, and otherwise clean house to make myself expendable. Miraculously, BQ doesn't fall apart, but both deals do. Back to Groundhog Day. Soon thereafter, both companies attempt to replicate my product and lose millions of dollars.

June 2004   I decide that, even if my company implodes, I need to escape before I go Howard Hughes. I turn everything upside down and—backpack in hand—go to JFK Airport in New York City, buying the first one-way ticket to Europe I can find. I land in London and intend to continue on to Spain for four weeks of recharging my batteries before returning to the salt mines. I start my relaxation by promptly having a nervous breakdown the first morning.

July 2004–2005 Four weeks turn into eight, and I decide to stay overseas indefinitely for a final exam in automation and experimental living, limiting e-mail to one hour each Monday morning. As soon as I remove myself as a bottleneck, profits increase 40%. What on earth do you do when you no longer have work as an excuse to be hyperactive and avoid the big questions? Be terrified and hold on to your ass with both hands, apparently.

September 2006 I return to the U.S. in an odd, Zen-like state after methodically destroying all of my assumptions about what can and cannot be done. "Drug Dealing for Fun and Profit" has evolved into a class on ideal lifestyle design. The new message is simple: I've seen the promised land, and there is good news. You can have it all.

Step I:
D is for Definition

Reality is merely an illusion,
albeit a very persistent one.

—ALBERT EINSTEIN

1

Cautions and Comparisons

►HOW TO BURN $1,000,000 A NIGHT

These individuals have riches just as we say that we "have a fever," when really the fever has us.

—SENECA (4 B.C.–A.D. 65)

I also have in mind that seemingly wealthy, but most terribly impoverished class of all, who have accumulated dross, but know not how to use it, or get rid of it, and thus have forged their own golden or silver fetters.

—HENRY DAVID THOREAU (1817–1862)

1:00 A.M. CST | 30,000 FEET OVER LAS VEGAS

His friends, drunk to the point of speaking in tongues, were asleep. It was just the two of us now in first-class. He extended his hand to introduce himself, and an enormous—Looney Tunes enormous—diamond ring appeared from the ether as his fingers crossed under my reading light.

Mark was a legitimate magnate. He had, at different times, run practically all the gas stations, convenience stores, and gambling in South Carolina. He confessed with a half smile that, in an average trip to Sin City, he and his fellow weekend warriors might lose an average of $500,000 to $1,000,000—each. Nice.

He sat up in his seat as the conversation drifted to my travels, but I was more interested in his astounding record of printing money.

"So, of all your businesses, which did you like the most?"

The answer took less than a second of thought.

"None of them."

He explained that he had spent more than 30 years with people he didn't like to buy things he didn't need. Life had become a succession of trophy wives—he was on lucky number three—expensive cars, and other empty bragging rights. Mark was one of the living dead.

This is exactly where we don't want to end up.

Apples and Oranges: A Comparison

So, what makes the difference? What separates the New Rich, characterized by options, from the Deferrers (D), those who save it all for the end only to find that life has passed them by?

It begins at the beginning. The New Rich can be separated from the crowd based on their goals, which reflect very distinct priorities and life philosophies.

Note how subtle differences in wording completely change the necessary actions for fulfilling what at a glance appear to be similar goals. These are not limited to business owners. Even the first, as I will show later, applies to employees.

> **D:** To work for yourself.
> **NR:** To have others work for you.

> **D:** To work when you want to.
> **NR:** To prevent work for work's sake, and to do the minimum necessary for maximum effect ("minimum effective load").

> **D:** To retire early or young.
> **NR:** To distribute recovery periods and adventures (mini-retirements) throughout life on a regular basis and recognize that inactivity is not the goal. Doing that which excites you is.

D: To buy all the things you want to have.

NR: To do all the things you want to do, and be all the things you want to be. If this includes some tools and gadgets, so be it, but they are either means to an end or bonuses, not the focus.

D: To be the boss instead of the employee; to be in charge.

NR: To be neither the boss nor the employee, but the owner. To own the trains and have someone else ensure they run on time.

D: To make a ton of money.

NR: To make a ton of money with specific reasons and defined dreams to chase, timelines and steps included. What are you working for?

D: To have more.

NR: To have more quality and less clutter. To have huge financial reserves but recognize that most material wants are justifications for spending time on the things that don't really matter, including buying things and preparing to buy things. You spent two weeks negotiating your new Infiniti with the dealership and got $10,000 off? That's great. Does your life have a purpose? Are you contributing anything useful to this world, or just shuffling papers, banging on a keyboard, and coming home to a drunken existence on the weekends?

D: To reach the big pay-off, whether IPO, acquisition, retirement, or other pot of gold.

NR: To think big but ensure payday comes every day: cash flow first, big payday second.

D: To have freedom from doing that which you dislike.

NR: To have freedom from doing that which you dislike, but also the freedom and resolve to pursue your dreams without reverting to work for work's sake (W4W). After years of repetitive work, you will often need to dig hard to find your passions, redefine your dreams, and revive hobbies that you let atrophy to near extinction. The goal is not to simply eliminate the bad, which does nothing more than leave you with a vacuum, but to pursue and experience the best in the world.

Getting Off the Wrong Train

> The first principle is that you must not fool yourself, and you are the easiest person to fool.
> —RICHARD P. FEYNMAN, Nobel Prize–winning physicist

Enough is enough. Lemmings no more. The blind quest for cash is a fool's errand.

I've chartered private planes over the Andes, enjoyed many of the best wines in the world in between world-class ski runs, and lived like a king, lounging by the infinity pool of a private villa. Here's the little secret I rarely tell: It all cost less than rent in the U.S. If you can free your time and location, your money is automatically worth 3–10 times as much.

This has nothing to do with currency rates. Being financially rich and having the ability to live like a millionaire are fundamentally two very different things.

Money is multiplied in practical value depending on the number of W's you control in your life: **what** you do, **when** you do it, **where** you do it, and with **whom** you do it. I call this the "freedom multiplier."

Using this as our criterion, the 80-hour-per-week, $500,000-per-year investment banker is less "powerful" than the employed **NR** who works ¼ the hours for $40,000, but has complete freedom of when, where, and how to live. The former's $500,000 may be worth less than $40,000 and the latter's $40,000 worth more than

$500,000 when we run the numbers and look at the lifestyle output of their money.

Options—the ability to choose—is real power. This book is all about how to see and create those options with the least effort and cost. It just so happens, paradoxically, that you can make more money—a lot more money—by doing half of what you are doing now.

So, Who Are the NR?

► The employee who rearranges his schedule and negotiates a remote work agreement to achieve 90% of the results in one-tenth of the time, which frees him to practice cross-country skiing and take road trips with his family two weeks per month.

► The business owner who eliminates the least profitable customers and projects, outsources all operations entirely, and travels the world collecting rare documents, all while working remotely on a website to showcase her own illustration work.

► The student who elects to risk it all—which is nothing—to establish an online video rental service that delivers $5,000 per month in income from a small niche of Blu-ray aficionados, a two-hour-per-week side project that allows him to work full-time as an animal rights lobbyist.

The options are limitless, but each path begins with the same first step: replacing assumptions.

To join the movement, you will need to learn a new lexicon and recalibrate direction using a compass for an unusual world. From inverting responsibility to jettisoning the entire concept of "success," we need to change the rules.

New Players for a New Game: Global and Unrestricted

TURIN, ITALY

Civilization had too many rules for me, so I did my best to rewrite them.   —BILL COSBY

As he rotated 360 degrees through the air, the deafening noise turned to silence. Dale Begg-Smith executed the backflip perfectly—skis crossed in an X over his head—and landed in the record books as he slid across the finish.

It was February 16, 2006, and he was now a mogul-skiing gold medalist at the Turin Winter Olympics. Unlike other full-time athletes, he will never have to return to a dead-end job after his moment of glory, nor will he look back at this day as the climax of his only passion. After all, he was only 21 years old and drove a black Lamborghini.

Born a Canadian and something of a late bloomer, Dale found his calling, an Internet-based IT company, at the age of 13. Fortunately, he had a more-experienced mentor and partner to guide him: his 15-year-old brother, Jason. Created to fund their dreams of standing atop the Olympic podium, it would, only two years later, become the third-largest company of its kind in the world.

While Dale's teammates were hitting the slopes for extra sessions, he was often buying sake for clients in Tokyo. In a world of "work harder, not smarter," it came to pass that his coaches felt he was spending too much time on his business and not enough time in training, despite his results.

Rather than choose between his business or his dream, Dale chose to move laterally with both, from either/or to both/and. He wasn't spending too much time on his business; he and his brother were spending too much time with Canucks.

In 2002, they moved to the ski capital of the world, Australia, where the team was smaller, more flexible, and coached by a legend. Three short years later, he received citizenship, went head-to-head against former teammates, and became the third "Aussie" in history to win winter gold.

In the land of wallabies and big surf, Dale has since gone postal. Literally. Right next to the Elvis Presley commemorative edition, you can buy stamps with his face on them.

Fame has its perks, as does looking outside the choices presented to you. There are always lateral options.

NEW CALEDONIA, SOUTH PACIFIC OCEAN

Once you say you're going to settle for second, that's what
happens to you in life.   —JOHN F. KENNEDY

Some people remain convinced that just a bit more money will make things right. Their goals are arbitrary moving targets: $300,000 in the bank, $1,000,000 in the portfolio, $100,000 a year instead of $50,000, etc. Julie's goal made intrinsic sense: come back with the same number of children she had left with.

She reclined in her seat and glanced across the aisle past her sleeping husband, Marc, counting as she had done thousands of times—one, two, three. So far so good. In 12 hours, they would all be back in Paris, safe and sound. That was assuming the plane from New Caledonia held together, of course.

New Caledonia?

Nestled in the tropics of the Coral Sea, New Caledonia was a French territory and where Julie and Marc had just sold the sailboat that took them 15,000 miles around the world. Of course, recouping their initial investment had been part of the plan. All said and done, their 15-month exploration of the globe, from the gondola-rich waterways of Venice to the tribal shores of Polynesia, had cost between $18,000 and $19,000. Less than rent and baguettes in Paris.

Most people would consider this impossible. Then again, most people don't know that more than 300 families set sail from France each year to do the same.

The trip had been a dream for almost two decades, relegated to the back of the line behind an ever-growing list of responsibilities. Each passing moment brought a new list of reasons for putting it off.

One day, Julie realized that if she didn't do it now, she would never do it. The rationalizations, legitimate or not, would just continue to add up and make it harder to convince herself that escape was possible.

One year of preparation and one 30-day trial run with her husband later, they set sail on the trip of a lifetime. Julie realized almost as soon as the anchor lifted that, far from being a reason not to travel and seek adventure, children are perhaps the best reason of all to do both.

Pre-trip, her three little boys had fought like banshees at the drop of a hat. In the process of learning to coexist in a floating bedroom, they learned patience, as much for themselves as for the sanity of their parents. Pre-trip, books were about as appealing as eating sand. Given the alternative of staring at a wall on the open sea, all three learned to love books. Pulling them out of school for one academic year and exposing them to new environments had proven to be the best investment in their education to date.

Now sitting in the plane, Julie looked out at the clouds as the wing cut past them, already thinking of their next plans: to find a place in the mountains and ski all year long, using income from a sail-rigging workshop to fund the slopes and more travel.

Now that she had done it once, she had the itch.

►LIFESTYLE DESIGN IN ACTION

I was done with driving across town to collect my son from childcare only to slide across icy highways trying to get back to work with him in tow to finish my work. My mini-retirement brought us both to live at an alternative boarding school full of creative lifestyle redesigning children and staff in a gorgeous Florida forest with a spring-fed pond and plenty of sunshine. You can easily search for alternative schools or traditional schools that might accept your children during your stay. Alternative schools often see themselves as supportive communities and are exceptionally welcoming. You might even find an opportunity to work at a school where you could experience a new environment with your child.   —*DEB*

• • •

Tim,

Your book and blog have inspired me to quit my job, write two
e-books, sky dive, backpack through South America, sell all the clutter in my life, and host an annual convention of the world's top
dating instructors (my primary business venture, third year running).
The best part? I can't even buy a drink yet.

Thank you so much, bro! —*ANTHONY*

2

Rules That Change the Rules

►EVERYTHING POPULAR IS WRONG

I can't give you a surefire formula for success, but I can give you a formula for failure: try to please everybody all the time.
—HERBERT BAYARD SWOPE, American editor and journalist; first recipient of the Pulitzer Prize

Everything popular is wrong.
—OSCAR WILDE, *The Importance of Being Earnest*

Beating the Game, Not Playing the Game

In 1999, sometime after quitting my second unfulfilling job and eating peanut-butter sandwiches for comfort, I won the gold medal at the Chinese Kickboxing (Sanshou) National Championships.

It wasn't because I was good at punching and kicking. God forbid. That seemed a bit dangerous, considering I did it on a dare and had four weeks of preparation. Besides, I have a watermelon head—it's a big target.

I won by reading the rules and looking for unexploited opportunities, of which there were two:

1. **Weigh-ins were the day prior to competition:** Using dehydration techniques commonly practiced by elite powerlifters and Olympic wrestlers, I lost 28 pounds in 18 hours, weighed in at

165 pounds, and then hyperhydrated back to 193 pounds.[2] It's hard to fight someone from three weight classes above you. Poor little guys.

2. There was a technicality in the fine print: If one combatant fell off the elevated platform three times in a single round, his opponent won by default. I decided to use this technicality as my principal technique and push people off. As you might imagine, this did not make the judges the happiest Chinese I've ever seen.

The result? I won all of my matches by technical knock-out (TKO) and went home national champion, something 99% of those with 5–10 years of experience had been unable to do.

But, isn't pushing people out of the ring pushing the boundaries of ethics? Not at all—it's no more than doing the uncommon within the rules. The important distinction is that between official rules and self-imposed rules. Consider the following example, from the official website of the Olympic movement (www.olympic.org).

> The 1968 Mexico City Olympics marked the international debut of Dick Fosbury and his celebrated "Fosbury flop," which would soon revolutionize high-jumping. At the time, jumpers . . . swung their outside foot up and over the bar [called the "straddle," much like a hurdle jump, it allowed you to land on your feet]. Fosbury's technique began by racing up to the bar at great speed and taking off from his right (or outside) foot. Then he twisted his body so that he went over the bar head-first with his back to the bar. While the coaches of the world shook their heads in disbelief, the Mexico City audience was absolutely captivated by Fosbury and shouted, "Olé!" as he cleared the bar. Fosbury cleared every height through 2.22 metres without a miss

---

2. Most people will assume this type of weight manipulation is impossible, so I've provided sample photographs at www.fourhourblog.com. Do NOT try this at home. I did it all under medical supervision.

and then achieved a personal record of 2.24 metres to win the gold medal.

By 1980, 13 of the 16 Olympic finalists were using the Fosbury flop.

The weight-cutting techniques and off-platform throwing I used are now standard features of Sanshou competition. I didn't cause it, I just foresaw it as inevitable, as did others who tested this superior approach. Now it's par for the course.

Sports evolve when sacred cows are killed, when basic assumptions are tested.

The same is true in life and in lifestyles.

Challenging the Status Quo vs. Being Stupid

Most people walk down the street on their legs. Does that mean I walk down the street on my hands? Do I wear my underwear outside of my pants in the name of being different? Not usually, no. Then again, walking on my legs and keeping my thong on the inside have worked just fine thus far. I don't fix it if it isn't broken.

Different is better when it is more effective or more fun.

If everyone is defining a problem or solving it one way and the results are subpar, this is the time to ask, What if I did the opposite? Don't follow a model that doesn't work. If the recipe sucks, it doesn't matter how good a cook you are.

When I was in data storage sales, my first gig out of college, I realized that most cold calls didn't get to the intended person for one reason: gatekeepers. If I simply made all my calls from 8:00–8:30 A.M. and 6:00–6:30 P.M., for a total of one hour, I was able to avoid secretaries and book more than twice as many meetings as the senior sales executives who called from 9–5. In other words, I got twice the results for 1/8 the time.

From Japan to Monaco, from globetrotting single mothers to multimillionaire racecar drivers, the basic rules of successful **NR** are surprisingly uniform and predictably divergent from what the rest of the world is doing.

The following rules are the fundamental differentiators to keep in mind throughout this book.

1. Retirement Is Worst-Case-Scenario Insurance.

Retirement planning is like life insurance. It should be viewed as nothing more than a hedge against the absolute worst-case scenario: in this case, becoming physically incapable of working and needing a reservoir of capital to survive.

Retirement as a goal or final redemption is flawed for at least three solid reasons:

a. It is predicated on the assumption that you dislike what you are doing during the most physically capable years of your life. This is a nonstarter—nothing can justify that sacrifice.

b. Most people will never be able to retire and maintain even a hotdogs-for-dinner standard of living. Even one million is chump change in a world where traditional retirement could span 30 years and inflation lowers your purchasing power 2–4% per year. The math doesn't work.[3] The golden years become lower-middle-class life revisited. That's a bittersweet ending.

c. If the math does work, it means that you are one ambitious, hardworking machine. If that's the case, guess what? One week into retirement, you'll be so damn bored that you'll want to stick bicycle spokes in your eyes. You'll probably opt to look for a new job or start another company. Kinda defeats the purpose of waiting, doesn't it?

I'm not saying don't plan for the worst case—I have maxed out 401(k)s and IRAs I use primarily for tax purposes—but don't mistake retirement for the goal.

---

3. "Living Well" (*Barron's,* March 20, 2006, Suzanne McGee).

2. Interest and Energy Are Cyclical.

If I offered you $10,000,000 to work 24 hours a day for 15 years and then retire, would you do it? Of course not—you couldn't. It is unsustainable, just as what most define as a career: doing the same thing for 8+ hours per day until you break down or have enough cash to permanently stop.

How else can my 30-year-old friends all look like a cross between Donald Trump and Joan Rivers? It's horrendous—premature aging fueled by triple bypass frappuccinos and impossible workloads.

Alternating periods of activity and rest is necessary to survive, let alone thrive. Capacity, interest, and mental endurance all wax and wane. Plan accordingly.

The **NR** aims to distribute "mini-retirements" throughout life instead of hoarding the recovery and enjoyment for the fool's gold of retirement. By working only when you are most effective, life is both more productive and more enjoyable. It's the perfect example of having your cake and eating it, too.

Personally, I now aim for one month of overseas relocation or high-intensity learning (tango, fighting, whatever) for every two months of work projects.

3. Less Is Not Laziness.

Doing less meaningless work, so that you can focus on things of greater personal importance, is NOT laziness. This is hard for most to accept, because our culture tends to reward personal sacrifice instead of personal productivity.

Few people choose to (or are able to) measure the results of their actions and thus measure their contribution in time. More time equals more self-worth and more reinforcement from those above and around them. The **NR**, despite fewer hours in the office, produce more meaningful results than the next dozen non-**NR** combined.

Let's define "laziness" anew—to endure a non-ideal existence, to let circumstance or others decide life for you, or to amass a fortune while passing through life like a spectator from an office window. The size of your bank account doesn't change this, nor does the number of hours you log in handling unimportant e-mail or minutiae.

Focus on being productive instead of busy.

4. The Timing Is Never Right.

I once asked my mom how she decided when to have her first child, little ol' me. The answer was simple: "It was something we wanted, and we decided there was no point in putting it off. The timing is never right to have a baby." And so it is.

For all of the most important things, the timing always sucks. Waiting for a good time to quit your job? The stars will never align and the traffic lights of life will never all be green at the same time. The universe doesn't conspire against you, but it doesn't go out of its way to line up all the pins either. Conditions are never perfect. "Someday" is a disease that will take your dreams to the grave with you. Pro and con lists are just as bad. If it's important to you and you want to do it "eventually," just do it and correct course along the way.

5. Ask for Forgiveness, Not Permission.

If it isn't going to devastate those around you, try it and then justify it. People—whether parents, partners, or bosses—deny things on an emotional basis that they can learn to accept after the fact. If the potential damage is moderate or in any way reversible, don't give people the chance to say no. Most people are fast to stop you before you get started but hesitant to get in the way if you're moving. Get good at being a troublemaker and saying sorry when you really screw up.

6. Emphasize Strengths, Don't Fix Weaknesses.

Most people are good at a handful of things and utterly miserable at most. I am great at product creation and marketing but terrible at most of the things that follow.

My body is designed to lift heavy objects and throw them, and that's it. I ignored this for a long time. I tried swimming and looked like a drowning monkey. I tried basketball and looked like a caveman. Then I became a fighter and took off.

It is far more lucrative and fun to leverage your strengths instead of attempting to fix all the chinks in your armor. The choice is between *multiplication* of results using strengths or *incremental* improvement fixing weaknesses that will, at best, become mediocre. Focus on better use of your best weapons instead of constant repair.

7. Things in Excess Become Their Opposite.

It is possible to have too much of a good thing. In excess, most endeavors and possessions take on the characteristics of their opposite. Thus:

> Pacifists become militants.
> Freedom fighters become tyrants.
> Blessings become curses.
> Help becomes hindrance.
> More becomes less.[4]

Too much, too many, and too often of what you want becomes what you don't want. This is true of possessions and even time. Lifestyle Design is thus not interested in creating an excess of idle time, which is poisonous, but the positive use of free time, defined simply as doing what you want as opposed to what you feel obligated to do.

---

4. Goldian VandenBroeck, ed. From *Less Is More: An Anthology of Ancient and Modern Voices Raised in Praise of Simplicity* (Inner Traditions, 1996).

8. Money Alone Is Not the Solution.

There is much to be said for the power of money as currency (I'm a fan myself), but adding more of it just isn't the answer as often as we'd like to think. In part, it's laziness. "If only I had more money" is the easiest way to postpone the intense self-examination and decision-making necessary to create a life of enjoyment—now and not later. By using money as the scape-goat and work as our all-consuming routine, we are able to conveniently disallow ourselves the time to do otherwise: "John, I'd love to talk about the gaping void I feel in my life, the hopelessness that hits me like a punch in the eye every time I start my computer in the morning, but I have so much work to do! I've got at least three hours of unimportant e-mail to reply to before calling the prospects who said 'no' yesterday. Gotta run!"

Busy yourself with the routine of the money wheel, pretend it's the fix-all, and you artfully create a constant distraction that prevents you from seeing just how pointless it is. Deep down, you know it's all an illusion, but with everyone participating in the same game of make-believe, it's easy to forget.

The problem is more than money.

9. Relative Income Is More Important Than Absolute Income.

Among dietitians and nutritionists, there is some debate over the value of a calorie. Is a calorie a calorie, much like a rose is a rose? Is fat loss as simple as expending more calories than you consume, or is the source of those calories important? Based on work with top athletes, I know the answer to be the latter.

What about income? Is a dollar is a dollar is a dollar? The New Rich don't think so.

Let's look at this like a fifth-grade math problem. Two hard-working chaps are headed toward each other. Chap A moving at 80 hours per week and Chap B moving at 10 hours per week.

They both make $50,000 per year. Who will be richer when they pass in the middle of the night? If you said B, you would be correct, and this is the difference between **absolute** and **relative** income.

Absolute income is measured using one holy and inalterable variable: the raw and almighty dollar. Jane Doe makes $100,000 per year and is thus twice as rich as John Doe, who makes $50,000 per year.

Relative income uses two variables: the dollar and time, usually hours. The whole "per year" concept is arbitrary and makes it easy to trick yourself. Let's look at the real trade. Jane Doe makes $100,000 per year, $2,000 for each of 50 weeks per year, and works 80 hours per week. Jane Doe thus makes $25 per hour. John Doe makes $50,000 per year, $1,000 for each of 50 weeks per year, but works 10 hours per week and hence makes $100 per hour. In relative income, John is *four times* richer.

Of course, relative income has to add up to the minimum amount necessary to actualize your goals. If I make $100 per hour but only work one hour per week, it's going to be hard for me to run amuck like a superstar. Assuming that the total absolute income is where it needs to be to live my dreams (not an arbitrary point of comparison with the Joneses), relative income is the real measurement of wealth for the New Rich.

The top New Rich mavericks make at least $5,000 per hour. Out of college, I started at about $5. I'll get you closer to the former.

10. Distress Is Bad, Eustress Is Good.

Unbeknownst to most fun-loving bipeds, not all stress is bad. Indeed, the New Rich don't aim to eliminate all stress. Not in the least. There are two separate types of stress, each as different as euphoria and its seldom-mentioned opposite, *dys*phoria.

*Dis*tress refers to harmful stimuli that make you weaker, less confident, and less able. Destructive criticism, abusive bosses, and smashing your face on a curb are examples of this. These are things we want to avoid.

*Eu*stress, on the other hand, is a word most of you have probably never heard. *Eu-,* a Greek prefix for "healthy," is used in the same sense in the word "euphoria." Role models who push us to exceed our limits, physical training that removes our spare tires, and risks that expand our sphere of comfortable action are all examples of eustress—stress that is healthful and the stimulus for growth.

People who avoid all criticism fail. It's destructive criticism we need to avoid, not criticism in all forms. Similarly, there is no progress without eustress, and the more eustress we can create or apply to our lives, the sooner we can actualize our dreams. The trick is telling the two apart.

The New Rich are equally aggressive in removing distress and finding eustress.

►Q&A: QUESTIONS AND ACTIONS

1. How has being "realistic" or "responsible" kept you from the life you want?

2. How has doing what you "should" resulted in subpar experiences or regret for not having done something else?

3. Look at what you're currently doing and ask yourself, "What would happen if I did the opposite of the people around me? What will I sacrifice if I continue on this track for 5, 10, or 20 years?"

Dodging Bullets

►FEAR-SETTING AND ESCAPING PARALYSIS

Many a false step was made by standing still.
—FORTUNE COOKIE

Named must your fear be before banish it you can.
—YODA, from *Star Wars: The Empire Strikes Back*

RIO DE JANEIRO, BRAZIL

Twenty feet and closing.

"Run! Ruuuuuuuuuun!" Hans didn't speak Portuguese, but the meaning was clear enough—haul ass. His sneakers gripped firmly on the jagged rock, and he drove his chest forward toward 3,000 feet of nothing.

He held his breath on the final step, and the panic drove him to near unconsciousness. His vision blurred at the edges, closing to a single pinpoint of light, and then . . . he floated. The all-consuming celestial blue of the horizon hit his visual field an instant after he realized that the thermal updraft had caught him and the wings of the paraglider. Fear was behind him on the mountaintop, and thousands of feet above the resplendent green rain forest and pristine white beaches of Copacabana, Hans Keeling had seen the light.

That was Sunday.

On Monday, Hans returned to his law office in Century City, Los Angeles's posh corporate haven, and promptly handed in his three-week notice. For nearly five years, he had faced his alarm clock with the same dread: I have to do *this* for another 40–45 years? He had once slept under his desk at the office after a punishing half-done project, only to wake up and continue on it the next morning. That same morning, he had made himself a promise: two more times and I'm out of here. Strike number three came the day before he left for his Brazilian vacation.

We all make these promises to ourselves, and Hans had done it before as well, but things were now somehow different. He was different. He had realized something while arcing in slow circles toward the earth—risks weren't that scary once you took them. His colleagues told him what he expected to hear: He was throwing it all away. He was an attorney on his way to the top—what the hell did he want?

Hans didn't know exactly what he wanted, but he had tasted it. On the other hand, he did know what bored him to tears, and he was done with it. No more passing days as the living dead, no more dinners where his colleagues compared cars, riding on the sugar high of a new BMW purchase until someone bought a more expensive Mercedes. It was over.

Immediately, a strange shift began—Hans felt, for the first time in a long time, at peace with himself and what he was doing. He had always been terrified of plane turbulence, as if he might die with the best inside of him, but now he could fly through a violent storm sleeping like a baby. Strange indeed.

More than a year later, he was still getting unsolicited job offers from law firms, but by then had started Nexus Surf,[5] a premier surf-adventure company based in the tropical paradise of Florianopolis, Brazil. He had met his dream girl, a Carioca with caramel-colored skin named Tatiana, and spent most of his time relaxing under palm trees or treating clients to the best times of their lives.

Is this what he had been so afraid of?

---

5. www.nexussurf.com

These days, he often sees his former self in the underjoyed and overworked professionals he takes out on the waves. Waiting for the swell, the true emotions come out: "God, I wish I could do what you do." His reply is always the same: "You can."

The setting sun reflects off the surface of the water, providing a Zen-like setting for a message he knows is true: It's not giving up to put your current path on indefinite pause. He could pick up his law career exactly where he left off if he wanted to, but that is the furthest thing from his mind.

As they paddle back to shore after an awesome session, his clients get ahold of themselves and regain their composure. They set foot on shore, and reality sinks its fangs in: "I would, but I can't really throw it all away."

He has to laugh.

The Power of Pessimism: Defining the Nightmare

> Action may not always bring happiness, but there is no happiness without action.
>
> —BENJAMIN DISRAELI, former British Prime Minister

To do or not to do? To try or not to try? Most people will vote no, whether they consider themselves brave or not. Uncertainty and the prospect of failure can be very scary noises in the shadows. Most people will choose unhappiness over uncertainty. For years, I set goals, made resolutions to change direction, and nothing came of either. I was just as insecure and scared as the rest of the world.

The simple solution came to me accidentally four years ago. At that time, I had more money than I knew what to do with—I was making $70K or so per month—and I was completely miserable, worse than ever. I had no time and was working myself to death. I had started my own company, only to realize it would be nearly impossible to sell.[6] Oops. I felt trapped and stupid at the same time. I should be able to figure this out, I thought. Why am I such an idiot? Why can't I make this work?! Buckle up and stop being such a (insert expletive)! What's wrong with me? The truth was, nothing was wrong with me. I hadn't reached my limit; I'd reached the limit of my business model at the time. It wasn't the driver, it was the vehicle.

Critical mistakes in its infancy would never let me sell it. I could hire magic elves and connect my brain to a supercomputer—it didn't matter. My little baby had some serious birth defects. The question then became, How do I free myself from this Frankenstein while making it self-sustaining? How do I pry myself from the tentacles of workaholism and the fear that it would fall to pieces without my 15-hour days? How do I escape this self-made prison? A trip, I decided. A sabbatical year around the world.

So I took the trip, right? Well, I'll get to that. First, I felt it prudent to dance around with my shame, embarrassment, and anger for six months, all the while playing an endless loop of reasons why my cop-out fantasy trip could never work. One of my more productive periods, for sure.

Then, one day, in my bliss of envisioning how bad my future suffering would be, I hit upon a gem of an idea. It was surely a highlight of my "don't happy, be worry" phase: Why don't I decide exactly what my nightmare would be—the worst thing that could possibly happen as a result of my trip?

Well, my business could fail while I'm overseas, for sure. Probably would. A legal warning letter would accidentally not get forwarded and I would get sued. My business would be shut down, and inventory would spoil on the shelves while I'm picking my toes in solitary misery on some cold shore in Ireland. Crying in the rain, I

---

6. This turned out to be yet another self-imposed limitation and false construct. BrainQUICKEN was acquired by a private equity firm in 2009. The process is described on www.fourhourblog.com.

imagine. My bank account would crater by 80% and certainly my car and motorcycle in storage would be stolen. I suppose someone would probably spit on my head from a high-rise balcony while I'm feeding food scraps to a stray dog, which would then spook and bite me squarely on the face. God, life is a cruel, hard bitch.

Conquering Fear = Defining Fear

> Set aside a certain number of days, during which you shall be content with the scantiest and cheapest fare, with course and rough dress, saying to yourself the while: "Is this the condition that I feared?"
> —SENECA

Then a funny thing happened. In my undying quest to make myself miserable, I accidentally began to backpedal. As soon as I cut through the vague unease and ambiguous anxiety by defining my nightmare, the worst-case scenario, I wasn't as worried about taking a trip. Suddenly, I started thinking of simple steps I could take to salvage my remaining resources and get back on track if all hell struck at once. I could always take a temporary bartending job to pay the rent if I had to. I could sell some furniture and cut back on eating out. I could steal lunch money from the kindergarteners who passed by my apartment every morning. The options were many. I realized it wouldn't be that hard to get back to where I was, let alone survive. None of these things would be fatal—not even close. Mere panty pinches on the journey of life.

I realized that on a scale of 1–10, 1 being nothing and 10 being permanently life-changing, my so-called worst-case scenario might have a *temporary* impact of 3 or 4. I believe this is true of most people and most would-be "holy sh*t, my life is over" disasters. Keep in mind that this is the one-in-a-million disaster nightmare. On the other hand, if I realized my best-case scenario, or even a probable-case scenario, it would easily have a *permanent* 9 or 10 positive life-changing effect.

In other words, I was risking an unlikely and temporary 3 or 4 for a probable and permanent 9 or 10, and I could easily recover my baseline workaholic prison with a bit of extra work if I wanted to. This all equated to a significant realization: There was practically no risk, only huge life-changing upside potential, and I could resume my previous course without any more effort than I was already putting forth.

That is when I made the decision to take the trip and bought a one-way ticket to Europe. I started planning my adventures and eliminating my physical and psychological baggage. None of my disasters came to pass, and my life has been a near fairy tale since. The business did better than ever, and I practically forgot about it as it financed my travels around the world in style for 15 months.

Uncovering Fear Disguised as Optimism

> There's no difference between a pessimist who says, "Oh, it's hopeless, so don't bother doing anything," and an optimist who says, "Don't bother doing anything, it's going to turn out fine anyway." Either way, nothing happens.
> —YVON CHOUINARD,[7] founder of Patagonia

Fear comes in many forms, and we usually don't call it by its four-letter name. Fear itself is quite fear-inducing. Most intelligent people in the world dress it up as something else: optimistic denial.

Most who avoid quitting their jobs entertain the thought that their course will improve with time or increases in income. This seems valid and is a tempting hallucination when a job is boring or

7. http://www.tpl.org/tier3_cd.cfm?content_item_id=5307&folder_id=1545.

uninspiring instead of pure hell. Pure hell forces action, but anything less can be endured with enough clever rationalization.

Do you really think it will improve or is it wishful thinking and an excuse for inaction? If you were confident in improvement, would you really be questioning things so? Generally not. This is fear of the unknown disguised as optimism.

Are you better off than you were one year ago, one month ago, or one week ago?

If not, things will not improve by themselves. If you are kidding yourself, it is time to stop and plan for a jump. Barring any James Dean ending, your life is going to be LONG. Nine to five for your working lifetime of 40–50 years is a long-ass time if the rescue doesn't come. About 500 months of solid work.

How many do you have to go? It's probably time to cut your losses.

Someone Call the Maître D'

You have comfort. You don't have luxury. And don't tell me that money plays a part. The luxury I advocate has nothing to do with money. It cannot be bought. It is the reward of those who have no fear of discomfort.
— JEAN COCTEAU, French poet, novelist, boxing manager, and filmmaker, whose collaborations were the inspiration for the term "surrealism"

Sometimes timing is perfect. There are hundreds of cars circling a parking lot, and someone pulls out of a spot 10 feet from the entrance just as you reach his or her bumper. Another Christmas miracle!

Other times, the timing could be better. The phone rings during sex and seems to ring for a half hour. The UPS guy shows up 10 minutes later. Bad timing can spoil the fun.

Jean-Marc Hachey landed in West Africa as a volunteer, with high hopes of lending a helping hand. In that sense, his timing was great.

He arrived in Ghana in the early 1980s, in the middle of a coup d'état, at the peak of hyperinflation, and just in time for the worst drought in a decade. For these same reasons, some people would consider his timing quite poor from a more selfish survival standpoint.

He had also missed the memo. The national menu had changed, and they were out of luxuries like bread and clean water. He would be surviving for four months on a slushlike concoction of corn meal and spinach. Not what most of us would order at the movie theater.

"WOW, I CAN SURVIVE."

Jean-Marc had passed the point of no return, but it didn't matter. After two weeks of adjusting to the breakfast, lunch, and dinner (Mush à la Ghana), he had no desire to escape. The most basic of foods and good friends proved to be the only real necessities, and what would seem like a disaster from the outside was the most life-affirming epiphany he'd ever experienced: The worst really wasn't that bad. To enjoy life, you don't need fancy nonsense, but you do need to control your time and realize that most things just aren't as serious as you make them out to be.

Now 48, Jean-Marc lives in a nice home in Ontario, but could live without it. He has cash, but could fall into poverty tomorrow and it wouldn't matter. Some of his fondest memories still include nothing but friends and gruel. He is dedicated to creating special moments for himself and his family and is utterly unconcerned with retirement. He's already lived 20 years of partial retirement in perfect health.

Don't save it all for the end. There is every reason not to.

►Q&A: QUESTIONS AND ACTIONS

> I am an old man and have known a great many troubles, but most of them never happened.   —MARK TWAIN

If you are nervous about making the jump or simply putting it off out of fear of the unknown, here is your antidote. Write down your answers, and keep in mind that thinking a lot will not prove as fruitful or as prolific as simply brain vomiting on the page. Write and do not edit—aim for volume. Spend a few minutes on each answer.

1. **Define your nightmare, the absolute worst that could happen if you did what you are considering.** What doubt, fears, and "what-ifs" pop up as you consider the big changes you can—or need—to make? Envision them in painstaking detail. Would it be the end of your life? What would be the permanent impact, if any, on a scale of 1–10? Are these things really permanent? How likely do you think it is that they would actually happen?

2. **What steps could you take to repair the damage or get things back on the upswing, even if temporarily?** Chances are, it's easier than you imagine. How could you get things back under control?

3. **What are the outcomes or benefits, both temporary and permanent, of more probable scenarios?** Now that you've defined the nightmare, what are the more probable or definite positive outcomes, whether internal (confidence, self-esteem, etc.) or external? What would the impact of these more-likely outcomes be on a scale of 1–10? How likely is it that you could produce at least a moderately good outcome? Have less intelligent people done this before and pulled it off?

4. **If you were fired from your job today, what would you do to get things under financial control?** Imagine this scenario and run through questions 1–3 above. If you quit your job to test other options, how could you later get back on the same career track if you absolutely had to?

5. **What are you putting off out of fear?** Usually, what we most fear doing is what we most need to do. That phone call, that conversation, whatever the action might be—it is fear of unknown

outcomes that prevents us from doing what we need to do. Define the worst case, accept it, and do it. I'll repeat something you might consider tattooing on your forehead: *What we fear doing most is usually what we most need to do.* As I have heard said, a person's success in life can usually be measured by the number of uncomfortable conversations he or she is willing to have. Resolve to do one thing every day that you fear. I got into this habit by attempting to contact celebrities and famous businesspeople for advice.

6. **What is it costing you—financially, emotionally, and physically—to postpone action?** Don't only evaluate the potential downside of action. It is equally important to measure the atrocious cost of inaction. If you don't pursue those things that excite you, where will you be in one year, five years, and ten years? How will you feel having allowed circumstance to impose itself upon you and having allowed ten more years of your finite life to pass doing what you know will not fulfill you? If you telescope out 10 years and know with 100% certainty that it is a path of disappointment and regret, and if we define risk as "the likelihood of an irreversible negative outcome," inaction is the greatest risk of all.

7. **What are you waiting for?** If you cannot answer this without resorting to the previously rejected concept of good timing, the answer is simple: You're afraid, just like the rest of the world. Measure the cost of inaction, realize the unlikelihood and repairability of most missteps, and develop the most important habit of those who excel and enjoy doing so: action.

4

System Reset

►BEING UNREASONABLE AND UNAMBIGUOUS

"Would you tell me, please, which way I ought to go from
here?"

"That depends a good deal on where you want to get to,"
said the Cat.

"I don't much care where . . ." said Alice.

"Then it doesn't matter which way you go," said the Cat.

—LEWIS CARROLL, *Alice in Wonderland*

The reasonable man adapts himself to the world; the unreasonable one persists in trying to adapt the world to himself. Therefore all progress depends on the unreasonable
man.

—GEORGE BERNARD SHAW, *Maxims for Revolutionists*

SPRING 2005 / PRINCETON, NEW JERSEY

I had to bribe them. What other choice did I have?

They formed a circle around me, and, while the names dif-
fered, the question was one and the same: "What's the challenge?"
All eyes were on me.

My lecture at Princeton University had just ended with excitement and enthusiasm. At the same time, I knew that most students
would go out and promptly do the opposite of what I preached.
Most of them would be putting in 80-hour weeks as high-paid coffee fetchers unless I showed that the principles from class could
actually be applied.

Hence the challenge.

I was offering a round-trip ticket anywhere in the world to anyone who could complete an undefined "challenge" in the most impressive fashion possible. Results plus style. I told them to meet me after class if interested, and here they were, nearly 20 out of 60 students.

The task was designed to test their comfort zones while forcing them to use some of the tactics I teach. It was simplicity itself: Contact three seemingly impossible-to-reach people—J.Lo, Bill Clinton, J. D. Salinger, I don't care—and get at least one to reply to three questions.

Of 20 students, all frothing at the mouth to win a free spin across the globe, how many completed the challenge?

Exactly . . . none. Not a one.

There were many excuses: "It's not that easy to get someone to . . ." "I have a big paper due, and . . ." "I would love to, but there's no way I can. . . ." There was but one real reason, however, repeated over and over again in different words: It was a difficult challenge, perhaps impossible, and the other students would outdo them. Since all of them overestimated the competition, no one even showed up.

According to the rules I had set, if someone had sent me no more than an illegible one-paragraph response, I would have been obligated to give them the prize. This result both fascinated and depressed me.

The following year, the outcome was quite different.

I told the above cautionary tale and 6 out of 17 finished the challenge in less than 48 hours. Was the second class better? No. In fact, there were more capable students in the first class, but they did nothing. Firepower up the wazoo and no trigger finger.

The second group just embraced what I told them before they started, which was . . .

Doing the Unrealistic Is Easier Than Doing the Realistic

From contacting billionaires to rubbing elbows with celebrities—the second group of students did both—it's as easy as believing it can be done.

It's lonely at the top. Ninety-nine percent of people in the world are convinced they are incapable of achieving great things, so they aim for the mediocre. The level of competition is thus fiercest for "realistic" goals, paradoxically making them the most time- and energy-consuming. It is easier to raise $1,000,000 than it is $100,000. It is easier to pick up the one perfect 10 in the bar than the five 8s.

If you are insecure, guess what? The rest of the world is, too. Do not overestimate the competition and underestimate yourself. You are better than you think.

Unreasonable and unrealistic goals are easier to achieve for yet another reason.

Having an unusually large goal is an adrenaline infusion that provides the endurance to overcome the inevitable trials and tribulations that go along with any goal. Realistic goals, goals restricted to the average ambition level, are uninspiring and will only fuel you through the first or second problem, at which point you throw in the towel. If the potential payoff is mediocre or average, so is your effort. I'll run through walls to get a catamaran trip through the Greek islands, but I might not change my brand of cereal for a weekend trip through Columbus, Ohio. If I choose the latter because it is "realistic," I won't have the enthusiasm to jump even the smallest hurdle to accomplish it. With beautiful, crystal-clear Greek waters and delicious wine on the brain, I'm prepared to do battle for a dream that is worth dreaming. Even though their difficulty of achievement on a scale of 1–10 appears to be a 10 and a 2 respectively, Columbus is more likely to fall through.

The fishing is best where the fewest go, and the collective insecurity of the world makes it easy for people to hit home runs while everyone else is aiming for base hits. There is just less competition for bigger goals.

Doing big things begins with asking for them properly.

What Do You Want? A Better Question, First of All

Most people will never know what they want. I don't know what I want. If you ask me what I want to do in the next five months for language learning, on the other hand, I do know. It's a matter of specificity. "What do you want?" is too imprecise to produce a meaningful and actionable answer. Forget about it.

"What are your goals?" is similarly fated for confusion and guesswork. To rephrase the question, we need to take a step back and look at the bigger picture.

Let's assume we have 10 goals and we achieve them—what is the desired outcome that makes all the effort worthwhile? The most common response is what I also would have suggested five years ago: happiness. I no longer believe this is a good answer. Happiness can be bought with a bottle of wine and has become ambiguous through overuse. There is a more precise alternative that reflects what I believe the actual objective is.

Bear with me. What is the opposite of happiness? Sadness? No. Just as love and hate are two sides of the same coin, so are happiness and sadness. Crying out of happiness is a perfect illustration of this. The opposite of love is indifference, and the opposite of happiness is—here's the clincher—boredom.

Excitement is the more practical synonym for happiness, and it is precisely what you should strive to chase. It is the cure-all. When people suggest you follow your "passion" or your "bliss," I propose that they are, in fact, referring to the same singular concept: excitement.

This brings us full circle. The question you should be asking isn't, "What do I want?" or "What are my goals?" but "What would excite me?"

Adult-Onset ADD: Adventure Deficit Disorder

Somewhere between college graduation and your second job, a chorus enters your internal dialogue: Be realistic and stop pretending. Life isn't like the movies.

If you're five years old and say you want to be an astronaut, your parents tell you that you can be anything you want to be. It's harmless, like telling a child that Santa Claus exists. If you're 25 and announce you want to start a new circus, the response is different: Be realistic; become a lawyer or an accountant or a doctor, have babies, and raise them to repeat the cycle.

If you do manage to ignore the doubters and start your own business, for example, ADD doesn't disappear. It just takes a different form.

When I started BrainQUICKEN LLC in 2001, it was with a clear goal in mind: Make $1,000 per day whether I was banging my head on a laptop or cutting my toenails on the beach. It was to be an automated source of cash flow. If you look at my chronology, it is obvious that this didn't happen until a meltdown forced it, despite the requisite income. Why? The goal wasn't specific enough. I hadn't defined *alternate activities* that would replace the initial workload. Therefore, I just continued working, even though there was no financial need. I needed to feel productive and had no other vehicles.

This is how most people work until death: "I'll just work until I have X dollars and then do what I want." If you don't define the "what I want" alternate activities, the X figure will increase indefinitely to avoid the fear-inducing uncertainty of this void.

This is when both employees and entrepreneurs become fat men in red BMWs.

The Fat Man in the Red BMW Convertible

There have been several points in my life—among them, just before I was fired from TrueSAN and just before I escaped the U.S. to avoid taking an Uzi into McDonald's—at which I saw my future as another fat man in a midlife-crisis BMW. I simply looked at those who were 15–20 years ahead of me on the same track, whether a director of sales or an entrepreneur in the same industry, and it scared the hell out of me.

It was such an acute phobia, and such a perfect metaphor for the sum of all fears, that it became a pattern interrupt between myself and fellow lifestyle designer and entrepreneur Douglas Price. Doug and I traveled parallel paths for nearly five years, facing the same challenges and self-doubt and thus keeping a close psychological eye on each other. Our down periods seem to alternate, making us a good team.

Whenever one of us began to set our sights lower, lose faith, or "accept reality," the other would chime in via phone or e-mail like an AA sponsor: "Dude, are you turning into the bald fat man in the red BMW convertible?" The prospect was terrifying enough that we always got our asses and priorities back on track immediately. The worst that could happen wasn't crashing and burning, it was accepting terminal boredom as a tolerable status quo.

Remember—boredom is the enemy, not some abstract "failure."

Correcting Course: Get Unrealistic

There is a process that I have used, and still use, to reignite life or correct course when the Fat Man in the BMW rears his ugly head. In some form or another, it is the same process used by the most impressive **NR** I have met around the world: dreamlining. Dreamlining is so named because it applies timelines to what most would consider dreams.

It is much like goal-setting but differs in several fundamental respects:

1. The goals shift from ambiguous wants to defined steps.
2. The goals have to be unrealistic to be effective.
3. It focuses on activities that will fill the vacuum created when work is removed. *Living* like a millionaire requires *doing* interesting things and not just owning enviable things.

Now it's your turn to think big.

How to Get George Bush Sr. or the CEO of Google on the Phone

The article below, titled "Fail Better" and written by Adam Gottesfeld, explores how I teach Princeton students to connect with luminary-level business mentors and celebrities of various types. I've edited it for length in a few places.

People are fond of using the "it's not what you know, it's who you know" adage as an excuse for inaction, as if all successful people are born with powerful friends.

Nonsense.

Here's how normal people build supernormal networks.

Fail Better
BY ADAM GOTTESFELD

MOST PRINCETON students love to procrastinate in writing their dean's date [term] papers. Ryan Marrinan '07, from Los Angeles, was no exception. But while the majority of undergraduates fill their time by updating their Facebook profiles or watching videos on YouTube, Marrinan was discussing Soto Zen Buddhism via e-mail with Randy Komisar, a partner at the venture capital firm Kleiner Perkins Caufield and Byers, and asking Google CEO Eric Schmidt via e-mail when he had been happiest in his life. (Schmidt's answer: "Tomorrow.")

Prior to his e-mail, Marrinan had never contacted Komisar. He had met Schmidt, a Princeton University trustee, only briefly at an academic affairs meeting of the trustees in November. A self-described "naturally shy kid," Marrinan said he would never have dared to randomly e-mail two of the most powerful men in Silicon Valley if it weren't for Tim Ferriss, who offered a guest lecture in Professor Ed Zschau's "High-Tech Entrepreneurship" class. Ferriss challenged Marrinan and his fellow seniors to contact high-profile celebrities and CEOs and get their answers to questions they have always wanted to ask.

For extra incentive, Ferriss promised the student who could contact the most hard-to-reach name and ask the most intriguing question a round-trip plane ticket anywhere in the world.

"I believe that success can be measured in the number of uncomfortable conversations you're willing to have. I felt that if I could help students overcome the fear of rejection with cold-calling and cold e-mail, it would serve them forever," Ferriss said. "It's easy to sell yourself short, but when you see classmates getting responses from people like [former president] George Bush, the CEOs of Disney, Comcast, Google, and HP, and dozens of other impossible-to-reach people, it forces you to reconsider your self-set limitations." . . . Ferriss lectures to the students of "High-Tech Entrepreneurship" each semester about creating a startup and designing the ideal lifestyle.

"I participate in this contest every day," said Ferriss. "I do what I always do: find a personal e-mail if possible, often through their little-known personal blogs, send a two- to three-paragraph e-mail which explains that I am familiar with their work, and ask one simple-to-answer but thought-provoking question in that e-mail related to their work or life philosophies. The goal is to start a dialogue so they take the time to answer future e-mails—not to ask for help. That can only come after at least three or four genuine e-mail exchanges."

With "textbook execution of the Tim Ferriss Technique," as he put it, Marrinan was able to strike up a bond with Komisar. In his initial e-mail, he talked about reading one of Komisar's *Harvard Business Review* articles and feeling inspired to ask him, "When were you happiest in your life?" After Komisar replied with references to Tibetan Buddhism, Marrinan responded, "Just as words are inadequate to explain true happiness, so too are words inadequate to express my thanks." His e-mail included his personal translation of a French poem by Taisen Deshimaru, the former European head of Soto Zen. An e-mail relationship was formed, and Komisar even e-mailed Marrinan a few days later with a link to a *New York Times* article on happiness.

Contacting Schmidt proved more challenging. For Marrinan, the toughest part was getting Schmidt's personal e-mail address. He e-mailed a Princeton dean asking for it. No response. Two weeks later, he e-mailed the same dean again, defending his request by reminding her that he had previously met Schmidt. The dean said no, but Marrinan refused to give up. He e-mailed her a third time. "Have you ever made an exception?" he asked. The dean finally gave in, he said, and provided him with Schmidt's e-mail.

"I know some of my classmates pursued the alternative scattershot technique with some success, but that's not my bag," Marrinan said, explaining his perseverance. "I deal with rejection by persisting, not by taking my business elsewhere. My maxim comes from Samuel Beckett, a personal hero of mine: 'Ever tried. Ever failed. No matter. Try again. Fail again. Fail better.' You won't believe what you can accomplish by attempting the impossible with the courage to repeatedly fail better."

Nathan Kaplan, another participant in the contest, was most proud of the way that he was able to contact former Newark mayor Sharpe James. Because James had made a campaign contribution to Al Sharpton, the website www.fundrace.org listed James's home address. Kaplan then input James's address into an online serach-by-address phone directory, through which he received the former mayor's phone number. Kaplan left a message for James, and a few days later finally got to ask him about childhood education.

Ferriss is proud of the effort students have put into his contest. "Most people can do absolutely awe-inspiring things," he said. "Sometimes they just need a little nudge."

►Q&A: QUESTIONS AND ACTIONS

The existential vacuum manifests itself mainly in a state of boredom.
—VIKTOR FRANKL, Auschwitz survivor and founder of Logotherapy, *Man's Search for Meaning*

Life is too short to be small.   —BENJAMIN DISRAELI

Dreamlining will be fun, and it will be hard. The harder it is, the more you need it. To save time, I recommend using the automatic calculators and forms at www.fourhourblog.com. Refer to the model worksheet on page 60 as you complete the following steps:

1. **What would you do if there were no way you could fail? If you were 10 times smarter than the rest of the world?**
Create two timelines—6 months and 12 months—and list up to five things you dream of *having* (including, but not limited to, material wants: house, car, clothing, etc.), *being* (be a great cook, be fluent in Chinese, etc.), and *doing* (visiting Thailand, tracing your roots overseas, racing ostriches, etc.) in that order. If you have difficulty identifying what you want in some categories, as most will, consider what you hate or fear in each and write down the opposite. Do not limit yourself, and do not concern yourself with how these things will be accomplished. For now, it's unimportant. This is an exercise in reversing repression.

Be sure not to judge or fool yourself. If you really want a Ferrari, don't put down solving world hunger out of guilt. For some, the dream will be fame, for others fortune or prestige. All people have their vices and insecurities. If something will improve your feeling of self-worth, put it down. I have a racing motorcycle, and quite apart from the fact that I love speed, it just makes me feel like a cool dude. There is nothing wrong with that. Put it all down.

2. **Drawing a blank?**

   For all their bitching about what's holding them back, most people have a lot of trouble coming up with the defined dreams they're being held from. This is particularly true with the "doing" category. In that case, consider these questions:

   a. What would you do, day to day, if you had $100 million in the bank?

   b. What would make you most excited to wake up in the morning to another day?

   Don't rush—think about it for a few minutes. If still blocked, fill in the five "doing" spots with the following:

   one place to visit
   one thing to do before you die (a memory of a lifetime)
   one thing to do daily
   one thing to do weekly
   one thing you've always wanted to learn

3. **What does "being" entail doing?**

   Convert each "being" into a "doing" to make it actionable. Identify an action that would characterize this state of being or a task that would mean you had achieved it. People find it easier to brainstorm "being" first, but this column is just a temporary holding spot for "doing" actions. Here are a few examples:

   > Great cook ➡ make Christmas dinner without help
   > Fluent in Chinese ➡ have a five-minute conversation
   >   with a Chinese co-worker

4. **What are the four dreams that would change it all?**

   Using the 6-month timeline, star or otherwise highlight the four most exciting and/or important dreams from all columns. Repeat the process with the 12-month timeline if desired.

5. **Determine the cost of these dreams and calculate your Target Monthly Income (TMI) for both timelines.**

If financeable, what is the cost per month for each of the four dreams (rent, mortgage, payment plan installments, etc.)? Start thinking of income and expense in terms of monthly cash flow—dollars in and dollars out—instead of grand totals. Things often cost much, much less than expected. For example, a Lamborghini Gallardo Spyder, fresh off the showroom floor at $260,000, can be had for $2,897.80 per month. I found my personal favorite, an Aston Martin DB9 with 1,000 miles on it, through eBay for $136,000—$2,003.10 per month. How about a Round-the-World trip (Los Angeles → Tokyo → Singapore → Bangkok → Delhi or Bombay → London → Frankfurt → Los Angeles) for $1,399?

For some of these costs, the Tools and Tricks at the end of Chapter 14 will help.

Last, calculate your Target Monthly Income (TMI) for realizing these dreamlines. This is how to do it: First, total each of the columns A, B, and C, counting only the four selected dreams. Some of these column totals could be zero, which is fine. Next, add your total monthly expenses × 1.3 (the 1.3 represents your expenses plus a 30% buffer for safety or savings). This grand total is your TMI and the target to keep in mind for the rest of the book. I like to further divide this TMI by 30 to get my TDI—Target Daily Income. I find it easier to work with a daily goal. Online calculators on our companion site do all the work for you and make this step a cinch.

Chances are that the figure is lower than expected, and it often decreases over time as you trade more and more "having" for once-in-a-lifetime "doing." Mobility encourages this trend. Even if the total is intimidating, don't fret in the least. I have helped students get to more than $10,000 per month in extra income within three months.

Sample Dreamline

TARGET MONTHLY INCOME
A + B + C + (1.3 x monthly expenses)
=

TMI: $3,337 + ($2,600) = $5,937

÷ 30

=

TDI: $197.90

	STEP ① : HAVING	STEP ⑤ : COST
*	1. Aston Martin DB9	1. $2,003/month
	2. Go Board from 1800s	2.
*	3. Personal assistant	3. $5/hr. x 80 = $400
	4. Full Kendo armor	4.
	5.	5.

A = $2,403

IN 6 MONTHS I DREAM OF:

	STEP ② : BEING		STEP ④ : DOING
	1. flexible	→	1. full side splits
*	2. best-selling author	→	2. sell 20,000 per week
	3. fluent in Greek	→	3. have 15-minute conversation w/ native
	4. excellent cook	→	4. make Thanksgiving dinner for six people
	5.	→	5.

	STEP ③ : DOING	STEP ⑤ : COST
	1. sell a TV show	1.
*	2. visit Croatian coast	2. $514 roundtrip airfare, $420 rent
	3. find smart & gorgeous girlfriend	3.
	4.	4.
	5.	5.

C = $934

STEP ⑤ : COST
1.
2. $0 (3 free interns for media calls & own time)
3.
4.
5.

B = $0

STEPS NOW
1. Find showroom, schedule test drive
2. Post bullet-point job description on 3 major sites
3. Send top 3 questions to five best-selling authors from 2–3 years ago
4. Visit Virtual Tourist and determine best season and to-do top 5

TOMORROW
1. Take test drive
2. Assign 1- to 2-hour task to top 3
3. Formulate plan around responses (marketing/PR)
4. Research tickets & housing for 3 weeks and invite friend to go

DAY AFTER
1. Decide on desired details & extras
2. Choose top 1 for 20 hrs. per week
3. Send intern recruitment e-mail to nearby college English departments
4. Reserve tickets (for yourself even if friend refuses)

Dreamline

(Go to www.fourhourblog.com for larger printable worksheets and online calculators.)

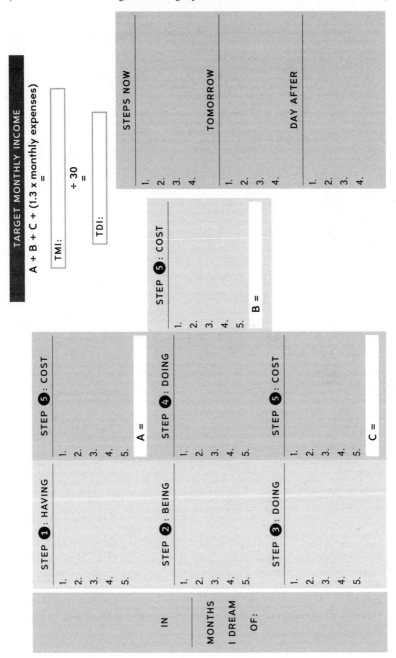

TARGET MONTHLY INCOME

A + B + C + (1.3 x monthly expenses) =

TMI:

÷ 30 =

TDI:

STEPS NOW
1.
2.
3.
4.

TOMORROW
1.
2.
3.
4.

DAY AFTER
1.
2.
3.
4.

STEP 1 : HAVING
1.
2.
3.
4.
5.

STEP 5 : COST
1.
2.
3.
4.
5.

A =

STEP 2 : BEING
1.
2.
3.
4.
5.

STEP 4 : DOING
1.
2.
3.
4.
5.

STEP 5 : COST
1.
2.
3.
4.
5.

B =

STEP 3 : DOING
1.
2.
3.
4.
5.

STEP 5 : COST
1.
2.
3.
4.
5.

C =

IN

MONTHS

I DREAM

OF:

Dreamline Math—Another Good Option

There could be a different way of handling monthly and one-time goals. I'll use your example of an Aston Martin's monthly payment, a personal assistant's monthly payment, and a trip to the Croatian coast. While the first two should certainly be totaled and included in your target monthly income, the trip is something that should be divided by the number of months between now and the dreamline's total time.

Thus if you had a six-month dreamline:

Aston Martin = 2,003 per month
Personal assistant = 400 per month
Croatian trip = 934 total, and thus 934/6 per month

Right now in the book and in the spreadsheet we have (2003 + 400 + 934) × 1.3 monthly expenses = Target Monthly Income (or TMI).

But I think it should be (2003 + 400 + 934/6 × 1.3 monthly expenses = TMI.

Or, more generally: [Monthly Goals + (One-Time Goals / Total Months)] × 1.3 monthly expenses = TMI.

—*JARED, president, SET Consulting*

6. Determine *three steps* for each of the *four dreams* in just the 6-month timeline and take the first step *now*.

I'm not a big believer in long-term planning and far-off goals. In fact, I generally set 3-month and 6-month dreamlines. The variables change too much and in-the-future distance becomes an excuse for postponing action. The objective of this exercise isn't, therefore, to outline every step from start to finish, but to define the end goal, the required vehicle to achieve them (TMI, TDI), and build momentum with critical first steps. From that point, it's a matter of freeing time and generating the TMI, which the following chapters cover.

First, let's focus on those critical first steps. Define three steps for each dream that will get you closer to its actualization. Set actions—simple, well-defined actions—for now, tomorrow (complete before II A.M.) and the day after (again completed before II A.M.).

Once you have three steps for each of the four goals, complete the three actions in the "now" column. Do it now. Each should be simple enough to do in five minutes or less. If not, rachet it down. If it's the middle of the night and you can't call someone, do something else now, such as send an e-mail, and set the call for first thing tomorrow.

If the next stage is some form of research, get in touch with someone who knows the answer instead of spending too much time in books or online, which can turn into paralysis by analysis. The best first step, the one I recommend, is finding someone who's done it and ask for advice on how to do the same. It's not hard.

Other options include setting a meeting or phone call with a trainer, mentor, or salesperson to build momentum. Can you schedule a private class or a commitment that you'll feel bad about canceling? Use guilt to your advantage.

Tomorrow becomes never. No matter how small the task, take the first step now!

►COMFORT CHALLENGE

The most important actions are never comfortable.

Fortunately, it is possible to condition yourself to discomfort and overcome it. I've trained myself to propose solutions instead of ask for them, to elicit desired responses instead of react, and to be assertive without burning bridges. To have an uncommon lifestyle, you need to *develop the uncommon habit of making decisions, both for yourself and for others.*

From this chapter forward, I'll take you through progressively more uncomfortable exercises, simple and small. Some of the exercises will appear deceptively easy and even irrelevant (such as the next) until you try them. Look at it as a game and expect some butterflies and sweat—that's the whole point. For most of these exercises, the duration is two days. Mark the exercise of the day on your calendar so you don't forget, and don't attempt more than one Comfort Challenge at a time.

Remember: There is a direct correlation between an increased sphere of comfort and getting what you want.

Here we go.

Learn to Eye Gaze (2 days)

My friend Michael Ellsberg invented a singles event called Eye Gazing. It is similar to speed dating but different in one fundamental respect—no speaking is permitted. It involves gazing into the eyes of each partner for three minutes at a time. If you go to such an event, it becomes clear how uncomfortable most people are doing this. For the next two days, practice gazing into the eyes of others—whether people you pass on the street or conversational partners—until they break contact. Hints:

1. Focus on one eye and be sure to blink occasionally so you don't look like a psychopath or get your ass kicked.

2. In conversation, maintain eye contact when you are speaking. It's easy to do while listening.

3. Practice with people bigger or more confident than yourself. If a passerby asks you what the hell you're staring at, just smile and respond, "Sorry about that. I thought you were an old friend of mine."

Step II:
E is for Elimination

One does not accumulate but eliminate. It is not daily increase but daily decrease. The height of cultivation always runs to simplicity.

—BRUCE LEE

The End of Time Management

►ILLUSIONS AND ITALIANS

Perfection is not when there is no more to add, but no more to take away.

—ANTOINE DE SAINT-EXUPÉRY, pioneer of international postal flight and author of *Le Petit Prince (The Little Prince)*

It is vain to do with more what can be done with less.

—WILLIAM OF OCCAM (1300–1350), originator of "Occam's Razor"

Just a few words on time management: Forget all about it.

In the strictest sense, you shouldn't be trying to do more in each day, trying to fill every second with a work fidget of some type. It took me a long time to figure this out. I used to be very fond of the results-by-volume approach.

Being busy is most often used as a guise for avoiding the few critically important but uncomfortable actions. The options are almost limitless for creating "busyness": You could call a few hundred unqualified sales leads, reorganize your Outlook contacts, walk across the office to request documents you don't really need, or fuss with your BlackBerry for a few hours when you should be prioritizing.

In fact, if you want to move up the ladder in most of corporate America, and assuming they don't really check what you are doing (let's be honest), just run around the office holding a cell phone to your head and carrying papers. Now, that is one busy employee! Give them a raise. Unfortunately for the **NR**, this behavior won't get you out of the office or put you on an airplane to Brazil. Bad dog. Hit yourself with a newspaper and cut it out.

After all, there is a far better option, and it will do more than simply increase your results—it will multiply them. Believe it or not, it is not only possible to accomplish more by doing less, it is mandatory.

Enter the world of elimination.

How You Will Use Productivity

Now that you have defined what you want to do with your time, you have to free that time. The trick, of course, is to do so while maintaining or increasing your income.

The intention of this chapter, and what you will experience if you follow the instructions, is an increase in personal productivity between 100 and 500%. The *principles* are the same for both employees and entrepreneurs, but the *purpose* of this increased productivity is completely different.

First, the employee. The employee is increasing productivity to increase negotiating leverage for two simultaneous objectives: pay raises and a remote working arrangement.

Recall that, as indicated in the first chapter of this book, the general process of joining the New Rich is **D-E-A-L**, in that order, but that employees intent on remaining employees for now need to implement the process as **D-E-L-A**. The reason relates to environment. They need to **Liberate** themselves from the office environment before they can work ten hours a week, for example, because the expectation in that environment is that you will be in constant motion from 9–5. Even if you produce twice the results you had in the past, if you're working a quarter of the hours of your colleagues, there is a good chance of receiving a pink slip. Even if you work 10 hours a week and produce twice the results of people working 40, the collective request will be, "Work 40 hours a week and produce 8 times the results." This is an endless game and one you want to avoid. Hence the need for **Liberation** first.

If you're an employee, this chapter will increase your value and make it more painful for the company to fire you than to grant raises and a remote working agreement. That is your goal. Once the latter is accomplished, you can drop hours without bureaucratic interference and use the resultant free time to fulfill dreamlines.

The entrepreneur's goals are less complex, as he or she is generally the direct beneficiary of increased profit. The goal is to decrease the amount of work you perform while increasing revenue. This will set the stage for replacing yourself with **Automation,** which in turn permits **Liberation.**

For both tracks, some definitions are in order.

Being Effective vs. Being Efficient

Effectiveness is doing the things that get you closer to your goals. Efficiency is performing a given task (whether important or not) in the most economical manner possible. Being efficient without regard to effectiveness is the default mode of the universe.

I would consider the best door-to-door salesperson efficient—that is, refined and excellent at selling door-to-door without wasting time—but utterly ineffective. He or she would sell more using a better vehicle such as e-mail or direct mail.

This is also true for the person who checks e-mail 30 times per day and develops an elaborate system of folder rules and sophisticated techniques for ensuring that each of those 30 brain farts moves as quickly as possible. I was a specialist at such professional wheel-spinning. It is efficient on some perverse level, but far from effective.

Here are two truisms to keep in mind:

1. Doing something unimportant well does not make it important.
2. Requiring a lot of time does not make a task important.

From this moment forward, remember this: *What* you do is infinitely more important than *how* you do it. Efficiency is still important, but it is useless unless applied to the right things.

To find the right things, we'll need to go to the garden.

Pareto and His Garden: 80/20 and Freedom from Futility

> What gets measured gets managed.
>
> —PETER DRUCKER, management theorist, author of
> 31 books, recipient of Presidential Medal of Freedom

Four years ago, an economist changed my life forever. It's a shame I never had a chance to buy him a drink. My dear Vilfredo died almost 100 years ago.

Vilfredo Pareto was a wily and controversial economist-cum-sociologist who lived from 1848 to 1923. An engineer by training, he started his varied career managing coal mines and later succeeded Léon Walras as the chair of political economy at the University of Lausanne in Switzerland. His seminal work, *Cours d'economie politique,* included a then little-explored "law" of income distribution that would later bear his name: "Pareto's Law" or the "Pareto Distribution," in the last decade also popularly called the "80/20 Principle."

The mathematical formula he used to demonstrate a grossly uneven but predictable distribution of wealth in society—80% of the wealth and income was produced and possessed by 20% of the population—also applied outside of economics. Indeed, it could be found almost everywhere. Eighty percent of Pareto's garden peas were produced by 20% of the peapods he had planted, for example.

Pareto's Law can be summarized as follows: 80% of the outputs result from 20% of the inputs. Alternative ways to phrase this, depending on the context, include:

80% of the consequences flow from 20% of the causes.
80% of the results come from 20% of the effort and time.
80% of company profits come from 20% of the products and customers.
80% of all stock market gains are realized by 20% of the investors and 20% of an individual portfolio.

The list is infinitely long and diverse, and the ratio is often skewed even more severely: 90/10, 95/5, and 99/1 are not uncommon, but the minimum ratio to seek is 80/20.

When I came across Pareto's work one late evening, I had been slaving away with 15-hour days seven days per week, feeling completely overwhelmed and generally helpless. I would wake up before dawn to make calls to the United Kingdom, handle the U.S. during the normal 9–5 day, and then work until near midnight making calls to Japan and New Zealand. I was stuck on a runaway freight train with no brakes, shoveling coal into the furnace for lack of a better option. Faced with certain burnout or giving Pareto's ideas a trial run, I opted for the latter. The next morning, I began a dissection of my business and personal life through the lenses of two questions:

1. Which 20% of sources are causing 80% of my problems and unhappiness?
2. Which 20% of sources are resulting in 80% of my desired outcomes and happiness?

For the entire day, I put aside everything seemingly urgent and did the most intense truth-baring analysis possible, applying these questions to everything from my friends to customers and advertising to relaxation activities. Don't expect to find you're doing everything right—the truth often hurts. The goal is to find your inefficiencies in order to eliminate them and to find your strengths so you can multiply them. In the 24 hours that followed, I made several simple but emotionally difficult decisions that literally changed my life forever and enabled the lifestyle I now enjoy.

The first decision I made is an excellent example of how dramatic and fast the ROI of this analytical fat-cutting can be: I stopped contacting 95% of my customers and fired 2%, leaving me with the top 3% of producers to profile and duplicate.

Out of more than 120 wholesale customers, a mere 5 were bringing in 95% of the revenue. I was spending 98% of my time chasing the remainder, as the aforementioned 5 ordered regularly without any follow-up calls, persuasion, or cajoling. In other words, I was working because I felt as though I should be doing something from 9–5. I didn't realize that working every hour from 9–5 isn't the goal; it's simply the structure most people use, whether it's necessary or not. I had a severe case of work-for-work (W4W), the most-hated acronym in the **NR** vocabulary.

All, and I mean 100%, of my problems and complaints came from this unproductive majority, with the exception of two large customers who were simply world-class experts of the "here is the fire I started, now you put it out" approach to business. I put all of these unproductive customers on passive mode: If they ordered, great—let them fax in the order. If not, I would do absolutely no chasing: no phone calls, no e-mail, nothing. That left the two larger customers to deal with, who were professional ball breakers but contributed about 10% to the bottom line at the time.

You'll always have a few of these, and it is a quandary that causes all sorts of problems, not the least of which are self-hatred and depression. Up to that point, I had taken their browbeating, insults, time-consuming arguments, and tirades as a cost of doing business.

I realized during the 80/20 analysis that these two people were the source of nearly all my unhappiness and anger throughout the day, and it usually spilled over into my personal time, keeping me up at night with the usual "I should have said X, Y, and Z to that penis" self-flagellation. I finally concluded the obvious: The effect on my self-esteem and state of mind just wasn't worth the financial gain. I didn't need the money for any precise reason, and I had assumed I needed to take it. The customers are always right, aren't they? Part of doing business, right? Hell, no. Not for the **NR**, anyway. I fired their asses and enjoyed every second of it. The first conversation went like this:

Customer: What the &#@$? I ordered two cases and they arrived two days late. [Note: He had sent the order to the wrong person via the wrong medium, despite repeated reminders.] You guys are the most disorganized bunch of idiots I've ever worked with. I have 20 years of experience in this industry, and this is the worst.

Any NR—in this case, me: I will kill you. Be afraid, be very afraid.

I wish. I did rehearse that a million times in my mental theater, but it actually went something more like this:

I'm sorry to hear that. You know, I've been taking your insults for a while now, and it's unfortunate that it seems we won't be able to do business anymore. I'd recommend you take a good look at where this unhappiness and anger is actually coming from. In any case, I wish you well. If you would like to order product, we'll be happy to supply it, but only if you can conduct yourself without profanity and unnecessary insults. You have our fax number. All the best and have a nice day. [Click.]

I did this once via phone and once through e-mail. So what happened? I lost one customer, but the other corrected course and simply faxed orders, again and again and again. Problem solved, minimum revenue lost. I was immediately 10 times happier.

I then identified the common characteristics of my top-five customers and secured three or so similarly profiled buyers in the following week. Remember, more customers is not automatically more income. More customers is not the goal and often translates into 90% more housekeeping and a paltry 1–3% increase in income. Make no mistake, maximum income from minimal necessary effort (including minimum number of customers) is the primary goal. I duplicated my strengths, in this case my top producers, and focused on increasing the size and frequency of their orders.

The end result? I went from chasing and appeasing 120 customers to simply receiving large orders from 8, with absolutely no pleading phone calls or e-mail haranguing. My monthly income increased from $30K to $60K in four weeks and my weekly hours immediately dropped from over 80 to approximately 15. Most important, I was happy with myself and felt both optimistic and liberated for the first time in over two years.

In the ensuing weeks, I applied the 80/20 Principle to dozens of areas, including the following:

1. Advertising

I identified the advertising that was generating 80% or more of revenue, identified the commonalities among them, and multiplied them, eliminating all the rest at the same time. My advertising costs dropped over 70% and my direct sales income nearly doubled from a monthly $15K to $25K in 8 weeks. It would have doubled immediately had I been using radio, newspapers, or television instead of magazines with long lead times.

2. Online Affiliates and Partners

I fired more than 250 low-yield online affiliates or put them in holding patterns to focus instead on the *two* affiliates who were generating 90% of the income. My management time decreased from 5–10 hours per week to 1 hour per month. Online partner income increased more than 50% in that same month.

Slow down and remember this: Most things make no difference. *Being busy is a form of laziness—lazy thinking and indiscriminate action.*

Being overwhelmed is often as unproductive as doing nothing, and is far more unpleasant. Being selective—doing less—is the path of the productive. Focus on the important few and ignore the rest.

Of course, before you can separate the wheat from the chaff and eliminate activities in a new environment (whether a new job or an entrepreneurial venture), you will need to try a lot to identify what pulls the most weight. Throw it all up on the wall and see what sticks. That's part of the process, but it should not take more than a month or two.

It's easy to get caught in a flood of minutiae, and the key to not feeling rushed is remembering that *lack of time is actually lack of priorities.* Take time to stop and smell the roses, or—in this case—to count the pea pods.

The 9–5 Illusion and Parkinson's Law

> I saw a bank that said "24-Hour Banking," but I don't have that much time. —STEVEN WRIGHT, comedian

If you're an employee, spending time on nonsense is, to some extent, not your fault. There is often no incentive to use time well unless you are paid on commission. The world has agreed to shuffle papers between 9:00 A.M. and 5:00 P.M., and since you're trapped in the office for that period of servitude, you are compelled to create activities to fill that time. Time is wasted because there is so much time available. It's understandable. Now that you have the new goal of negotiating a remote work arrangement instead of just collecting a paycheck, it's time to revisit the status quo and become effective. The best employees have the most leverage.

For the entrepreneur, the wasteful use of time is a matter of bad habit and imitation. I am no exception. Most entrepreneurs were once employees and come from the 9–5 culture. Thus they adopt the same schedule, whether or not they function at 9:00 A.M. or need 8 hours to generate their target income. This schedule is a collective social agreement and a dinosaur legacy of the results-by-volume approach. How is it possible that all the people in the world need exactly 8 hours to accomplish their work? It isn't. 9–5 is arbitrary.

You don't need 8 hours per day to become a legitimate million-aire—let alone have the means to live like one. Eight hours per week is often excessive, but I don't expect all of you to believe me just yet. I know you probably feel as I did for a long time: There just aren't enough hours in the day.

But let's consider a few things we can probably agree on.

Since we have 8 hours to fill, we fill 8 hours. If we had 15, we would fill 15. If we have an emergency and need to suddenly leave work in 2 hours but have pending deadlines, we miraculously complete those assignments in 2 hours.

It is all related to a law that was introduced to me by Ed Zschau in the spring of 2000.

I had arrived to class nervous and unable to concentrate. The final paper, worth a full 25% of the semester's grade, was due in 24 hours. One of the options, and that which I had chosen, was to interview the top executives of a start-up and provide an in-depth analysis of their business model. The corporate powers that be had decided last minute that I couldn't interview two key figures or use their information due to confidentiality issues and pre-IPO precautions. Game over.

I approached Ed after class to deliver the bad news.

"Ed, I think I'm going to need an extension on the paper." I explained the situation, and Ed smiled before he replied without so much as a hint of concern.

"I think you'll be OK. Entrepreneurs are those who make things happen, right?"

Twenty-four hours later and one minute before the deadline, as his assistant was locking the office, I handed in a 30-page final paper. It was based on a different company I had found, interviewed, and dissected with an intense all-nighter and enough caffeine to get an entire Olympic track team disqualified. It ended up being one of the best papers I'd written in four years, and I received an A.

Before I left the classroom the previous day, Ed had given me some parting advice: Parkinson's Law.

Parkinson's Law dictates that a task will swell in (perceived) importance and complexity in relation to the time allotted for its completion. It is the magic of the imminent deadline. If I give you 24 hours to complete a project, the time pressure forces you to focus on execution, and you have no choice but to do only the bare essentials. If I give you a week to complete the same task, it's six days of making a mountain out of a molehill. If I give you two months, God forbid, it becomes a mental monster. The end product of the shorter deadline is almost inevitably of equal or higher quality due to greater focus.

This presents a very curious phenomenon. There are two synergistic approaches for increasing productivity that are inversions of each other:

1. Limit tasks to the important to shorten work time (80/20).
2. Shorten work time to limit tasks to the important (Parkinson's Law).

The best solution is to use both together: Identify the few critical tasks that contribute most to income and schedule them with *very short* and clear deadlines.

If you haven't identified the mission-critical tasks and set aggressive start and end times for their completion, the unimportant becomes the important. Even if you know what's critical, without deadlines that create focus, the minor tasks forced upon you (or invented, in the case of the entrepreneur) will swell to consume time until another bit of minutiae jumps in to replace it, leaving you at the end of the day with nothing accomplished. How else could dropping off a package at UPS, setting a few appointments, and checking e-mail consume an entire 9–5 day? Don't feel bad. I spent months jumping from one interruption to the next, feeling run by my business instead of the other way around.

THE 80/20 PRINCIPLE and Parkinson's Law are the two cornerstone concepts that will be revisited in different forms throughout this entire section. Most inputs are useless and time is wasted in proportion to the amount that is available.

Fat-free performance and time freedom begins with limiting intake overload. In the next chapter, we'll put you on the real breakfast of champions: the Low-Information Diet.

A Dozen Cupcakes and One Question

Love of bustle is not industry.   —SENECA

MOUNTAIN VIEW, CALIFORNIA

"Saturdays are my days off," I offered to the crowd of strangers staring at me, friends of a friend. It was true. Can you eat All-Bran and chicken seven days a week? Me neither. Don't be so judgmental.

Between my tenth and twelfth cupcakes, I plopped down on the couch to revel in the sugar high until the clock struck midnight and sent me back to my adultsville Sunday–Friday diet. There was another party guest seated next to me on a chair, nursing a glass of wine, not his twelfth but certainly not his first, and we struck up a conversation. As usual, I had to struggle to answer "What do you do?" and, as usual, my answer left someone to wonder whether I was a pathological liar or a criminal.

How was it possible to spend so little time on income generation? It's a good question. It's THE question.

In almost all respects, Charney had it all. He was happily married with a two-year-old son and another due to arrive in three months. He was a successful technology salesman, and though he wanted to earn $500,000 more per year as all do, his finances were solid.

He also asked good questions. I had just returned from another trip overseas and was planning a new adventure to Japan. He drilled me for two hours with a refrain: How is it possible to spend so little time on income generation?

"If you're interested, we can make you a case study and I'll show you how," I offered.

Charney was in. The one thing he didn't have was time.

One e-mail and five weeks of practice later, Charney had good news: He had accomplished more in the last week than he had in the previous four combined. He did so while taking Monday and Friday off and spending at least 2 more hours per day with his family. From 40 hours per week, he was down to 18 and producing four times the results.

Was it from mountaintop retreats and secret kung fu training? Nope. Was it a new Japanese management secret or better software? Nein. I just asked him to do one simple thing consistently without fail.

At least three times per day at scheduled times, he had to ask himself the following question:

Am I being productive or just active?

Charney captured the essence of this with less-abstract wording:

Am I inventing things to do to avoid the important?

He eliminated all of the activities he used as crutches and began to focus on demonstrating results instead of showing dedication. Dedication is often just meaningless work in disguise. Be ruthless and cut the fat.

It is possible to have your cupcake and eat it, too.

►Q&A: QUESTIONS AND ACTIONS

> We create stress for ourselves because you feel like you
> have to do it. You *have* to. I don't feel that anymore.
> —OPRAH WINFREY, actress and talk-show host, *The Oprah
> Winfrey Show*

The key to having more time is doing less, and there are two paths to getting there, both of which should be used together: (1) Define a to-do list and (2) define a not-to-do list. In general terms, there are but two questions:

What 20% of sources are causing 80% of my problems and
  unhappiness?
What 20% of sources are resulting in 80% of my desired
  outcome and happiness?

Hypothetical cases help to get us started:

1. **If you had a heart attack and had to work two hours per day, what would you do?**
   Not five hours, not four hours, not three—two hours. It's not where I want you to ultimately be, but it's a start. Besides, I can hear your brain bubbling already: That's ridiculous. Impossible! I know, I know. If I told you that you could survive for months, functioning quite well, on four hours of sleep per night, would you believe me? Probably not. Notwithstanding, millions of new mothers do it all the time. This exercise is not optional. The doctor has warned you, after triple-bypass surgery, that if you don't cut down your work to two hours per day for the first three months post-op, you will die. How would you do it?

2. **If you had a second heart attack and had to work two hours per *week*, what would you do?**

3. **If you had a gun to your head and *had* to stop doing 4/5 of different time-consuming activities, what would you remove?**

Simplicity requires ruthlessness. If you had to stop ⅘ of time-consuming activities—e-mail, phone calls, conversations, paperwork, meetings, advertising, customers, suppliers, products, services, etc.—what would you eliminate to keep the negative effect on income to a minimum? Used even once per month, this question alone can keep you sane and on track.

4. **What are the top-three activities that I use to fill time to feel as though I've been productive?**
These are usually used to postpone more important actions (often uncomfortable because there is a chance of failure or rejection). Be honest with yourself, as we all do this on occasion. What are your crutch activities?

5. **Who are the 20% of people who produce 80% of your enjoyment and propel you forward, and which 20% cause 80% of your depression, anger, and second-guessing?**
Identify:

   ► Positive friends versus time-consuming friends: Who is helping versus hurting you, and how do you increase your time with the former while decreasing or eliminating your time with the latter?
   ► Who is causing me stress disproportionate to the time I spend with them? What will happen if I simply stop interacting with these people? Fear-setting helps here.
   ► When do I feel starved for time? What commitments, thoughts, and people can I eliminate to fix this problem?

Exact numbers aren't needed to realize that we spend too much time with those who poison us with pessimism, sloth, and low expectations of themselves and the world. It is often the case that you have to fire certain friends or retire from particular social circles to have the life you want. This isn't being mean; it is being practical. Poisonous people do not deserve your time. To think otherwise is masochistic.

The best way to approach a potential break is simple: Confide in them honestly but tactfully and explain your concerns. If they bite back, your conclusions have been confirmed. Drop them like any other bad habit. If they promise to change, first spend at least two weeks apart to develop other positive influences in your life and diminish psychological dependency. The next trial period should have a set duration and consist of pass-or-fail criteria.

If this approach is too confrontational for you, just politely refuse to interact with them. Be in the middle of something when the call comes, and have a prior commitment when the invitation to hang out comes. Once you see the benefits of decreased time with these people, it will be easier to stop communication altogether.

I'm not going to lie: It sucks. It hurts like pulling out a splinter. But you are the average of the five people you associate with most, so do not underestimate the effects of your pessimistic, unambitious, or disorganized friends. If someone isn't making you stronger, they're making you weaker.

Remove the splinters and you'll thank yourself for it.

6. **Learn to ask, "If this is the only thing I accomplish today, will I be satisfied with my day?"**
    Don't ever arrive at the office or in front of your computer without a clear list of priorities. You'll just read unassociated e-mail and scramble your brain for the day. Compile your to-do list for tomorrow no later than this evening. I don't recommend using Outlook or computerized to-do lists, because it is possible to add an infinite number of items. I use a standard piece of paper folded in half three times, which fits perfectly in the pocket and limits you to noting only a few items.

    There should never be more than two mission-critical items to complete each day. Never. It just isn't necessary if they're actu-

ally high-impact. If you are stuck trying to decide between multiple items that all seem crucial, as happens to all of us, look at
each in turn and ask yourself, *If this is the only thing I accomplish
today, will I be satisfied with my day?*

To counter the seemingly urgent, ask yourself: What will
happen if I don't do this, and is it worth putting off the important to do it? If you haven't already accomplished at least one
important task in the day, don't spend the last business hour returning a DVD to avoid a $5 late charge. Get the important task
done and pay the $5 fine.

7. **Put a Post-it on your computer screen or set an Outlook reminder to alert you at least three times daily with the question: Are you inventing things to do to avoid the important?**
I also use free time-tracking software called RescueTime (www
.rescuetime.com) to alert me when I spend more than an allotted
time on certain websites or programs often used to avoid the important (Gmail, Facebook, Outlook, etc.). It also summarizes
your time use each week and compares your performance to
peers.

8. **Do not multitask.**
I'm going to tell you what you already know. Trying to brush
your teeth, talk on the phone, and answer e-mail at the same time
just doesn't work. Eating while doing online research and instant messaging? Ditto.

If you prioritize properly, there is no need to multitask. It is
a symptom of "task creep"—doing more to feel productive while
actually accomplishing less. As stated, you should have, at most,
two primary goals or tasks per day. Do them separately from
start to finish without distraction. Divided attention will result
in more frequent interruptions, lapses in concentration, poorer
net results, and less gratification.

9. **Use Parkinson's Law on a Macro and Micro Level.**

   Use Parkinson's Law to accomplish more in less time. Shorten schedules and deadlines to necessitate focused action instead of deliberation and procrastination.

   On a weekly and daily macro level, attempt to take Monday and/or Friday off, as well as leave work at 4 P.M. This will focus you to prioritize more effectively and quite possibly develop a social life. If you're under the hawklike watch of a boss, we'll discuss the nuts and bolts of how to escape in later chapters.

   On a micro task level, limit the number of items on your to-do list and use impossibly short deadlines to force immediate action while ignoring minutiae.

   If doing work online or near an online computer, http://e.ggtimer.com/ is a convenient countdown timer. Just type the desired time limit directly into the URL field and hit enter. The http:// can often be omitted. For example:

   > http://e.ggtimer.com/5minutes (or just "e.ggtimer.com/5min" in some browsers)
   > http://e.ggtimer.com/1hour30minutes30seconds
   > http://e.ggtimer.com/30 (if you just put in a number, it assumes seconds)

►COMFORT CHALLENGE

Learn to Propose (2 Days)

Stop asking for opinions and start proposing solutions. Begin with the small things. If someone is going to ask, or asks, "Where should we eat?" "What movie should we watch?" "What should we do tonight?" or anything similar, do NOT reflect it back with, "Well, what do you want to . . . ?" *Offer a solution.* Stop the back-and-forth and make a decision. Practice this in both personal and professional environments. Here are a few lines that help (my favorites are the first and last):

"Can I make a suggestion?"

"I propose . . ."

"I'd like to propose . . ."

"I suggest that . . . What do you think?"

"Let's try . . . and then try something else if that doesn't work."

►LIFESTYLE DESIGN IN ACTION

I'm a musician who got your book because Derek Sivers at CD Baby recommended it. Checking Pareto's Law I realized that 78% of my downloads came from just one of my CDs and that 55% of my total download income came from only five songs! It showed me what my fans are looking for and allowed me to showcase those on my web-site. Downloads are the way to go. iTunes sells the song and CD Baby direct deposits it to my account. Fully automated once the recording is done. There are some months I can live off download income. Once I finish paying off debt, it should be no problem to travel as an artist and create new fans all over the world and have a cyber income stream.   **—VICTOR JOHNSON**

• • •

As for "outsourcing" your banking, any company that needs to take checks (cheques) should consider a lock box solution. Just about any bank that does business banking offers it. All checks go to a PO box at the bank, the bank processes the checks and deposits them, and according to your instructions can send you a file of all the checks that are deposited. Normally this can be done in either a flat, Excel or other file type that can interface with any accounting systems from Excel, to Quicken to SAP. Quite cost effective.

—ANONYMOUS

6

The Low-Information Diet

►CULTIVATING SELECTIVE IGNORANCE

What information consumes is rather obvious: it consumes the attention of its recipients. Hence, a wealth of information creates a poverty of attention and a need to allocate that attention efficiently among the overabundance of information sources that might consume it.

—HERBERT SIMON, recipient of Nobel Memorial Prize in Economics[8] and the A.M. Turing Award, the "Nobel Prize of Computer Science"

Reading, after a certain age, diverts the mind too much from its creative pursuits. Any man who reads too much and uses his own brain too little falls into lazy habits of thinking.

—ALBERT EINSTEIN

I hope you're sitting down. Take that sandwich out of your mouth so you don't choke. Cover the baby's ears. I'm going to tell you something that upsets a lot of people.

I never watch the news and have bought one single newspaper in the last five years, in Stansted Airport in London, and only because it gave me a discount on a Diet Pepsi.

I would claim to be Amish, but last time I checked, Pepsi wasn't on the menu.

---

8. Simon received the Nobel Prize in 1978 for his contribution to organizational decision making: It is impossible to have perfect and complete information at any given time to make a decision.

How obscene! I call myself an informed and responsible citizen? How do I stay up-to-date with current affairs? I'll answer all of that, but wait—it gets better. I usually check business e-mail for about an hour each Monday, and I never check voicemail when abroad. Never ever.

But what if someone has an emergency? It doesn't happen. My contacts now know that I don't respond to emergencies, so the emergencies somehow don't exist or don't come to me. Problems, as a rule, solve themselves or disappear if you remove yourself as an information bottleneck and empower others.

Cultivating Selective Ignorance

There are many things of which a wise man might wish to be ignorant.   —RALPH WALDO EMERSON (1803–1882)

From this point forward, I'm going to propose that you develop an uncanny ability to be selectively ignorant. Ignorance may be bliss, but it is also practical. It is imperative that you learn to ignore or redirect all information and interruptions that are irrelevant, unimportant, or unactionable. Most are all three.

The first step is to develop and maintain a low-information diet. Just as modern man consumes both too many calories and calories of no nutritional value, information workers eat data both in excess and from the wrong sources.

Lifestyle design is based on massive action—output. Increased output necessitates decreased input. Most information is time-consuming, negative, irrelevant to your goals, and outside of your influence. I challenge you to look at whatever you read or watched today and tell me that it wasn't at least two of the four.

I read the front-page headlines through the newspaper machines as I walk to lunch each day and nothing more. In five years, I haven't had a single problem due to this selective ignorance. It gives you something new to ask the rest of the population in lieu of small talk: "Tell me, what's new in the world?" And, if it's that important, you'll hear people talking about it. Using my crib notes approach to world affairs, I also retain more than someone who loses the forest for the trees in a sea of extraneous details.

From an actionable information standpoint, I consume a maximum of one-third of one industry magazine (*Response* magazine) and one business magazine *(Inc.)* per month, for a grand total of approximately four hours. That's it for results-oriented reading. I read an hour of fiction prior to bed for relaxation.

How on earth do I act responsibly? Let me give an example of how I and other **NR** both consider and obtain information. I voted in the last presidential election,[9] despite having been in Berlin. I made my decision in a matter of hours. First, I sent e-mails to educated friends in the U.S. who share my values and asked them who they were voting for and why. Second, I judge people based on actions and not words; thus, I asked friends in Berlin, who had more perspective outside of U.S. media propaganda, how they judged the candidates based on their historical behavior. Last, I watched the presidential debates. That was it. I let other dependable people synthesize hundreds of hours and thousands of pages of media for me. It was like having dozens of personal information assistants, and I didn't have to pay them a single cent.

That's a simple example, you say, but what if you need to learn to do something your friends haven't done? Like, say, sell a book to the world's largest publisher as a first-time author? Funny you should ask. There are two approaches I used:

1. I picked one book out of dozens based on reader reviews and the fact that the authors had actually done what I wanted to do. If the task is how-to in nature, I only read accounts that are "how

---

9. 2004 at the time this was written.

I did it" and autobiographical. No speculators or wannabes are worth the time.

2. Using the book to generate intelligent and specific questions, I contacted 10 of the top authors and agents in the world via e-mail and phone, with a response rate of 80%.

I only read the sections of the book that were relevant to immediate next steps, which took less than two hours. To develop a template e-mail and call script took approximately four hours, and the actual e-mails and phone calls took less than an hour. This personal contact approach is not only more effective and more efficient than all-you-can-eat info buffets, it also provided me with the major league alliances and mentors necessary to sell this book. Rediscover the power of the forgotten skill called "talking." It works.

Once again, less is more.

How to Read 200% Faster in 10 Minutes

There will be times when, it's true, you will have to read. Here are four simple tips that will lessen the damage and increase your speed at least 200% in 10 minutes with no comprehension loss:

1. *Two Minutes:* Use a pen or finger to trace under each line as you read as fast as possible. Reading is a series of jumping snapshots (called saccades), and using a visual guide prevents regression.

2. *Three Minutes:* Begin each line focusing on the third word in from the first word, and end each line focusing on the third word in from the last word. This makes use of peripheral vision that is otherwise wasted on margins. For example, even when the highlighted words in the next line are your beginning and ending focal points, the entire sentence is "read," just with less eye movement:

"Once upon a time, an information addict **decided** to detox."

Move in from both sides further and further as it gets easier.

3. *Two Minutes:* Once comfortable indenting three or four words from both sides, attempt to take only two snapshots—also known as fixations—per line on the first and last indented words.

4. *Three Minutes:* Practice reading too fast for comprehension but with good technique (the above three techniques) for five pages prior to reading at a comfortable speed. This will heighten perception and reset your speed limit, much like how 50 mph normally feels fast but seems like slow motion if you drop down from 70 mph on the freeway.

To calculate reading speed in words per minute (wpm)—and thus progress—in a given book, add up the number of words in ten lines and divide by ten to get the average words per line. Multiply this by the number of lines per page and you have the average words per page. Now it's simple. If you initially read 1.25 pages in one minute at 330 average words per page, that's 412.5 words per minute. If you then read 3.5 pages after training, it's 1,155 words per minute and you're in the top 1% of the world's fastest readers.

►Q&A: QUESTIONS AND ACTIONS

> Learning to ignore things is one of the great paths to inner
> peace.   —ROBERT J. SAWYER, *Calculating God*

I. **Go on an immediate one-week media fast.**

The world doesn't even hiccup, much less end, when you cut the information umbilical cord. To realize this, it's best to use the Band-Aid approach and do it quickly: a one-week media fast. Information is too much like ice cream to do otherwise. "Oh, I'll just have a half a spoonful" is about as realistic as "I just want to jump online for a minute." Go cold turkey.

If you want to go back to the 15,000-calorie potato chip information diet afterward, fine, but beginning tomorrow and for at least five full days, here are the rules:

No newspapers, magazines, audiobooks, or nonmusic radio. Music is permitted at all times.

No news websites whatsoever (cnn.com, drudgereport.com, msn.com,[10] etc.).

No television at all, except for one hour of pleasure viewing each evening.

No reading books, except for this book and one hour of *fiction*[11] pleasure reading prior to bed.

No web surfing at the desk unless it is necessary to complete a work task for *that day*. Necessary means necessary, not nice to have.

Unnecessary reading is public enemy number one during this one-week fast.

What do you do with all the extra time? Replace the newspaper at breakfast with speaking to your spouse, bonding with your children, or learning the principles in this book. Between 9–5, complete your top priorities as per the last chapter. If you complete them with time to spare, do the exercises in this book. Recommending this book might seem hypocritical, but it's not: The information in these pages is both important and to be applied now, not tomorrow or the day after.

Each day at lunch break, and no earlier, get your five-minute news fix. Ask a well-informed colleague or a restaurant waiter, "Anything important happening in the world today? I couldn't get the paper today." Stop this as soon as you realize that the answer doesn't affect your actions at all. Most people won't even remember what they spent one to two hours absorbing that morning.

---

10. LOL.

11. As someone who read exclusively nonfiction for nearly 15 years, I can tell you two things: It's not productive to read two fact-based books at the same time (this is one), and fiction is better than sleeping pills for putting the happenings of the day behind you.

Be strict with yourself. I can prescribe the medicine, but you need to take it.

Download the Firefox web browser (www.firefox.com) and use **LeechBlock** to block certain sites entirely for set periods. From their site (http://www.proginosko.com/leechblock.html):

> You can specify up to six sets of sites to block, with different times and days for each set. You can block sites within fixed time periods (e.g., between 9am and 5pm), after a time limit (e.g., 10 minutes in every hour), or with a combination of time periods and time limit (e.g., 10 minutes in every hour between 9am and 5pm). You can also set a password for access to the extension options, just to slow you down in moments of weakness!

2. **Develop the habit of asking yourself, "Will I definitely use this information for something immediate and important?"** It's not enough to use information for "something"—it needs to be immediate and important. If "no" on either count, don't consume it. Information is useless if it is not applied to something important or if you will forget it before you have a chance to apply it.

    I used to have the habit of reading a book or site to prepare for an event weeks or months in the future, and I would then need to reread the same material when the deadline for action was closer. This is stupid and redundant. Follow your to-do short list and fill in the information gaps as you go.

    Focus on what digerati Kathy Sierra calls "just-in-time" information instead of "just-in-case" information.

3. **Practice the art of nonfinishing.**
    This is another one that took me a long time to learn. Starting something doesn't automatically justify finishing it.

    If you are reading an article that sucks, put it down and don't pick it back up. If you go to a movie and it's worse than *Matrix III,* get the hell out of there before more neurons die. If you're full after half a plate of ribs, put the damn fork down and don't order dessert.

More is not better, and stopping something is often 10 times better than finishing it. Develop the habit of nonfinishing that which is boring or unproductive if a boss isn't demanding it.

►COMFORT CHALLENGE

Get Phone Numbers (2 Days)

Being sure to maintain eye contact, ask for the phone numbers of at least two (the more you attempt, the less stressful it will be) attractive members of the opposite sex on each day. Girls, this means you're in the game as well, and it doesn't matter if you're 50+. Remember that the real goal is not to get numbers, but to get over the fear of asking, so the outcome is unimportant. If you're in a relationship, sign up to (or pretend to) gather information for Greenpeace. Just toss the numbers if you get them.

Go to a mall if you want to get some rapid-fire practice—my preference for getting over the discomfort quickly—and aim to ask three people in a row within five minutes. Feel free to use some variation of the following script:

"Excuse me. I know this is going to sound strange, but if I don't ask you now, I'll be kicking myself for the rest of the day. I'm running to meet a friend [i.e., I have friends and am not a stalker], but I think you're really [extremely, drop-dead] cute [gorgeous, hot]. Could I have your phone number? I'm not a psycho—I promise. You can give me a fake one if you're not interested."

7

Interrupting Interruption and the Art of Refusal

Do your own thinking independently. Be the chess player, not the chess piece.   —RALPH CHARELL

Meetings are an addictive, highly self-indulgent activity that corporations and other organizations habitually engage in only because they cannot actually masturbate.

—DAVE BARRY, Pulitzer Prize–winning American humorist

SPRING 2000, PRINCETON, NEW JERSEY

1:35 P.M.

"I think I understand. Moving on. In the next paragraph, it explains that . . ." I had detailed notes and didn't want to miss a single point.

3:45 P.M.

"OK. That makes sense, but if we look at the following example . . ." I paused for a moment mid-sentence. The teaching assistant had both hands on his face.

"Tim, let's end here for now. I'll be sure to keep these points in mind." He had had enough. Me too, but I knew I'd only have to do it once.

For all four years of school, I had a policy. If I received anything less than an A on the first paper or non-multiple-choice test in a given class, I would bring 2–3 hours of questions to the grader's office hours and not leave until the other had answered them all or stopped out of exhaustion.

This served two important purposes:

1. I learned exactly how the grader evaluated work, including his or her prejudices and pet peeves.
2. The grader would think long and hard about ever giving me less than an A. He or she would never consider giving me a bad grade without exceptional reasons for doing so, as he or she knew I'd come a'knocking for another three-hour visit.

Learn to be difficult when it counts. In school as in life, having a reputation for being assertive will help you receive preferential treatment without having to beg or fight for it every time.

Think back to your days on the playground. There was always a big bully and countless victims, but there was also that one small kid who fought like hell, thrashing and swinging for the fences. He or she might not have won, but after one or two exhausting exchanges, the bully chose not to bother him or her. It was easier to find someone else.

Be that kid.

Doing the important and ignoring the trivial is hard because so much of the world seems to conspire to force crap upon you. Fortunately, a few simple routine changes make bothering you much more painful than leaving you in peace.

It's time to stop taking information abuse.

Not All Evils Are Created Equal

For our purposes, an interruption is anything that prevents the start-to-finish completion of a critical task, and there are three principal offenders:

1. **Time wasters:** those things that can be ignored with little or no consequence. Common time wasters include meetings, discussions, phone calls, web surfing, and e-mail that are *unimportant.*

2. **Time consumers:** repetitive tasks or requests that need to be completed but often interrupt high-level work. Here are a few you might know intimately: reading and responding to e-mail, making and returning phone calls, customer service (order status, product assistance, etc.), financial or sales reporting, personal errands, all necessary repeated actions and tasks.

3. **Empowerment failures:** instances where someone needs approval to make something small happen. Here are just a few: fixing customer problems (lost shipments, damaged shipments, malfunctions, etc.), customer contact, cash expenditures of all types.

Let's look at the prescriptions for all three in turn.

Time Wasters: Become an Ignoramus

The best defense is a good offense.
—DAN GABLE, Olympic gold medalist in wrestling and the most successful coach in history; personal record: 299–6–3, with 182 pins

Time wasters are the easiest to eliminate and deflect. It is a matter of limiting access and funneling all communication toward immediate action.

First, limit e-mail consumption and production. This is the greatest single interruption in the modern world.

1. Turn off the audible alert if you have one on Outlook or a similar program and turn off automatic send/receive, which delivers e-mail to your inbox as soon as someone sends them.

2. Check e-mail twice per day, once at 12:00 noon or just prior to lunch, and again at 4:00 P.M. 12:00 P.M. and 4:00 P.M. are times that ensure you will have the most responses from previously sent e-mail. Never check e-mail first thing in the morning.[12] Instead, complete your most important task before 11:00 A.M. to avoid using lunch or reading e-mail as a postponement excuse.

Before scheduled e-mail/phone   After scheduled e-mail/phone

LIGHT GRAY INDICATES TIME AVAILABLE FOR HIGH-PRIORITY TASKS.

Courtesy of SANDIA

Before implementing the twice-daily routine, you must create an e-mail autoresponse that will train your boss, co-workers, suppliers, and clients to be more effective. I would recommend that you do not ask to implement this. Remember one of our ten commandments: Beg for forgiveness; don't ask for permission.

If this gives you heart palpitations, speak with your immediate supervisor and propose to trial the approach for one to three days.

---

12. This habit alone can change your life. It seems small but has an enormous effect.

Cite pending projects and frustration with constant interruptions as the reasons. Feel free to blame it on spam or someone outside of the office.

Here is a simple e-mail template that can be used:

> Greetings, Friends [or Esteemed Colleagues],
>
> Due to high workload, I am currently checking and responding to e-mail twice daily at 12:00 P.M. ET [or your time zone] and 4:00 P.M. ET.
>
> If you require urgent assistance (please ensure it is urgent) that cannot wait until either 12:00 P.M. or 4:00 P.M., please contact me via phone at 555-555-5555.
>
> Thank you for understanding this move to more efficiency and effectiveness. It helps me accomplish more to serve you better.
>
> Sincerely,
>
> Tim Ferriss

MOVE TO ONCE-PER-DAY as quickly as possible. Emergencies are seldom that. People are poor judges of importance and inflate minutiae to fill time and feel important. This autoresponse is a tool that, far from decreasing collective effectiveness, forces people to re-evaluate their reason for interrupting you and helps them decrease meaningless and time-consuming contact.

I was initially terrified of missing important requests and inviting disaster, just as you might be upon reading this recommendation. Nothing happened. Give it a shot and work out the small bumps as you progress.

For an extreme example of a personal autoresponder that has never prompted a complaint and allowed me to check e-mail once per week, send an e-mail to template@fourhourworkweek.com. It has been revised over three years and works like a charm.

The second step is to screen incoming and limit outgoing phone calls.

1. Use two telephone numbers if possible—one office line (non-urgent) and one cellular (urgent). This could also be two cell phones, or the non-urgent line could be an Internet phone number that routes calls to online voicemail (www.skype.com, for example).

Use the cell number in the e-mail autoresponse and answer it at all times unless it is an unknown caller or it is a call you don't want to answer. If in doubt, allow the call to go to voicemail and listen to the voicemail immediately afterward to gauge importance. If it can wait, let it wait. The offending parties have to learn to wait.

The office phone should be put on silent mode and allowed to go to voicemail at all times. The voicemail recording should sound familiar:

> You've reached the desk of Tim Ferriss.
> I am currently checking and responding to voicemail twice daily at 12:00 P.M. ET [or your time zone] and 4:00 P.M. ET.
> If you require assistance with a truly urgent matter that cannot wait until either 12:00 P.M. or 4:00 P.M., please contact me on my cell at 555-555-5555. Otherwise, please leave a message and I will return it at the next of those two times. Be sure to leave your e-mail address, as I am often able to respond faster that way.
> Thank you for understanding this move to more efficiency and effectiveness. It helps me accomplish more to serve you better.
> Have a wonderful day.

2. If someone does call your cell phone, it is presumably urgent and should be treated as such. Do not allow them to consume time otherwise. It's all in the greeting. Compare the following:

Jane (receiver): Hello?
John (caller): Hi, is this Jane?
Jane: This is Jane.
John: Hi, Jane, it's John.

> **Jane:** Oh, hi, John. How are you? (or) Oh, hi, John. What's
> going on?

John will now digress and lead you into a conversation about nothing, from which you will have to recover and then fish out the ultimate purpose of the call. There is a better approach:

> **Jane:** This is Jane speaking.
> **John:** Hi, it's John.
> **Jane:** Hi, John. I'm right in the middle of something. How
> can I help you out?

Potential continuation:

> **John:** Oh, I can call back.
> **Jane:** No, I have a minute. What can I do for you?

Don't encourage people to chitchat and don't let them chitchat. Get them to the point immediately. If they meander or try to postpone for a later undefined call, reel them in and get them to come to the point. If they go into a long description of a problem, cut in with, "[Name], sorry to interrupt, but I have a call in five minutes. What can I do to help out?" You might instead say, "[Name], sorry to interrupt, but I have a call in five minutes. Can you send me an e-mail?"

The third step is to master the art of refusal and avoiding meetings.

THE FIRST DAY our new Sales VP arrived at TrueSAN in 2001, he came into the all-company meeting and made an announcement in just about this many words: "I am not here to make friends. I have been hired to build a sales team and sell product, and that's what I intend to do. Thanks." So much for small talk.

He proceeded to deliver on his promise. The office socializers disliked him for his no-nonsense approach to communication, but everyone respected his time. He wasn't rude without reason, but he was direct and kept the people around him focused. Some didn't consider him charismatic, but no one considered him anything less than spectacularly effective.

I remember sitting down in his office for our first one-on-one meeting. Fresh off four years of rigorous academic training, I immediately jumped into explaining the prospect profiles, elaborate planning I'd developed, responses to date, and so forth and so on. I had spent at least two hours preparing to make this first impression a good one. He listened with a smile on his face for no more than two minutes and then held up a hand. I stopped. He laughed in a kind-hearted manner and said, "Tim, I don't want the story. Just tell me what we need to do."

Over the following weeks, he trained me to recognize when I was unfocused or focused on the wrong things, which meant anything that didn't move the top two or three clients one step closer to signing a purchase order. Our meetings were now no more than five minutes long.

From this moment forward, resolve to keep those around you focused and avoid all meetings, whether in person or remote, that do not have clear objectives. It is possible to do this tactfully, but expect that some time wasters will be offended the first few times their advances are rejected. Once it is clear that remaining on task is your policy and not subject to change, they will accept it and move on with life. Hard feelings pass. Don't suffer fools or you'll become one.

It is your job to train those around you to be effective and efficient. No one else will do it for you. Here are a few recommendations:

1. Decide that, given the non-urgent nature of most issues, you will steer people toward the following means of communication, in order of preference: e-mail, phone, and in-person meetings. If

someone proposes a meeting, request an e-mail instead and then use the phone as your fallback offer if need be. Cite other immediately pending work tasks as the reason.

2. Respond to voicemail via e-mail whenever possible. This trains people to be concise. Help them develop the habit.

Similar to our opening greeting on the phone, e-mail communication should be streamlined to prevent needless back-and-forth. Thus, an e-mail with "Can you meet at 4:00 P.M.?" would become "Can you meet at 4:00 P.M.? If so. . . . If not, please advise three other times that work for you."

This "if . . . then" structure becomes more important as you check e-mail less often. Since I only check e-mail once a week, it is critical that no one needs a "what if?" answered or other information within seven days of a given e-mail I send. If I suspect that a manufacturing order hasn't arrived at the shipping facility, for example, I'll send an e-mail to my shipping facility manager along these lines: "Dear Susan . . . Has the new manufacturing shipment arrived? If so, please advise me on . . . If not, please contact John Doe at 555-5555 or via e-mail at john@doe.com (he is also CC'd) and advise on delivery date and tracking. John, if there are any issues with the shipment, please coordinate with Susan, reachable at 555-4444, who has the authority to make decisions up to $500 on my behalf. In case of emergency, call me on my cell phone, but I trust you two. Thanks." This prevents most follow-up questions, avoids two separate dialogues, and takes me out of the problem-solving equation.

Get into the habit of considering what "if . . . then" actions can be proposed in any e-mail where you ask a question.

3. Meetings should only be held to make decisions about a predefined situation, not to define the problem. If someone proposes that you meet with them or "set a time to talk on the phone," ask that person to send you an e-mail with an agenda to define the purpose:

> That sounds doable. So I can best prepare, can you please send me an e-mail with an agenda? That is, the topics and questions we'll need to address? That would be great. Thanks in advance.

Don't give them a chance to bail out. The "thanks in advance" before a retort increases your chances of getting the e-mail.

The e-mail medium forces people to define the desired outcome of a meeting or call. Nine times out of ten, a meeting is unnecessary and you can answer the questions, once defined, via e-mail. Impose this habit on others. I haven't had an in-person meeting for my business in more than five years and have had fewer than a dozen conference calls, all lasting less than 30 minutes.

4. Speaking of 30 minutes, if you absolutely cannot stop a meeting or call from happening, *define the end time.* Do not leave these discussions open-ended, and keep them short. If things are well-defined, decisions should not take more than 30 minutes. Cite other commitments at odd times to make them more believable (e.g., 3:20 vs. 3:30) and force people to focus instead of socializing, commiserating, and digressing. If you must join a meeting that is scheduled to last a long time or that is open-ended, inform the organizer that you would like permission to cover your portion first, as you have a commitment in 15 minutes. If you have to, feign an urgent phone call. Get the hell out of there and have someone else update you later. The other option is to be completely transparent and voice your opinion of how unnecessary the meeting is. If you choose this route, be prepared to face fire and offer alternatives.

5. The cubicle is your temple—don't permit casual visitors. Some suggest using a clear "DO NOT DISTURB" sign of some type, but I have found that this is ignored unless you have an office. My approach was to put headphones on, even if I wasn't listening to anything. If someone approached me despite this discouragement, I would pretend to be on the phone. I'd put a finger to my lips, say something like, "I hear you," and then say into the mic, "Can you hold on a second?" Next, I'd turn to the invader and say, "Hi. What can I do for you?" I wouldn't let them "get back to me" but rather force the person to give me a five-second summary and then send me an e-mail if necessary.

If headphone games aren't your thing, the reflexive response to an invader should be the same as when answering the cell phone: "Hi, invader. I'm right in the middle of something. How can I be of help?" If it's not clear within 30 seconds, ask the person to send you an e-mail about the chosen issue; do not offer to send them an e-mail first: "I'll be happy to help, but I have to finish this first. Can you send me a quick e-mail to remind me?" If you still cannot deflect an invader, give the person a time limit on your availability, which can also be used for phone conversations: "OK, I only have two minutes before a call, but what's the situation and what can I do to help?"

6. Use the Puppy Dog Close to help your superiors and others develop the no-meeting habit. The Puppy Dog Close in sales is so named because it is based on the pet store sales approach: If someone likes a puppy but is hesitant to make the life-altering purchase, just offer to let them take the pup home and bring it back if they change their minds. Of course, the return seldom happens.

The Puppy Dog Close is invaluable whenever you face resistance to permanent changes. Get your foot in the door with a "let's just try it once" reversible trial.

Compare the following:

"I think you'd love this puppy. It will forever add to your responsibilities until he dies 10 years from now. No more care-free vacations, and you'll finally get to pick up poop all over the city—what do you think?"

vs.

"I think you'd love this puppy. Why don't you just take him home and see what you think? You can just bring him back if you change your mind."

Now imagine walking up to your boss in the hallway and clapping a hand on her shoulder:

"I'd like to go to the meeting, but I have a better idea. Let's never have another one, since all we do is waste time and not decide anything useful."

vs.

"I'd really like to go to the meeting, but I'm totally overwhelmed and really need to get a few important things done. Can I sit out just for today? I'd be distracted in the meeting otherwise. I promise I'll catch up afterward by reviewing the meeting with Colleague X. Is that OK?"

The second set of alternatives seem less permanent, and they're intended to appear so. Repeat this routine and ensure that you achieve more outside of the meeting than the attendees do within it; repeat the disappearing act as often as possible and cite improved productivity to convert this slowly into a permanent routine change.

Learn to imitate any good child: "Just this once! Please!!! I promise I'll do X!" Parents fall for it because kids help adults to fool themselves. It works with bosses, suppliers, customers, and the rest of the world, too.

Use it, but don't fall for it. If a boss asks for overtime "just this once," he or she will expect it in the future.

Time Consumers: Batch and Do Not Falter

A schedule defends from chaos and whim.
—ANNIE DILLARD, winner of Pulitzer Prize in
nonfiction, 1975

If you have never used a commercial printer before, the pricing and lead times could surprise you.

Let's assume it costs $310 and takes one week to print 20 customized T-shirts with 4-color logos. How much and how long does it take to print 3 of the same T-shirt?

$310 and one week.

How is that possible? Simple—the setup charges don't change. It costs the printer the same amount in materials for plate preparation ($150) and the same in labor to man the press itself ($100). The setup is the real time-consumer, and thus the job, despite its small size, needs to be scheduled just like the other, resulting in the same one-week delivery date. The lower economy of scale picks up the rest: The cost for 3 shirts is $20 per shirt × 3 shirts instead of $3 per shirt × 20 shirts.

The cost- and time-effective solution, therefore, is to wait until you have a larger order, an approach called "batching." Batching is also the solution to our distracting but necessary **time consumers**, those repetitive tasks that interrupt the most important.

If you check mail and make bill payments five times a week, it might take 30 minutes per instance and you respond to a total of 20 letters in two and a half hours. If you do this once per week instead, it might take 60 minutes total and you still respond to a total of 20 letters. People do the former out of fear of emergencies. First, there are seldom real emergencies. Second, of the urgent communication you will receive, missing a deadline is usually reversible and otherwise costs a minimum to correct.

There is an inescapable setup time for all tasks, large or minuscule in scale. It is often the same for one as it is for a hundred. There is a psychological switching of gears that can require up to 45 minutes to resume a major task that has been interrupted. More than a quarter of each 9–5 period (28%) is consumed by such interruptions.[13]

This is true of all recurring tasks and is precisely why we have already decided to check e-mail and phone calls twice per day at *specific predetermined times* (between which we let them accumulate).

From mid-2004 to 2007, I checked mail no more than once a week, often not for up to four weeks at a time. Nothing was irreparable, and nothing cost more than $300 to fix. This batching has saved me hundreds of hours of redundant work. How much is your time worth?

Let's use a hypothetical example:

1. $20 per hour is how much you are paid or value your time. This would be the case, for example, if you are paid $40,000 per year and get two weeks of vacation per year ($40,000 divided by [40 hours per week × 50 = 2,000] = $20/hour). Estimate your hourly income by cutting the last three zeroes off of your annual income and halving the remaining number (e.g., $50,000/year → $25/hour.

2. Estimate the amount of time you will save by grouping similar tasks together and batching them, and calculate how much you have earned by multiplying this hour number by your per-hour rate ($20 here):

1 × per week:	10 hours = $200
1 × per two weeks:	20 hours = $400
1 × per month:	40 hours = $800

---

13. Jonathan B. Spira and Joshua B. Feintuch, *The Cost of Not Paying Attention: How Interruptions Impact Knowledge Worker Productivity* (Basex, 2005).

3. Test each of the above batching frequencies and determine how much problems cost to fix in each period. If the cost is less than the above dollar amounts, batch even further apart.

For example, using our above math, if I check e-mail once per week and that results in an average loss of two sales per week, totaling $80 in lost profit, I will continue checking once per week because $200 (10 hours of time) minus $80 is still a $120 net gain, not to mention the enormous benefits of completing other main tasks in those 10 hours. If you calculate the financial and emotional benefit of completing just one main task (such as landing a major client or completing a life-changing trip), the value of batching is much more than the per-hour savings.

If the problems cost more than hours saved, scale back to the next-less-frequent batch schedule. In this case, I would drop from once per week to twice per week (not daily) and attempt to fix the system so that I can return to once per week. Do not work harder when the solution is working smarter. I have batched both personal and business tasks further and further apart as I've realized just how few real problems come up. Some of my scheduled batches in 2007 were e-mail (Mondays 10:00 A.M.), phone (completely eliminated), laundry (every other Sunday at 10:00 P.M.), credit cards and bills (most are on automatic payment, but I check balances every second Monday after e-mail), strength training (every 4th day for 30 minutes), etc.

Empowerment Failure: Rules and Readjustment

> The vision is really about empowering workers, giving them all the information about what's going on so they can do a lot more than they've done in the past.
> —BILL GATES, cofounder of Microsoft, richest man in the world

Empowerment failure refers to being unable to accomplish a task without first obtaining permission or information. It is often a case of being micromanaged or micromanaging someone else, both of which consume *your* time.

For the employee, the goal is to have full access to necessary information and as much independent decision-making ability as possible. For the entrepreneur, the goal is to grant as much information and independent decision-making ability to employees or contractors as possible.

Customer service is often the epitome of empowerment failure, and a personal example from BrainQUICKEN illustrates just how serious but easily solved the problem can be.

In 2002, I had outsourced customer service for order tracking and returns but still handled product-related questions myself. The result? I received more than 200 e-mail per day, spending all hours between 9–5 responding to them, and the volume was growing at a rate of more than 10% per week! I had to cancel advertising and limit shipments, as additional customer service would have been the final nail in the coffin. It wasn't a *scalable* model. Remember this word, as it will be important later. It wasn't scalable because there was an information and decision bottleneck: me.

The clincher? The bulk of the e-mail that landed in my inbox was not product-related at all but requests from the outsourced customer service reps seeking permission for different actions:

The customer claims he didn't receive the shipment. What should we do?

The customer had a bottle held at customs. Can we reship to a U.S. address?

The customer needs the product for a competition in two days. Can we ship overnight, and if so, how much should we charge?

It was endless. Hundreds upon hundreds of different situations made it impractical to write a manual, and I didn't have the time or experience to do so regardless.

Fortunately, someone did have the experience: the outsourced reps themselves. I sent one single e-mail to all the supervisors that immediately turned 200 e-mail per day into fewer than 20 e-mail per week:

> Hi All,
>
> I would like to establish a new policy for my account that overrides all others.
>
> Keep the customer happy. If it is a problem that takes less than $100 to fix, use your judgment and fix it yourself.
>
> This is official written permission and a request to fix all problems that cost under $100 without contacting me. I am no longer your customer; my customers are your customer. Don't ask me for permission. Do what you think is right, and we'll make adjustments as we go along.
>
> Thank you,
> Tim

Upon close analysis, it became clear that more than 90% of the issues that prompted e-mail could be resolved for less than $20. I reviewed the financial results of their independent decision-making on a weekly basis for four weeks, then a monthly basis, and then on a quarterly basis.

It's amazing how someone's IQ seems to double as soon as you give them responsibility and indicate that you trust them. The first month cost perhaps $200 more than if I had been micromanaging. In the meantime, I saved more than 100 hours of my own time per month, customers received faster service, returns dropped to less than 3% (the industry average is 10–15%), and outsourcers spent less time on my account, all of which resulted in rapid growth, higher profit margins, and happier people on all sides.

People are smarter than you think. Give them a chance to prove themselves.

If you are a micromanaged employee, have a heart-to-heart with your boss and explain that you want to be more productive and interrupt him or her less. "I hate that I have to interrupt you so much and pull you away from more important things I know you have on your plate. I was doing some reading and had some thoughts on how I might be more productive. Do you have a second?"

Before this conversation, develop a number of "rules" like the previous example that would allow you to work more autonomously with less approval-seeking. The boss can review the outcome of your decisions on a daily or weekly basis in the initial stages. Suggest a one-week trial and end with "I'd like to try it. Does that sound like something we could try for a week?" or my personal favorite, "Is that reasonable?" It's hard for people to label things unreasonable.

Realize that bosses are supervisors, not slave masters. Establish yourself as a consistent challenger of the status quo and most people will learn to avoid challenging you, particularly if it is in the interest of higher per-hour productivity.

If you are a micromanaging entrepreneur, realize that even if you can do something better than the rest of the world, it doesn't mean that's what you should be doing if it's part of the minutiae. Empower others to act without interrupting you.

SET THE RULES in your favor: Limit access to your time, force people to define their requests before spending time with them, and batch routine menial tasks to prevent postponement of more important projects. Do not let people interrupt you. Find your focus and you'll find your lifestyle.

The bottom line is that you only have the rights you fight for.

In the next section, **Automation**, we'll see how the New Rich create management-free money and eliminate the largest remaining obstacle of all: themselves.

►Q&A: QUESTIONS AND ACTIONS

> People think it must be fun to be a super genius, but they
> don't realize how hard it is to put up with all the idiots in
> the world.   —CALVIN, from Calvin and Hobbes

Blaming idiots for interruptions is like blaming clowns for scaring children—they can't help it. It's their nature. Then again, I had (who am I kidding—and have), on occasion, been known to create interruptions out of thin air. If you're anything like me, that makes us both occasional idiots. Learn to recognize and fight the interruption impulse.

This is infinitely easier when you have a set of rules, responses, and routines to follow. It is your job to prevent yourself and others from letting the unnecessary and unimportant prevent the start-to-finish completion of the important.

This chapter differs from the previous in that the necessary actions, due to the inclusion of examples and templates, have been presented throughout from start to finish. This Q & A will thus be a summary rather than a repetition. The devil is in the details, so be sure to reread this chapter for the specifics.

The 50,000-foot review is as follows:

1. **Create systems to limit your availability via e-mail and phone and deflect inappropriate contact.**
   Get the autoresponse and voicemail script in place now, and master the various methods of evasion. Replace the habit of "How are you?" with "How can I help you?" Get specific and remember—no stories. Focus on immediate actions. Set and practice interruption-killing policies.

   Avoid meetings whenever possible:

   ►Use e-mail instead of face-to-face meetings to solve problems.

►Beg-off going (this can be accomplished through the Puppy Dog Close).

If meetings are unavoidable, keep the following in mind:

►Go in with a clear set of objectives.
►Set an end time or leave early.

2. **Batch activities to limit setup cost and provide more time for dreamline milestones.**
   What can I routinize by batching? That is, what tasks (whether laundry, groceries, mail, payments, or sales reporting, for example) can I allot to a specific time each day, week, month, quarter, or year so that I don't squander time repeating them more often than is absolutely necessary?

3. **Set or request autonomous rules and guidelines with occasional review of results.**
   Eliminate the decision bottleneck for all things that are nonfatal if misperformed. If an employee, believe in yourself enough to ask for more independence on a trial basis. Have practical "rules" prepared and ask the boss for the sale after surprising him or her with an impromptu presentation. Remember the Puppy Dog Close—make it a one-time trial and reversible.

   For the entrepreneur or manager, give others the chance to prove themselves. The likelihood of irreversible or expensive problems is minimal and the time savings are guaranteed. Remember, profit is only profitable to the extent that you can use it. For that you need time.

►TOOLS AND TRICKS

Eliminating Paper Distractions, Capturing Everything

►Evernote (www.fourhourblog.com/evernote)
This is perhaps the most impressive tool I've found in the last year,

introduced to me by some of the most productive technologists in the world. Evernote has eliminated more than 90% of the paper in my life and eliminated nearly all of the multiple tabs I used to leave open in web browsers, both of which distracted me to no end. It can clear out your entire office clutter in one to three hours.

Evernote allows you to easily capture information from anywhere using whatever device is at hand, and everything is then searchable (read: findable) from anywhere. I use it to:

- ►Take photographs of everything I might want to remember or find later—business cards, handwritten notes, wine labels, receipts, whiteboard sessions, and more. Evernote identifies the text in all of these pictures automatically, so it's all searchable(!), whether from an iPhone, your laptop, or the web. Just as one example, I can store and find the contact information from any business card in seconds (often using the built in iSight camera on Mac to capture it), rather than spending hours inputting it all into contacts or searching through e-mail for that lost phone number. It's mind-numbing how much time this saves.
- ►Scan all agreements, paper articles, etc., that would otherwise sit in file folders or on my desk. I use the Mac Fujitsu ScanSnap miniscanner (http://bit.ly/scansnapmac), the best I've found, which scans all of it directly to Evernote in seconds with one button.
- ►Take snapshots of websites, capturing all text and links, so that I can read them offline when traveling or doing later research. Get rid of all those scattered bookmarks, favorites, and open tabs.

Screening and Avoiding Unwanted Calls

- ►GrandCentral (www.grandcentral.com) and
  YouMail (www.youmail.com)

In a world where your physical address will change more often than your cell phone number (and e-mail), it can be disastrous if your number becomes public or gets in the wrong hands. Enter GrandCentral, which will give you a number with the area code of your choosing that then forwards to your own phone(s). I now give a GrandCentral number to anyone besides family and close friends. Some of the benefits:

►Identify any incoming number as unwanted, and that caller will then hear a "number not in service" message when attempting to call you.

►Customize your voicemail message to individual callers (spouse, boss, colleague, client, etc.) and listen in on messages as they're being left, so you can "pick up" if the message is worth the interruption. Call recording is also an option.

►Use an area code outside of your hometown to prevent people and companies from finding and misusing addresses you'd prefer to keep private.

►Establish do-not-disturb hours, when calls are routed directly to voicemail with no ring.

►Have voicemail sent to your cell phone as SMS (text messages).

YouMail, another option, can also transcribe voicemails and send them to your phone as text messages. Getting calls while stuck in a time-wasting meeting? No problem: Respond to voicemails via SMS during the meeting so you're not stuck returning calls afterward.

One Shot, One Kill Scheduling Without E-mail Back-and-Forth

Few things are as time-consuming as scheduling via e-mail. Person A: "How about Tues. at 3 P.M.?" Person B: "I can make it." Person C: "I have a meeting. How about Thurs.?" Person D: "I'm on a con-call. How about 10 A.M. on Fri.?" Use these tools to make scheduling simple and fast instead of another part-time job.

►Doodle (www.doodle.com)

The best free tool I've found for herding cats (multiple people) for scheduling without excessive e-mail. Create and poll in 30 seconds with the proposed options and forward a link to everyone invited. Check back a few hours later and you'll have the best time for the most people.

►TimeDriver (www.timedriver.com)

Let colleagues and clients self-schedule with you based on your availability, which is determined by integration with Outlook or Google Calendar. Embed a "schedule now" button in e-mail messages and you'll never have to tell people when you can make a call or meeting. Let them see what's open and choose.

Choosing the Best E-mail Batching Times

►Xobni (www.xobni.com/special)

Xobni—*inbox* spelled backwards—is a free program for putting Outlook on steroids. It offers many features, but the most relevant to this chapter is its ability to identify "hotspots," or periods of time when you receive the bulk of e-mail from your most important contacts. These "hotspots" are batching times that will enable you to keep critical contacts (clients, bosses, etc.) smiling even while you reduce checking e-mail to 1–3 times per day. It will also populate your contacts automatically by pulling phone numbers, addresses, etc., from separate e-mail buried in the inbox.

E-mailing Without Entering the Black Hole of the Inbox

Don't enter the black hole of the inbox off hours because you're afraid you'll forget something. Use these services instead to keep focused, whether on completing a critical project or simply enjoying the weekend.

►Jott (www.jott.com)

Capture thoughts, create to-do's, and set reminders with a simple toll-free phone call. The service transcribes your message (15–30 seconds) and e-mails it to whomever you want, including yourself, or to your Google calendar for automatic scheduling. Jott also enables you to post voice message links to Twitter (www.twitter.com), Facebook (www.facebook.com), and other services that tend to consume hours if you visit the sites themselves.

►Copytalk (www.copytalk.com)

Dictate any message up to four minutes and have the transcription e-mailed to you within hours. Excellent for brainstorming, and the accuracy is astounding.

Preventing Web Browsing Completely

►Freedom (http://www.ibiblio.org/fred/freedom/)

Freedom is a free application that disables networking on an Apple computer for 1–480 mintues (up to eight hours) at a time. Freedom will free you from the distractions of the Internet, allowing you the focus to get real work done.

Freedom enforces freedom; a reboot is the only method for turning

Freedom off before the time limit you've set for yourself. The hassle of re-booting means you're less likely to cheat, and you'll be more productive. Experiment with the software for short periods of time at first (30–60 minutes.)

►COMFORT CHALLENGE

Revisit the Terrible Twos (2 Days)

For the next two days, do as all good two-year-olds do and say "no" to all requests. Don't be selective. Refuse to do all things that won't get you immediately fired. Be selfish. As with the last exercise, the objective isn't an outcome—in this case, eliminating just those things that waste time—but the process: getting comfortable with saying "no." Potential questions to decline include the following:

Do you have a minute?
Want to see a movie tonight/tomorrow?
Can you help me with X?

"No" should be your default answer to all requests. Don't make up elaborate lies or you'll get called on them. A simple "I really can't—sorry; I've got too much on my plate right now" will do as a catch-all response.

►LIFESTYLE DESIGN IN ACTION

Batching tool—PO Box: This might be stating the obvious, but one easy way to encourage batching of your mail is to use a PO Box versus getting mail delivered to your house. We got our PO Box to limit access to our physical address online, but it also encourages you to get the mail less and deal with it in batch. Our post office has recycling bins, so at least 60% of the mail doesn't even come home with us. For a while I was only getting and managing the mail once a week, and I found not only did it take less time overall, I did a better job managing it and getting it out of the way versus looking at it and setting it aside for future follow up.   —*LAURA TURNER*

• • •

For families, the four-hour workweek doesn't have to mean four months on a sailboat in the Caribbean unless that's their dream, but even the simple ideal of having time to take a walk in the park every evening or spending weekends together, makes taking actions to implement this program worthwhile.

[There are many different approaches for making this work]: Kids have to promise they won't bother Mommy in the evening while she works on the computer, the husband watches the kids in the evening, both parents make plans once a week to have someone take care of the kids, etc. Then close with the huge payoff for the family of having more time to spend with each other.   **—ADRIENNE JENKINS**

• • •

Why not combine a mini-retirement with dentistry (or medical) geoarbitrage and finance your trip with the savings? I lived in Thailand for four months and got root canal treatment and a crown for $1/3$ of the price that it costs in Australia. There are many upmarket clinics set up for "expats" and health travelers in Thailand, Philippines, Vietnam, Goa, etc., with English-speaking dentists. And in Europe many people go to Poland or Hungary. To research, just Google "dentist" and the country and you will come across practices advertising to foreigners. Talk to expats when you're in the country or on online chat forums for recommendations. Now I'm in Australia I still combine my travels with annual dentist checkups—and the savings often finance my airfare. Even between developed countries there are significant cost differences. For example France is far cheaper than the UK and Australia is cheaper than the U.S. [Note from Tim: Learn more about the incredible world of medical tourism and geoarbitrage at http://en.wikipedia.org/wiki/Medical_tourism. Even large insurers like AETNA often cover overseas treatments and surgeries.]   **—ANONYMOUS**

Step III:

A is for Automation

SCOTTY: She's all yours, sir. All systems automated and ready. A chimpanzee and two trainees could run her!

CAPTAIN KIRK: Thank you, Mr. Scott. I'll try not to take that personally.

—*STAR TREK*

8

Outsourcing Life

►OFF-LOADING THE REST AND A TASTE OF GEOARBITRAGE[14]

A man is rich in proportion to the number of things he can afford to let alone.   —HENRY DAVID THOREAU, naturalist

If I told you this story, you wouldn't believe me, so I'll let AJ tell it. It will set the stage for even more incredible things to come, all of which you will do yourself.

My Outsourced Life

A true account by AJ Jacobs, editor-at-large at *Esquire* magazine (ellipses represent passage of time between entries)

IT BEGAN a month ago. I was midway through *The World Is Flat,* the bestseller by Tom Friedman. I like Friedman, despite his puzzling decision to wear a mustache. His book is all about how outsourcing to India and China is not just for tech support and carmakers but is poised to transform every industry in America, from law to banking to accounting.

I don't have a corporation; I don't even have an up-to-date business card. I'm a writer and editor working from home, usually in my boxer shorts or, if I'm feeling formal, my penguin-themed pajama bottoms.

---

14. To leverage global pricing and currency differences for profit or lifestyle purposes.

Then again, I think, why should Fortune 500 firms have all the fun? Why can't I join in on the biggest business trend of the new century? Why can't I outsource my low-end tasks? Why can't I outsource my life?

The next day I e-mail Brickwork, one of the companies Friedman mentions in his book. Brickwork—based in Bangalore, India—offers "remote executive assistants," mostly to financial firms and health-care companies that want data processed. I explain that I'd like to hire someone to help with *Esquire*-related tasks—doing research, format-ting memos, like that. The company's CEO, Vivek Kulkarni, responds, "It would be a great pleasure to be talking to a person of your stature." Already I'm liking this. I've never had stature before. In America, I barely command respect from a Bennigan's maître d', so it's nice to know that in India I have stature.

A couple of days later, I get an e-mail from my new "remote execu-tive assistant."

> Dear Jacobs,
>   My name is Honey K. Balani. I would be assisting you in your editorial and personal job. . . . I would try to adapt myself as per your requirements that would lead to desired satisfaction.

Desired satisfaction. This is great. Back when I worked at an office, I had assistants, but there was never any talk of *desired satisfaction*. In fact, if anyone ever used the phrase "desired satisfaction," we'd all end up in a solemn meeting with HR.

• • •

I GO OUT to dinner with my friend Misha, who grew up in India, founded a software firm, and subsequently became nauseatingly rich. I tell him about Operation Outsource. "You should call Your Man in India," he says. Misha explains that this is a company for Indian businessmen who have moved overseas but who still have parents back in New Delhi or

Mumbai. YMII is their overseas concierge service—it buys movie tickets and cell phones and other sundries for abandoned moms.

Perfect. This could kick my outsourcing up to a new level. I can have a nice, clean division of labor: Honey will take care of my business affairs, and YMII can attend to my personal life—pay my bills, make vacation reservations, buy stuff online. Happily, YMII likes the idea, and just like that the support team at Jacobs Inc. has doubled.

• • •

HONEY HAS completed her first project for me: research on the person *Esquire* has chosen as the Sexiest Woman Alive. I've been assigned to write a profile of this woman, and I really don't want to have to slog through all the heavy-breathing fan websites about her. When I open Honey's file, I have this reaction: America is f*cked. There are charts. There are section headers. There is a well-organized breakdown of her pets, measurements, and favorite foods (e.g., swordfish). If all Bangalorians are like Honey, I pity Americans about to graduate college. They're up against a hungry, polite, Excel-proficient Indian army.

• • •

IN FACT, in the next few days, I outsource a whole mess of online errands to Asha (from the personal service YMII): paying my bills, getting stuff from drugstore.com, finding my son a Tickle Me Elmo. (Actually, the store was out of Tickle Me Elmos, so Asha bought a Chicken Dance Elmo—good decision.) I had her call Cingular to ask about my cell-phone plan. I'm just guessing, but I bet her call was routed from Bangalore to New Jersey and then back to a Cingular employee in Bangalore, which makes me happy for some reason.

• • •

IT'S THE fourth morning of my new, farmed-out life, and when I flip on my computer, my e-mail inbox is already filled with updates from my overseas aides. It's a strange feeling having people work for you while you sleep. Strange, but great. I'm not wasting time while I drool on my pillow; things are getting done.

• • •

HONEY IS my protector. Consider this: For some reason, the Colorado Tourism Board e-mails me all the time. (Most recently, they informed me about a festival in Colorado Springs featuring the world's most famous harlequin.) I request that Honey gently ask them to stop with the press releases. Here's what she sent:

> Dear All,
>   Jacobs often receives mails from Colorado news, too often. They are definitely interesting topics. However, these topics are not suitable for "Esquire."
>   Further, we do understand that you have taken a lot of initiatives working on these articles and sending it to us. We understand. Unfortunately, these articles and mails are too time consuming to be read.
>   Currently, these mails are not serving right purpose for both of us. Thus, we request to stop sending these mails.
>   We do not mean to demean your research work by this.
>   We hope you understand too.
>   Thanking you,
>
> >   Honey K B

That is the best rejection notice in journalism history. It's exceedingly polite, but there's a little undercurrent of indignation. Honey seems almost outraged that Colorado would waste the valuable time of Jacobs.

• • •

I DECIDE to test the next logical relationship: my marriage. These arguments with my wife are killing me—partly because Julie is a much better debater than I am. Maybe Asha can do better:

Hello Asha,

My wife got annoyed at me because I forgot to get cash at
the automatic bank machine . . . I wonder if you could tell
her that I love her, but gently remind her that she too forgets
things—she has lost her wallet twice in the last month. And
she forgot to buy nail clippers for Jasper.

AJ

I can't tell you what a thrill I got from sending that note. It's pretty
hard to get much more passive-aggressive than bickering with your
wife via an e-mail from a subcontinent halfway around the world.

The next morning, Asha CC'd me on the e-mail she sent to Julie.

Julie,

Do understand your anger that I forgot to pick up the
cash at the automatic machine. I have been forgetful and I
am sorry about that.

But I guess that doesn't change the fact that I love you
so much. . . .

Love
AJ

P. S. This is Asha mailing on behalf of Mr. Jacobs.

As if that weren't enough, she also sent Julie an e-card. I click on
it: two teddy bears embracing, with the words, "Anytime you need a
hug, I've got one for you. . . . I'm sorry."

Damn! My outsourcers are too friggin' nice! They kept the apology
part but took out my little jabs. They are trying to save me from myself. They are superegoing my id. I feel castrated.

Julie, on the other hand, seems quite pleased: "That's nice,
sweetie. I forgive you."

• • •

DESPITE THREE weeks with my support team, I'm still stressed. Perhaps it's the fault of Chicken Dance Elmo, whom my son loves to the

point of dry humping, but who is driving me slowly insane. Whatever the reason, I figure it's time to conquer another frontier: outsourcing my inner life.

First, I try to delegate my therapy. My plan is to give Asha a list of my neuroses and a childhood anecdote or two, have her talk to my shrink for 50 minutes, then relay the advice. Smart, right? My shrink refused. Ethics or something. Fine. Instead, I have Asha send me a meticulously researched memo on stress relief. It had a nice Indian flavor to it, with a couple of yogic postures and some visualization.

This was okay, but it didn't seem quite enough. I decided I needed to outsource my worry. For the last few weeks I've been tearing my hair out because a business deal is taking far too long to close. I asked Honey if she would be interested in tearing her hair out in my stead. Just for a few minutes a day. She thought it was a wonderful idea. "I will worry about this every day," she wrote. "Do not worry."

The outsourcing of my neuroses was one of the most successful experiments of the month. Every time I started to ruminate, I'd remind myself that Honey was already on the case, and I'd relax. No joke—this alone was worth it.

At a Glance: Where You Will Be

The future is here. It's just not widely distributed yet.
—WILLIAM GIBSON, author of *Neuromancer*; coined term "cyberspace" in 1984

Here is a sneak preview of full automation.
I woke up this morning, and given that it's Monday, I checked my e-mail for one hour after an exquisite Buenos Aires breakfast.

Sowmya from India had found a long-lost high school classmate of mine, and Anakool from YMII had put together Excel research reports for retiree happiness and the average annual hours worked in different fields. Interviews for this week had been set by a third Indian virtual assistant, who had also found contact information for the best Kendo schools in Japan and the top salsa teachers in Cuba. In the next e-mail folder, I was pleased to see that my fulfillment account manager in Tennessee, Beth, had resolved nearly two dozen problems in the last week—keeping our largest clients in China and South Africa smiling—and had also coordinated California sales tax filing with my accountants in Michigan. The taxes had been paid via my credit card on file, and a quick glance at my bank accounts confirmed that Shane and the rest of the team at my credit card processor were depositing more cash than last month. All was right in the world of automation.

It was a beautiful sunny day, and I closed my laptop with a smile. For an all-you-can-eat buffet breakfast with coffee and orange juice, I paid $4 U.S. The Indian outsourcers cost between $4–10 U.S. per hour. My domestic outsourcers are paid on performance or when product ships. This creates a curious business phenomenon: Negative cash flow is impossible.

Fun things happen when you earn dollars, live on pesos, and compensate in rupees, but that's just the beginning.

But I'm an Employee! How Does This Help Me?

> Nobody can give you freedom. Nobody can give you equality or justice or anything. If you're a man, you take it.
> —MALCOLM X, *Malcolm X Speaks*

Getting a remote personal assistant is a huge departure point and marks the moment that you learn how to give orders and be commander instead of the commanded. It is small-scale training wheels for the most critical of **NR** skills: remote management and communication.

It is time to learn how to be the boss. It isn't time-consuming. It's low-cost and it's low-risk. Whether or not you "need" someone at this point is immaterial. It is an exercise.

It is also a litmus test for entrepreneurship: Can you manage (direct and chastise) other people? Given the proper instruction and practice, I believe so. Most entrepreneurs fail because they jump into the deep end of the pool without learning to swim first. Using a virtual assistant (VA) as a simple exercise with no downside, the basics of management are covered in a 2–4-week test costing between $100–400. This is an investment, not an expense, and the ROI is astounding. It will be repaid in a maximum of 10–14 days, after which it is pure timesaving profit.

Becoming a member of the **NR** is not just about working smarter. It's about building a system to replace yourself.

This is the first exercise.

Even if you have no intention of becoming an entrepreneur, this is the ultimate continuation of our 80/20 and elimination process: Preparing someone to replace you (even if it never happens) will produce an ultrarefined set of rules that will cut remaining fat and redundancy from your schedule. Lingering unimportant tasks will disappear as soon as someone else is being paid to do them.

But what about the cost?

This is a hurdle that is hard for most. If I can do it better than an assistant, why should I pay them at all? *Because the goal is to free your time to focus on bigger and better things.*

This chapter is a low-cost exercise to get you past this lifestyle limiter. It is absolutely necessary that you realize that you can always do something more cheaply yourself. This doesn't mean you want to spend your time doing it. If you spend your time, worth $20–25 per hour, doing something that someone else will do for $10 per hour, it's simply a poor use of resources. It is important to take baby steps toward paying others to do work for you. Few do it, which is another reason so few people have their ideal lifestyles.

Even if the cost is occasionally more per hour than you currently earn, the trade is often worth it. Let's assume you make $50,000 and thus $25 per hour (working from 9–5, Monday through Friday, for 50 weeks per year). If you pay a top-notch assistant $30 per hour and he or she saves you one full 8-hour shift per week, your cost (subtracting what you're being paid) is $40 to free an extra day. Would you pay $40 per week to work Monday to Thursday? I would, and I do. Keep in mind that this is a worst-case cost scenario.

But what if your boss freaks out?

It's largely a non-issue, and prevention is better than cure. There is no ethical or legal reason for the boss to know if you choose non-sensitive tasks. The first option is to assign personal items. Time is time, and if you're spending time on chores and errands that could be spent better elsewhere, a VA will improve life and the management learning curve is similar. Second, you can delegate business tasks that don't include financial information or identify your company.

Ready to build an army of assistants? Let's first look at the dark side of delegation. A review is in order to prevent abuses of power and wasteful behavior.

Delegation Dangers: Before Getting Started

The first rule of any technology used in a business is that automation applied to an efficient operation will magnify the efficiency. The second is that automation applied to an inefficient operation will magnify the inefficiency.

—BILL GATES

Have you ever been given illogical assignments, handed unimportant work, or commanded to do something in the most inefficient fashion possible? Not fun and not productive.

Now it's your turn to show that you know better. Delegation is to be used as a further step in reduction, not as an excuse to create more movement and add the unimportant. Remember—unless something is well-defined and important, no one should do it.

Eliminate before you delegate.

Never automate something that can be eliminated, and never delegate something that can be automated or streamlined. Otherwise, you waste someone else's time instead of your own, which now wastes your hard-earned cash. How's that for incentive to be effective and efficient? Now you're playing with your own dough. It's something I want you to get comfortable with, and this baby step is small stakes.

Did I mention to eliminate before you delegate?

For example, it is popular among executives to have assistants read e-mail. In some cases this is valuable. In my case, I use spam filters, autoresponders with FAQs, and automatic forwarding to outsourcers to limit my e-mail obligation to 10–20 e-mail responses per week. It takes me 30 minutes per week because I used systems—elimination and automation—to make it so.

Nor do I use an assistant to set meetings and conference calls because I have eliminated meetings. If I need to set the odd 20-minute call for a given month, I'll send one two-sentence e-mail and be done with it.

Principle number one is to refine rules and processes before adding people. Using people to leverage a refined process multiplies production; using people as a solution to a poor process multiplies problems.

The Menu: A World of Possibilities

> I am not interested in picking up crumbs of compassion thrown from the table of someone who considers himself my master. I want the full menu of rights.
> —BISHOP DESMOND TUTU, South African cleric and activist

The next question then becomes, "What should you delegate?" It's a good question, but I don't want to answer it. I want to watch *Family Guy*.

The truth be told, it is a hell of a lot of work writing about not working. Ritika of Brickwork and Venky of YMII are more than capable of writing this section, so I'll just mention two guidelines and leave the mental hernia of detail work to them.

Golden Rule #1: Each delegated task must be both time-consuming *and well-defined*. If you're running around like a chicken with its head cut off and assign your VA to do that for you, it doesn't improve the order of the universe.

Golden Rule #2: On a lighter note, have some fun with it. Have someone in Bangalore or Shanghai send e-mails to friends as your personal concierge to set lunch dates or similar basics. Harass your boss with odd phone calls in strong accents from unknown numbers. Being effective doesn't mean being serious all the time. It's fun being in control for a change. Get a bit of repression off your chest so it doesn't turn into a complex later.

Getting Personal and Going Howard Hughes

Howard Hughes, the ultrarich filmmaker and eccentric from *The Aviator*, was notorious for assigning odd tasks to his assistants. Here are a few from Donald Bartlett's *Howard Hughes: His Life and Madness* you might want to consider.

1. After his first plane crash, Hughes confided in a friend that he believed his recovery was due to his consumption of orange juice and its healing properties. He believed that exposure to the air

diluted the juice's potency, so he demanded that fresh oranges be sliced and juiced in front of him.

2. When Hughes was partaking of the nightlife in Las Vegas, his aides were charged with approaching any girls he took a liking to. If a girl was invited to join the Hughes table and agreed, an aide would pull out a waiver and agreement for her to sign.

3. Hughes had a barber on call 24/7 but had his hair and nails trimmed about once a year.

4. In his hotel-bound years, Hughes was rumored to have instructed assistants to place a single cheeseburger in a specific tree outside his penthouse room at a 4:00 P.M. each day, whether he was there or not.

Such a world of possibilities! Just as the Model-T brought transportation to the masses, virtual assistants bring eccentric billionaire behavior within reach of each man, woman, and child. Now, that's progress.

Without further ado, let me pass the mic. Note that YMII performs both personal and business tasks, whereas Brickwork focuses solely on business projects. Let's start with the important but dull stuff and move quickly from the sublime to the ridiculous. To give a true taste of what to expect, I have not corrected non-native-sounding English.

Venky: Don't limit yourself. Just ask us if something is possible. We've arranged parties, organized caterers, researched summer courses, cleaned up accounting books, created 3D drafts based on blueprints. Just ask us. We could find the closest kid-friendly restaurant to your house for your son's birthday, finding out costs and organizing the birthday party. This frees up your time to work or hang out with your son.

What can we not do? We can't do anything that would require our physical presence. But you would be surprised as to how small a set of tasks that is in this day and age.

Here are the most common tasks we handle:

- scheduling interviews and meetings   - web-research
- following up on appointments, errands, and tasks
- online purchases   - creation of legal documents
- website maintenance (web design, publishing, uploading files) that doesn't require a professional designer
- monitoring, editing, and publishing comments for online discussions   - posting job vacancies on the web
- document creation   - proofreading and editing documents for spelling and formatting   - online research for updating blogs   - updating the database for Customer Relationship Management Software   - managing recruitment processes   - updating invoices and receiving payments   - voicemail transcription

Ritika at Brickwork added the following:

- market research   - financial research   - business plans   - industry analysis   - market assessment reports
- preparing presentations   - reports and newsletters
- legal research   - analytics   - website development
- search engine optimization   - maintaining and updating databases   - credit scoring   - managing procurement processes

Venky: We have a forgetful client who has us call him all the time with various reminders. One of our clients on a custom plan has us wake him up every morning. We've done the legwork and found people who fell out of contact after Katrina. Found jobs for clients! My favorite so far: One of our clients has a pair of trousers that he really likes that aren't in production anymore. He's sending them to Bangalore (from London) to have created exact replicas at a tiny fraction of the price.

Here are a few other YMII custom requests:

- ►Reminding an overzealous client to pay his current parking fines, as well as not speed and collect parking fines.
- ►Apologizing and sending flowers and cards to spouses of clients.
- ►Charting a diet plan, reminding client on it regularly, ordering groceries based on the specific diet plan.
- ►Getting a job for a person who lost his job due to outsourcing a year back. We did the job search, did the cover letters, did the resume tuning, and got the client a job in 30 days.
- ►Fixing a broken windowpane of a house in Geneva, Switzerland.
- ►Collecting homework information from teacher's voicemail and e-mailing it to the client (parents of the kid).
- ►Research on how to tie a shoelace meant for a kid (client's son).
- ►Find a parking slot for your car in some other city even before you make the trip.
- ►Ordered garbage bins for home.
- ►Get an authenticated weather forecast and weather report for a particular time in a particular place on a particular day, five years ago. This was to be used as supportive evidence for a lawsuit.
- ►Talking to parents in our client's stead.

Here's another real example of personal outsourcing from reader David Cross, who got a personal chef at home for less than $5 per meal. Just thinking of the possibilities is enough to make you start drooling. He explains:

I wanted to find someone to prepare food I love. I trained as a chef but I am often so busy and as I am the only one in the house who really cooks, I often don't have time to prepare the food that makes me feel the healthiest so I wrote the attached ad and dropped it on Craigslist.

This was a very tight focus—ultraspecific—I had just two applicants in two months—one who was a 2/10 match but the guy we just OK'd was a Hare Krishna follower for many years, lived in India, and his sample menu proved he knew what he's doing so we just started him.

The food is absolutely awesome. The hourly rate is *extremely reasonable,* he's a five-minute detour when either of us are in town to collect food and I now have delicious Indian food for less than $5 a meal and it's as good as anything I've ever eaten anywhere.

I'm going to progress to other cuisines now . . . Thai, Italian, Chinese, etc., and it means when I do have time to cook I'll enjoy doing it that much more as I am not the only one cooking!

Indian/Asian Vegetarian Cook Needed

Date: 2007-06-07, 12:25PM PDT

Hello.

We are a local, international family who love Indian and Asian vegetarian food. We are looking for a cook experienced in this wonderful cuisine to prepare delicious, fresh, healthy, authentic Indian/Asian vegetarian meals for us.

If you've cooked a curry once or twice or need to follow recipes, this position is probably not for you, but if you know Indian vegetarian cooking in depth and can prepare delicious, healthy, fresh, authentic Indian vegetarian food then we'd like to hear from you. This could be an ideal opportunity if you are Indian, Pakistani, Punjabi, etc., and are looking for a great way to apply your experience and love of Indian vegetarian food, cooking and culture. Knowledge of Ayurved and how this relates to food and diet is a plus though not essential.

Please reply with details of your experience and some dishes you could prepare. If we like what you have to offer, we'll arrange for you to cook a sample meal or two which we will pay you for and then we'll see what works out for us all.

This is a part-time position. You will be self-employed and responsible for your own taxes, etc. We'll pay you an hourly rate we will agree with you plus grocery bills for the food you prepare. You can prepare food in your own place and we can arrange to collect it from you, possibly for us to freeze for later eating. We will work with you to come up with menus and schedules that work out for you and us.

Thank you for your interest.

Basic Choices: New Delhi or New York?

There are tens of thousands of VAs—how on earth do you find the right one? The resources at the end of this chapter will show you where to look, but it is overwhelming and confusing unless you have a few criteria determined in advance.

It often helps to begin with the question "Where on Earth?"

Remote or Local?

"Made in the USA" doesn't have the ring it used to. The pros of jumping time zones and visiting third-world currency are twofold: People work while you sleep, and the per-hour expense is less. Time savings and cost savings. Ritika explains the former with an example.

> One can give the remote personal assistant in India their assignment when they are leaving work at the end of the day in New York City, and they will have the presentation ready the next morning. Because of the time difference with India, assistants can work on it while they are asleep and have it back in their morning. When they wake up, they will find the completed summary in their inbox. These assistants can also help them keep pace with what they want to read, for example.

Indian and Chinese VAs, as well as most from other developing countries, will run $4–15 per hour, the lower end being limited to simple tasks and the higher end including the equivalent of Harvard or Stanford M.B.A.s and Ph.D.s. Need a business plan to raise funding? Brickwork can provide it for between $2,500–5,000 instead of $15,000–20,000. Foreign assistance isn't just for the small time. I know from firsthand discussions that executives from big five accounting and management consulting firms routinely charge clients six figures for research reports that are then farmed to India for low four figures.

In the U.S. or Canada, the per-hour range is often $25–100.

Seems like an obvious choice, right? Bangalore 100%? It's not. The important metric is cost per completed task, not cost per hour.

The biggest challenge with overseas help will be the language barrier, which often quadruples back-and-forth discussion and the ultimate cost. The first time I hired an Indian VA, I made the fundamental mistake of not setting an hour cap for three simple tasks. I checked in later that week and found he had spent 23 hours chasing his tail. He had scheduled one tentative interview for the following week, set at the wrong time! Mind boggling. 23 hours? It ended up costing me, at $10 per hour, $230. The same tasks, assigned later that week to a native English speaker in Canada, were completed in two hours at $25 per hour. $50 for more than four times the results. That said, I later requested another Indian VA from the same firm who was able to duplicate the native speaker results.

How do you know which to choose? That's the beautiful part: You don't. It's a matter of testing a few assistants to both sharpen your communication skills and determine who is worth hiring and who is worth firing. Being a results-based boss isn't as simple as it looks.

There are a number of lessons to be learned here.

First, per-hour cost is not the ultimate determinant of cost. Look at per-task cost. If you need to spend time restating the task and otherwise managing the VA, determine the time required of you and add this (using your per-hour rate from earlier chapters) to the end sticker price of the task. It can be surprising. As cool as it is to say that you have people working for you in three countries, it's uncool to spend time babysitting people who are supposed to make your life easier.

Second, the proof is in the pudding. It is impossible to predict how well you will work with a given VA without a trial. Luckily, there are things you can do to improve your odds, and one of them is using a VA firm instead of a solo operator.

Solo vs. Support Team

Let's suppose you find the perfect VA. He or she is performing all of your noncritical tasks and you've decided to take a much-deserved vacation to Thailand. It's nice to know someone besides you will be manning the wheel and putting out fires for a change. Finally, some relief! Two hours before your flight from Bangkok to Phuket, you receive an e-mail: Your VA is out of commission and will be in the hospital for the next week. Not good. Vacation FUBAR.

I don't like being dependent on one person, and I don't recommend it in the least. In the world of high technology, this type of dependency would be referred to as a "single point of failure"—one fragile item upon which all else depends. In the world of IT,[15] the term "redundancy" is used as a selling point for systems that continue to function if there is a malfunction or mechanical failure in any given part. In the context of VAs, redundancy entails having fallback support.

I recommend that you hire a VA firm or VAs with backup teams instead of sole operators. Examples abound, of course, of people who have had a single assistant for decades without incident, but I suggest that this is the exception rather than the rule. Better safe than sorry. Besides simple disaster avoidance, a group structure provides a pool of talent that allows you to assign multiple tasks without bothering to find a new person with the qualifications. Brickwork and YMII both exemplify this type of structure and provide a single point of contact, a personal account manager, who then farms out your tasks to the most-capable people in the group and across different shifts. Need graphic design? Covered. Need database management? Covered. I don't like calling and coordinating multiple people. I want one-stop shopping and am willing to pay 10% more to have it. I encourage you to be similarly pound-wise and penny-foolish.

Team preference doesn't mean that bigger is better, just that

---

15. Information technology.

multiple people are better than one person. The best VA I have used to date is an Indian with five backup assistants under him. Three can be more than sufficient, but two is toeing the line.

The #1 Fear: "Sweetheart, Did You Buy a Porsche in China?"

I'm sure you might have your fears. AJ certainly did:

> My outsourcers now know an alarming amount about me—not just my schedule but my cholesterol, my infertility problems, my Social Security number, my passwords (including the one that is a particularly adolescent curse word). Sometimes I worry that I can't piss off my outsourcers or I'll end up with a $12,000 charge on my Master-Card bill from the Louis Vuitton in Anantapur.

The good news is that misuse of financial and confidential information is rare. In all of the interviews I conducted for this section, I could find only one case of information abuse, and I had to search long and hard. It involved an overworked U.S.-based VA who hired freelance help at the last moment.

Commit to memory the following—never use the new hire. Prohibit small-operation VAs from subcontracting work to untested freelancers without your written permission. The more established and higher-end firms, Brickwork in the below example, have security measures that border on excessive and make it simple to pinpoint abusers in the case of a breach:

- ►Employees undergo background checks and sign NDAs (nondisclosure agreements) in accordance with the company policy of maintaining confidentiality of client information
- ►Electronic access card for entry and exit
- ►Credit card information keyed only by select supervisors
- ►Removal of paper from the offices is prohibited

- ►VLAN-based access restrictions between different teams; this ensures that there is no unauthorized access of information between people of different teams in the organization
- ►Regular reporting on printer logs
- ►Floppy drives and USB ports disabled
- ►BS779 certification for accomplished international security standards
- ►128-bit encryption technology for all data exchange
- ►Secure VPN connection

I bet there is a fair chance that sensitive data is 100 times safer with Brickwork than on your own computer.

Still, information theft is best thought of as inevitable in a digital world, and precautions should be taken with damage control in mind. There are two rules that I use to minimize damage and allow for fast repair.

1. Never use debit cards for online transactions or with remote assistants. Reversing unauthorized credit card charges, particularly with American Express, is painless and near instantaneous. Recovering funds withdrawn from your checking account via unauthorized debit card use takes dozens of hours in paperwork alone and can take months to receive, if approved at all.

2. If your VA will be accessing websites on your behalf, create a new unique login and password to be used on those sites. Most of us reuse both logins and passwords on multiple sites, and taking this precaution limits possible damage. Instruct them to use these unique logins to create accounts on new sites if needed. Note that this is particularly important when using assistants who have access to live commercial websites (developers, programmers, etc.).

If information or identity theft hasn't hit you, it will. Use these guidelines and you'll realize when it happens that, just like most nightmares, it's not that big a deal and is reversible.

The Complicated Art of Simplicity: Common Complaints

M y assistant is an idiot! It took him 23 hours to book an inter-view! This was the first complaint I had, for sure. 23 hours! I was heated up for a shouting match. My original e-mail to this first assistant seemed clear enough.

> Dear Abdul,
>
> Here are the first tasks, due at the end of next Tuesday. Please call or e-mail with any questions:
>
> 1. Go to this article http://www.msnbc.msn.com/id/ 12666060/site/newsweek/, get the phone/e-mail/website contacts for Carol Milligan and Marc and Julie Szekely. Also find the same info for Rob Long here http://www.msnbc. msn.com/id/12652789/site/newsweek/.
>
> 2. Schedule 30-minute interviews for Carol, Marc/Julie, and Rob. Use www.myevents.com (username: notreal, pass-word: donttryit) to book them in my calendar for next week any time between 9–9 ET.
>
> 3. Find the name, e-mail, and phone (phone is least important) of workers in the U.S. who have negotiated remote work agreements (telecommuting) despite resistant bosses. Those who have traveled outside the U.S. are ideal. Other keywords could include "teleworking" and "telecom-muting." The important factor is that they negotiated with difficult bosses. Please send me links to their profiles or write a paragraph describing why they fit the profile above.
>
> Look forward to seeing what you can do. Please e-mail if you don't understand or have questions.
>
> Best,
> Tim

The truth is—I was at fault. This is not a good debut demand, and I made fatal mistakes even before composing it. If you are an effective person but unaccustomed to issuing commands, assume that most problems at the outset are your fault. It is tempting to immediately point the finger at someone else and huff and puff, but most beginner bosses repeat the same mistakes I made.

1. I accepted the first person the firm provided and made no special requests at the outset.

Request someone who has "excellent" English and indicate that phone calls will be required (even if not). Be fast to request a replacement if there are repeated communication issues.

2. I gave imprecise directions.

I asked him to schedule interviews but didn't indicate that it was for an article. He assumed, based on work with previous clients, that I wanted to hire someone and he misspent time compiling spreadsheets and combing online job sites for additional information I didn't need.

Sentences should have one possible interpretation and be suitable for a 2nd-grade reading level. This goes for native speakers as well and will make requests clearer. Ten-dollar words disguise imprecision.

Note that I asked him to respond *if* he didn't understand or had questions. This is the wrong approach. Ask foreign VAs to rephrase tasks to confirm understanding before getting started.

3. I gave him a license to waste time.

This brings us again to damage control. Request a status update after a few hours of work on a task to ensure that the task is both understood and achievable. Some tasks are, after initial attempts, impossible.

4. I set the deadline a week in advance.

Use Parkinson's Law and assign tasks that are to be completed within no more than 72 hours. I have had the best luck with 48 and 24 hours. This is another compelling reason to use a small group (three or more) rather than a single individual who can become overtaxed with last-minute requests from multiple clients.

Using short deadlines does not mean avoiding larger tasks (e.g., business plan), but rather breaking them into smaller milestones that can be completed in shorter time frames (outline, competitive research summaries, chapters, etc.).

5. I gave him too many tasks and didn't set an order of importance.

I advise sending one task at a time whenever possible and no more than two. If you want to cause your computer to hang or crash, open 20 windows and applications at the same time. If you want to do the same to your assistant, assign him or her a dozen tasks without prioritizing them. Recall our mantra: Eliminate before you delegate.

WHAT DOES A good VA task e-mail look like? The following example was recently sent to an Indian VA whose results have been nothing short of spectacular:

> Dear Sowmya,
>
> Thank you. I would like to start with the following task.
>
> TASK: I need to find the names and e-mails of editors of men's magazines in the US (for example: maxim, stuff, GQ, esquire, blender, etc.) who also have written books. An example of such a person would be AJ Jacobs who is Editor-at-Large of Esquire (www.ajjacobs.com). I already have his information and need more like him.
>
> Can you do this? If not, please advise. **Please reply and confirm what you will plan to do to complete this task.**
>
> DEADLINE: Since I'm in a rush, get started after your next e-mail and stop at 3 hours and tell me what results you have. Please begin this task now if possible. The deadline for these 3 hours and reported results is end-of-day ET Monday.
>
> Thank you for your fastest reply,
>
> Tim

Short, sweet, and to the point. Clear writing, and therefore clear commands, come from clear thinking. Think simple.

· · ·

IN THE NEXT several chapters, the communication skills you develop with our virtual assistant experiment will be applied to a much larger and obscenely profitable playing field: automation. The extent to which you will outsource next makes delegation look like finger painting.

In the world of automation, not all business models are created equal. How do you assemble a business and coordinate all its parts without lifting a finger? How do you automate cash deposits in your bank account while avoiding the most common problems? It begins with understanding the options, the art of dodging information flow, and what we will call "muses."

The next chapter is a blueprint for the first step: a product.

Go with the Flow

Here is a flowchart of 4HWW from reader Jed Wood, who has used it for faster decision making, more output with less input, and more time with his wife and children.

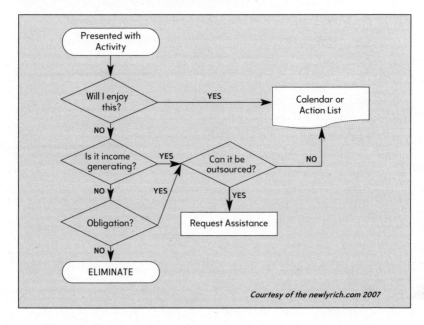

Courtesy of the newlyrich.com 2007

►Q&A: QUESTIONS AND ACTIONS

1. **Get an assistant—even if you don't need one.**

   Develop the comfort of commanding and not being commanded. Begin with a one-time test project or small repetitive task (daily preferred). I advise using domestic help for language-intensive tasks and using foreign assistants in the early stages to improve the general clarity of your communication. Pick one from each group and get started.

   The following sites, split up geographically, are useful resources.

   ### U.S. and Canada ($20/hour+)

   http://www.iavoa.com (International Association of
      Virtual Office Assistants). Global directory that
      includes the U.S.

   www.fourhourblog.com/cvac (Canadian Virtual Assistant
      Connection)

   http://www.canadianva.net/files/va-locator.html (Canada)

   www.fourhourblog.com/obm

   ### North America and International ($4/hour+)

   www.fourhourblog.com/elance (Search "virtual assistants,"
   "personal assistants," and "executive assistants.") The client
   feedback reviews on Elance enabled me to find my best VA to
   date, who costs $4/hour. Similar marketplaces with positive
   reviews include www.guru.com and www.fourhourblog.com/
   vworker

   ### India

   www.fourhourblog.com/asksunday ($20–60 per month
   for 24/7 concierge, free one-week trial). AskSunday is one of
   the sophisticated new kids on the personal outsourcing block.
   Their site was nominated the #2 website of the year in 2007
   by *Time* magazine. Just dial a 212 (NYC) area code and get
   routed to well-spoken assistants in India and the Philippines.
   I use this service 80% of the time, as most tasks take less

than 10 minues to complete. For longer projects, there are teams available for $12/hour.

www.b2kcorp.com ($15/hour+) From Fortune 10 oil companies and Fortune 500 clients to Big 5 accounting firms and U.S. congressmen, Brickwork can handle it all. This is reflected in the costs of this pure suit-and-tie operation—business only. No flowers for auntie.

www.taskseveryday.com ($6.98/hour for a dedicated virtual assistant) Based in Mumbai, available via phone and e-mail from the U.S., UK, and Australia. Must choose between 20 or 40 hours per week and pre-purchase hours.

www.yourmaninindia.com ($6.25/hour+) YMII handles both business and personal tasks and can work with you in real time (there are people on duty 24/7) and complete work while you sleep. English capability and effectiveness vary tremendously across VAs, so interview yours before getting started or assigning important tasks. Important: Following the publication of the first edition of this book, there have been some complaints of lower quality and up to four-week wait lists to become a client.

2. **Start small but think big.**
Tina Forsyth, an online business manager (higher-level VA) who helps six-figure-income clients achieve seven figures with business model redesigns, makes the following recommendations.

- ►Look at your to-do list—what has been sitting on it the longest?
- ►Each time you are interrupted or change tasks, ask, "Could a VA do this?"
- ►Examine pain points—what causes you the most frustration and boredom?

Here are a few common time-consumers in small businesses with online presences.

- ► Submitting articles to drive traffic to site and build mailing lists
- ► Participating in or moderating discussion forums and message boards
- ► Managing affiliate programs
- ► Creating content for and publishing newsletters and blog postings
- ► Background research components of new marketing initiatives or analysis of current marketing results

Don't expect miracles from a single VA, but don't expect too little, either. Let go of the controls a bit. Don't assign crap tasks that end up consuming rather than saving time. It makes little sense to spend 10–15 minutes sending an e-mail to India to get a price quote on a plane ticket when you could do the same online in 10 minutes and avoid all the subsequent back-and-forth.

Push outside your comfort zone—that is the entire point of the exercise.

It is always possible to reclaim a task for yourself if the VA proves incapable, so test the limits of their capabilities. Remember Brickwork's suggestion: Don't limit yourself.

3. **Identify your top five time-consuming non-work tasks and five personal tasks you could assign for sheer fun.**

4. **Keep in sync: scheduling and calendars.**
    If you decide to have an assistant schedule appointments and add things to your calendar, it will be important to ensure what you both see is updated. There are several options:

    BusySync (www.busysync.com) I have two Gmail accounts: one private account for me and one for my assistant, where general e-mail is sent. I use BusySync to synchronize her

Google Calendar with iCal (Mac calendar) on my laptop. I have also used **SpanningSync** (www.spanningsync.com) successfully for the same purpose.

WebEx Office (www.weboffice.com) Share your calendar online while masking personal appointments. Can be synchronized with Outlook, and also offers document sharing and other assistant- or team-friendly features. I suggest you compare this to synchronizing your Outlook with an assistant's Google Calendar.

►COMFORT CHALLENGE

Use the Criticism Sandwich (2 Days and Weekly)

Chances are good that someone—be it a co-worker, boss, customer, or significant other—does something irritating or at a subpar level. Rather than avoid the topic out of fear of confrontation, let's chocolate-coat it and ask them to fix it. Once per day for two days, and then each Thursday (M–W is too tense and Friday is too relaxed) for the next three weeks, resolve to use what I call the Criticism Sandwich with someone. It's called the Criticism Sandwich because you first *praise* the person for something, then *deliver the criticism,* and then close with topic-shifting *praise* to exit the sensitive topic. Here's an example with a superior or boss, with keywords and phrases in italics.

You: Hi, Mara. Do you have a second?
Mara: Sure. What's up?
You: *First, I wanted to thank you for* helping me with the Meelie Worm account [or whatever]. *I really appreciate* you showing me how to handle that. *You're really good at* fixing the technical issues.
Mara: No problem.

You: *Here's the thing.*[16] There is a lot of work coming down on everyone, and *I'm feeling*[17] a bit overwhelmed. *Normally, priorities are really clear to me,*[18] but I've been having trouble recently figuring out which tasks are highest on the list. *Could you help me by* pointing out the most important items when a handful need to be done? *I'm sure it's just me,*[19] *but I'd really appreciate it, and I think it would help.*

Mara: Uhh . . . I'll see what I can do.

You: *That means a lot to me. Thanks. Before I forget,*[20] last week's presentation was excellent.

Mara: Did you think so? Blah, blah, blah . . .

►LIFESTYLE DESIGN IN ACTION

THE BEST TIMES TO SEND E-MAIL

You've suggested people check e-mail only a few times a day. Here's a twist: I reply to e-mails when it's convenient, but I time it to arrive when it's also convenient for me. In Outlook you can delay e-mail delivery to any time of day. For example, when I return e-mails at 3 P.M., I don't want my staff instantly zinging me responses or clarifying questions. (This also prevents e-mail chats.) So I hit send, but it's delayed to arrive later in the evening or at 8 A.M. when my employees arrive the next day. This is how e-mail was meant to be! It's mail, not a chat service.　　　　**—JIM LARRANAGA**

---

16. Don't call it a problem if you can avoid it.

17. No one can argue with your feelings, so use this to avoid a debate about external circumstances.

18. Notice how I take "you" out of the sentence to avoid finger-pointing, even though it's implicit. "Normally, you make priorities clear" sounds like a back-handed insult. If this is a significant other, you can skip this formality, but never use "you always do X," which is just a fight starter.

19. Take a little bit of the heat off with this. The point has already been made.

20. "Before I forget" is a great segue to the closing compliment, which is also a topic shifter and gets you off the sensitive topic without awkwardness.

9

Income Autopilot I

►FINDING THE MUSE

Just set it and forget it!

—RON POPEIL, founder of RONCO; responsible for more than $1 billion in sales of rotisserie chicken roasters

As to methods there may be a million and then some, but principles are few. The man who grasps principles can successfully select his own methods. The man who tries methods, ignoring principles, is sure to have trouble.

—RALPH WALDO EMERSON

The Renaissance Minimalist

Douglas Price was waking up to another beautiful summer morning in his Brooklyn brownstone. First things first: coffee. The jet lag was minor, considering he had just returned from a two-week jaunt through the islands of Croatia. It was just one of six countries he had visited in the last 12 months. Japan was next on the agenda.

Buzzing with a smile and his coffee mug in hand, he ambled over to his Mac to check on personal e-mail first. There were 32 messages and all brought good news.

One of his friends and business partners, also a cofounder of Limewire, had an update: Last Bamboo, their start-up poised to reinvent peer-to-peer technology, was rounding the final corners of development. It could be their billion-dollar baby, but Doug was letting the engineers run wild first.

Samson Projects, one of the hottest contemporary art galleries in Boston, had compliments for Doug's latest work and requests for expanded involvement with new exhibits as their sound curator.

The last e-mail in his inbox was a fan letter addressed to "Demon Doc" and praise for his latest instrumental hip-hop album, *onliness v1.0.1*. Doug had released his album as what he termed "open source music"—anyone could download the album for free and use sounds from any track in his or her own compositions.

He smiled again, polished off his dark roast, and opened a window to deal with business e-mail next. It would take much less time. In fact, less than 30 minutes for the day and 2 hours for the week.

How much things change.

Two years earlier, in June of 2004, I was in Doug's apartment checking e-mail for what I hoped would be the last time for a long time. I was headed to JFK Airport in New York in a matter of hours and was preparing for an indefinite quest around the world. Doug looked on with amusement. He had similar plans for himself and was finally extricating himself from a venture-funded Internet start-up that had once been a cover story and his passion but was now just a job. The euphoria of the dot-com era was long dead, along with most chances for a sale or an IPO.

He bid me farewell and made a decision as the taxi pulled from the curb—enough of the complicated stuff. It was time to return to basics.

Prosoundeffects.com, launched in January of 2005 after one week of sales testing on eBay, was designed to do one thing: give Doug lots of cash with minimal time investment.

This brings us back to his business inbox in 2006.

There are 10 orders for sound libraries, CDs that film producers, musicians, video game designers, and other audio professionals use to add hard-to-find sounds—whether the purr of a lemur or an exotic instrument—to their own creations. These are Doug's products, but he doesn't own them, as that would require physical inventory and upfront cash. His business model is more elegant than that. Here is just one revenue stream:

1. A prospective customer sees his Pay-Per-Click (PPC) advertising on Google or other search engines and clicks through to his site, www.prosoundeffects.com.

2. The prospect orders a product for $325 (the average purchase price, though prices range from $29–7,500) on a Yahoo shopping cart, and a PDF with all their billing and shipping information is automatically e-mailed to Doug.

3. Three times a week, Doug presses a single button in the Yahoo management page to charge all his customers' credit cards and put cash in his bank account. Then he saves the PDFs as Excel purchase orders and e-mails the purchase orders to the manufacturers of the CD libraries. Those companies mail the products to Doug's customers—this is called drop-shipping—and Doug pays the manufacturers as little as 45% of the retail price of the products up to 90 days later (net-90 terms).

Let's look at the mathematical beauty of his system for full effect. For each $325 order at his cost of 55% off retail, Doug is entitled to $178.75. If we subtract 1% of the full retail price (1% of $325 = $3.25) for the Yahoo Store transaction fee and 2.5% for the credit card processing fee (2.5% of $325 = $8.13), Doug is left with a pre-tax profit of $167.38 for this one sale.

Multiply this by 10 and we have $1673.80 in profit for 30 minutes of work. Doug is making $3,347.60 per hour and purchases no product in advance. His initial start-up costs were $1,200 for the webpage design, which he recouped in the first week. His PPC advertising costs approximately $700 per month and he pays Yahoo $99 per month for their hosting and shopping cart.

He works less than two hours a week, often pulls more than $10,000 per month, and there is no financial risk whatsoever.

Now Doug spends his time making music, traveling, and exploring new businesses for excitement. Prosoundeffects.com is not his end-all-be-all, but it has removed all financial concerns and freed his mind to focus on other things.

What would you do if you didn't have to think about money? If you follow the advice in this chapter, you will soon have to answer this question.

It's time to find your muse.

THERE ARE A million and one ways to make a million dollars. From franchising to freelance consulting, the list is endless. Fortunately, most of them are unsuited to our purpose. This chapter is not for people who want to *run* businesses but for those who want to *own* businesses and spend no time on them.

The response I get when I introduce this concept is more or less universal: Huh?

People can't believe that most of the ultrasuccessful companies in the world do not manufacture their own products, answer their own phones, ship their own products, or service their own customers. There are hundreds of companies that exist to pretend to work for someone else and handle these functions, providing rentable infrastructure to anyone who knows where to find them.

Think Microsoft manufactures the Xbox 360 or that Kodak designs and distributes their digital cameras? Guess again. Flextronics, a Singapore-based engineering and manufacturing firm with locations in 30 countries and $15.3 billion in annual revenue, does both. Most popular brands of mountain bikes in the U.S. are all manufactured in the same three or four plants in China. Dozens of call centers press one button to answer calls for the JC Penneys of the world, another to answer calls for the Dell Computers of the world, and yet another to answer calls for the New Rich like me.

It's all beautifully transparent and cheap.

Before we create this virtual architecture, however, we need a *product* to sell. If you own a service business, this section will help you convert expertise into a downloadable or shippable good to escape the limits of a per-hour-based model. If starting from scratch, ignore service businesses for now, as constant customer contact makes absence difficult.[21]

To narrow the field further, our target product can't take more than $500 to test, it has to lend itself to automation *within four weeks,* and—when up and running—it can't require more than *one day per week* of management.

Can a business be used to change the world, like The Body Shop or Patagonia? Yes, but that isn't our goal here.

Can a business be used to cash out through an IPO or sale? Yes, but that isn't our goal either.

Our goal is simple: to create an automated vehicle for generating cash without consuming time. That's it.[22] I will call this vehicle a "muse" whenever possible to separate it from the ambiguous term "business," which can refer to a lemonade stand or a Fortune 10 oil conglomerate—our objective is more limited and thus requires a more precise label.

So first things first: cash flow and time. With these two currencies, all other things are possible. Without them, nothing is possible.

---

21. There are a few limited exceptions, such as online membership sites that don't require content generation, but as a general rule, products require much less maintenance and will get you to your TMI faster.
22. Muses will provide the time and financial freedom to realize your dreamlines in record time, after which one can (and often does) start additional companies to change the world or sell.

Why to Begin with the End in Mind:
A Cautionary Tale

S arah is excited.

It has been two weeks since her line of humorous T-shirts for golfers went online, and she is averaging 5 T-shirt sales per day at $15 each. Her cost per unit is $5, so she is grossing $50 in profit (minus 3% in credit card fees) per 24 hours, as she passes shipping and handling on to customers. She should soon recoup the cost of her initial order of 300 shirts (including plate charges, setup, etc.)—but wants to earn more.

It's a nice reversal of fortune, considering the fate of her first product. She had spent $12,000 to develop, patent, and manufacture a high-tech stroller for new moms (she has never been a new mom), only to find that no one was interested.

The T-shirts, in contrast, were actually selling, but sales were beginning to slow.

It appears she has reached her online sales ceiling, as well-funded and uneducated competitors are now spending too much for advertising and driving up costs. Then it strikes her—retail!

Sarah approaches the manager of her local golf shop, Bill, who immediately expresses interest in carrying the shirts. She's thrilled.

Bill asks for the customary 40% minimum discount for wholesale pricing. This means her sell price is now $9 instead of $15 and her profit has dropped from $10 to $4. Sarah decides to give it a shot and does the same with three other stores in surrounding towns. The shirts begin to move off the shelves, but she soon realizes that her small profit is being eaten by extra hours she spends handling invoices and additional administration.

She decides to approach a distributor[23] to alleviate this labor, a

---

23. Distributors are sometimes also referred to as "wholesalers," depending on the industry.

company that acts as a shipping warehouse and sells products from various manufacturers to golf stores nationwide. The distributor is interested and asks for its usual pricing—70% off of retail or $4.50—which would leave Sarah 50 cents in the hole on each unit. She declines.

To make matters worse, the four local stores have already started discounting her shirts to compete among one another and are killing their own profit margins. Two weeks later, reorders disappear. Sarah abandons retail and returns to her website demoralized. Sales online have dropped to almost nothing with new competition. She has not recouped her initial investment, and she still has 50 shirts in her garage.

Not good.

It all could have been prevented with proper testing and planning.

ED "MR. CREATINE" BYRD is no Sarah. He does not invest and hope for the best.

His San Francisco–based company, MRI, had the top-selling sports supplement in the U.S. from 2002–2005, NO2. It is still a top-seller despite dozens of imitators. He did it through smart testing, smart positioning, and brilliant distribution.

Prior to manufacturing, MRI first offered a low-priced book related to the product through ¼-page advertisements in men's health magazines. Once the need had been confirmed with a mountain of book orders, NO2 was priced at an outrageous $79.95, positioned as the premium product on the market, and sold exclusively through GNC stores nationwide. No one else was permitted to sell it.

How can it make sense to turn away business? There are a few good reasons.

First, the more competing resellers there are, the faster your product goes extinct. This was one of Sarah's mistakes.

It works like this: Reseller A sells the product for your recommended advertised price of $50, then reseller B sells it for $45 to compete with A, and then C sells it for $40 to compete with A and B. In no time at all, no one is making profit from selling your product and reorders disappear. Customers are now accustomed to the lower pricing and the process is irreversible. The product is dead and you need to create a new product. This is precisely the reason why so many companies need to create new product after new product month after month. It's a headache.

I had one single supplement, BrainQUICKEN® (also sold as BodyQUICK®) for six years and maintained a consistent profit margin by limiting wholesale distribution, particularly online, to the top one or two largest resellers who could move serious quantities of product and who agreed to maintain a minimum advertised pricing.[24] Otherwise, rogue discounters on eBay and mom-and-pop independents will drive you broke.

Second, if you offer someone exclusivity, which most manufacturers try to avoid, it can work in your favor. Since you are offering one company 100% of the distribution, it is possible to negotiate better profit margins (offering less of a discount off of retail price), better marketing support in-store, faster payment, and other preferential treatment.

It is critical that you decide how you will sell and distribute your product before you commit to a product in the first place. The more middlemen are involved, the higher your margins must be to maintain profitability for all the links in the chain.

Ed Byrd realized this and exemplifies how doing the opposite of what most do can reduce risk and increase profit. Choosing distribution before product is just one example.

Ed drives a Lamborghini down the California coast when not

---

24. It is illegal to control how much someone sells your product for, but you can dictate how much they advertise it for. This is done by including a Minimum Advertised Pricing (MAP) policy in your General Terms and Conditions (GTC), which are agreed to automatically when a written wholesale order is placed. Sample GTC and order forms are available at www.fourhourblog.com.

traveling or in the office with his small focused staff and his two Australian shepherds. This outcome is not accidental. His product-creation methods—and those of the New Rich in general—can be emulated.

Here's how you do it in the fewest number of steps.

Step One: Pick an Affordably Reachable Niche Market

When I was younger . . . I [didn't] want to be pigeonholed . . . Basically, now you want to be pigeonholed. It's your niche.

—JOAN CHEN, actress; appeared in *The Last Emperor* and *Twin Peaks*

Creating demand is hard. Filling demand is much easier. Don't create a product, then seek someone to sell it to. Find a market—define your customers—then find or develop a product for them.

I have been a student and an athlete, so I developed products for those markets, focusing on the male demographic whenever possible. The audiobook I created for college guidance counselors failed because I have never been a guidance counselor. I developed the subsequent speed-reading seminar after realizing that I had free access to students, and the business succeeded because—being a student myself—I understood their needs and spending habits. Be a member of your target market and don't speculate what others need or will be willing to buy.

Start Small, Think Big

Some people are just into lavish dwarf entertainment.

—DANNY BLACK (4'2"), part-owner of Shortdwarf.com[25]

---

25. *The Wall Street Journal,* July 18, 2005 (http://www.technologyinvestor.com/login/2004/Jul18-05.php).

Danny Black rents dwarfs as entertainment for $149 per hour. How is that for a niche market?

It is said that if everyone is your customer, then no one is your customer. If you start off aiming to sell a product to dog- or car-lovers, stop. It's expensive to advertise to such a broad market, and you are competing with too many products and too much free information. If you focus on how to train German shepherds or a restoration product for antique Fords, on the other hand, the market and competition shrink, making it less expensive to reach your customers and easier to charge premium pricing.

BrainQUICKEN was initially designed for students, but the market proved too scattered and difficult to reach. Based on positive feedback from student-athletes, I relaunched the product as BodyQUICK and tested advertising in magazines specific to martial artists and powerlifters. These are minuscule markets compared to the massive student market, but not small. Low media cost and lack of competition enabled me to dominate with the first "neural accelerator"[26] in these niches. It is more profitable to be a big fish in a small pond than a small undefined fish in a big pond. How do you know if it's big enough to meet your TMI? For a detailed real-life example of how I determined the market size of a recent product, see "Muse Math" on this book's companion site.

Ask yourself the following questions to find profitable niches.

1. Which social, industry, and professional groups do you belong to, have you belonged to, or do you understand, whether dentists, engineers, rock climbers, recreational cyclists, car restoration aficionados, dancers, or other?
Look creatively at your resume, work experience, physical habits, and hobbies and compile a list of all the groups, past and present,

26. This was a new product category that I created to eliminate and preempt the competition. Strive to be the largest, best, or first in a precise category. I prefer being first.

that you can associate yourself with. Look at products and books you own, include online and offline subscriptions, and ask yourself, "What groups of people purchase the same?" Which magazines, websites, and newsletters do you read on a regular basis?

2. Which of the groups you identified have their own magazines?

Visit a large bookstore such as Barnes & Noble and browse the magazine rack for smaller specialty magazines to brainstorm additional niches. There are literally thousands of occupation- and interest/hobby-specific magazines to choose from. Use *Writer's Market* to identify magazine options outside the bookstores. Narrow the groups from question 1 above to those that are reachable through one or two small magazines. It's not important that these groups all have a lot of money (e.g., golfers)—only that they spend money (amateur athletes, bass fishermen, etc.) on products of some type. Call these magazines, speak to the advertising directors, and tell them that you are considering advertising; ask them to e-mail their current advertising rate card and include both readership numbers and magazine back-issue samples. Search the back issues for repeat advertisers who sell direct-to-consumer via 800 numbers or websites—the more repeat advertisers, and the more frequent their ads, the more profitable a magazine is for them . . . and will be for us.

Step Two: Brainstorm (Do Not Invest In) Products

> Genius is only a superior power of seeing.
> —JOHN RUSKIN, famed art and social critic

Pick the two markets that you are most familiar with that have their own magazines with full-page advertising that costs less than $5,000. There should be no fewer than 15,000 readers.

This is the fun part. Now we get to brainstorm or find products with these two markets in mind.

The goal is come up with well-formed product ideas and spend nothing; in Step 3, we will create advertising for them and test responses from real customers before investing in manufacturing. There are several criteria that ensure the end product will fit into an automated architecture.

The Main Benefit Should Be Encapsulated in One Sentence.

People can dislike you—and you often sell more by offending some—but they should never misunderstand you.

The main benefit of your product should be explainable in one sentence or phrase. How is it different and why should I buy it? ONE sentence or phrase, folks. Apple did an excellent job of this with the iPod. Instead of using the usual industry jargon with GB, bandwidth, and so forth, they simply said, "1,000 songs in your pocket." Done deal. Keep it simple and do not move ahead with a product until you can do this without confusing people.

It Should Cost the Customer $50–200.

The bulk of companies set prices in the midrange, and that is where the most competition is. Pricing low is shortsighted, because someone else is always willing to sacrifice more profit margin and drive you both bankrupt. Besides perceived value, there are three main benefits to creating a premium, high-end image and charging more than the competition.

1. Higher pricing means that we can sell fewer units—and thus manage fewer customers—and fulfill our dreamlines. It's faster.
2. Higher pricing attracts lower-maintenance customers (better credit, fewer complaints/questions, fewer returns, etc.). It's less headache. This is HUGE.
3. Higher pricing also creates higher profit margins. It's safer.

I personally aim for an *8–10× markup,* which means a $100 product can't cost me more than $10–12.50.[27] If I had used the commonly recommended 5× markup with BrainQUICKEN, it would have gone bankrupt within 6 months due to a dishonest supplier and late magazine. The profit margin saved it, and within 12 months it was generating up to $80,000 per month.

High has its limits, however. If the per-unit price is above a certain point, prospects need to speak to someone on the phone before they are comfortable enough to make the purchase. This is contraindicated on our low-information diet.

I have found that a price range of $50–200 per sale provides the most profit for the least customer service hassle. Price high and then justify.

It Should Take No More Than 3 to 4 Weeks to Manufacture.

This is critically important for keeping costs low and adapting to sales demand without stockpiling product in advance. I will not pursue any product that takes more than three to four weeks to manufacture, and I recommend aiming for one to two weeks from order placement to shippable product.

How do you know how long something takes to manufacture?

Contact contract manufacturers who specialize in the type of products you're considering: http://www.thomasnet.com/. Call a related manufacturer (e.g., toilet bowls) if you need a referral to a related manufacturer you cannot find (e.g., toilet cleaning solutions). Still no luck? Google different synonyms for your product in combination with "organization" and "association" to contact the appropriate industry organizations. Ask them for referrals to contract manufacturers and for the names of their trade magazines, which

---

27. If you decide to resell someone else's higher-end products like Doug, especially with drop-shipping, the risk is lower and smaller margins can suffice.

often contain advertisements for contract manufacturers and related service providers we'll need for your virtual architecture later.

Request pricing from the contract manufacturers to ensure the proper markup is possible. Determine the per-unit costs of production for 100, 500, 1,000, and 5,000 units.

It Should Be Fully Explainable in a Good Online FAQ.

Here is where I really screwed up in my product choice with Brain-QUICKEN.

Even though ingestibles have enabled my **NR** life, I would not wish them on anyone. Why not? You get 1,000 questions from every customer: Can I eat bananas with your product? Will it make me fart during dinner? On and on, ad nauseam. Choose a product that you can fully explain in a good online FAQ. If not, the task of travelling and otherwise forgetting about work becomes very difficult or you end up spending a fortune on call center operators.

Understanding these criteria, a question remains: "How does one obtain a good muse product that satisfies them?" There are three options we'll cover in ascending order of recommendation.

Option One: Resell a Product

Purchasing an existing product at wholesale and reselling it is the easiest route but also the least profitable. It is the fastest to set up but the fastest to die off due to price competition with other resellers. The profitable life span of each product is short unless an exclusivity agreement prevents others from selling it. Reselling is, however, an excellent option for secondary back-end[28] products that

---

28. "Back-end" products are products sold to customers once the sale of a primary product has been made. iPod covers and car GPS systems are two examples. These products can have lower margins, because there is no advertising cost to acquire the customer.

can be sold to existing customers or cross-sold[29] to new customers online or on the phone.

To purchase at wholesale, use these steps.

1.   Contact the manufacturer and request a "wholesale pricelist" (generally 40% off retail) and terms.
2.   If a business tax ID number is needed, print out the proper forms from your state's Secretary of State website and file for an LLC (which I prefer) or similar protective business structure for $100–200.

Do NOT purchase product until you have completed Step 3 in the next chapter. It is enough at this point to confirm the profit margin and have product photos and sales literature.

That's reselling. Not much more to it.

Option Two: License a Product

> I not only use all the brains that I have, but all that I can borrow.   —WOODROW WILSON

Some of the world's best-known brands and products have been borrowed from someone or somewhere else.

The basis for the energy drink Red Bull came from a tonic in Thailand, and the Smurfs were brought from Belgium. Pokémon came from the land of Honda. The band KISS made millions in record and concert sales, but the real profit has been in licensing— granting others the right to produce hundreds of products with their name and image in exchange for a percentage of sales.

There are two parties involved in a licensing deal, and a member

---

29. "Cross-selling" is selling a related product to a customer while they're still on the phone or in an online shopping cart after the sale of a primary product has been made. For a full marketing and direct response (DR) glossary, visit www.fourhourblog.com.

of the New Rich could be either. First, there is the inventor of the product,[30] called the "licensor," who can sell others the right to manufacture, use, or sell his or her product, usually for 3–10% of the wholesale price (usually around 40% off retail) for each unit sold. Invent, let someone else do the rest, and cash checks. Not a bad model.

The other side of the equation is the person interested in manufacturing and selling the inventor's product for 90–97% of the profit: the licensee. This is, for me and most **NR**, more interesting.

Licensing is, however, dealmaking-intensive on both sides and a science unto itself. Creative contract negotiation is essential and most readers will run into problems if it's their first product. For real-world case studies on both sides, ranging from Teddy Ruxpin to Tae-Bo, and full agreements with actual dollar amounts, visit www.fourhourblog.com. From how to sell inventions without prototypes or patents to how to secure rights to products as a no-name beginner, it's all there. The economics are fascinating and the profits can be astounding.

In the meantime, we will focus on the least complicated and most profitable option open to the most people: product creation.

Option Three: Create a Product

Creation is a better means of self-expression than possession; it is through creating, not possessing, that life is revealed.
—VIDA D. SCUDDER, *The Life of the Spirit in the Modern English Poets*

C reating a product is not complicated.
   "Create" sounds more involved than it actually is. If the idea is a hard product—an invention—it is possible to hire mechanical engineers or industrial designers on www.fourhourblog.com/elance

---

30. This also refers to owners of copyrights or trademarks.

to develop a prototype based on your description of its function and appearance, which is then taken to a contract manufacturer. If you find a generic or stock product made by a contract manufacturer that can be repurposed or positioned for a special market, it's even easier: Have them manufacture it, stick a custom label on it for you, and presto—new product. This latter example is often referred to as "private labeling." Have you ever seen a massage therapist's office with its own line of vitamin products or the Kirkland brand at Costco? Private labeling in action.

It is true that we'll be testing market response without manufacturing, but if the test is successful, manufacturing is the next step. This means we need to keep in mind setup costs, per-unit costs, and order minimums. Innovative gadgets and devices are great but often require special tooling, which makes the manufacturing start-up costs too expensive to meet our criteria.

Putting mechanical devices aside and forgetting about welding and engineering, there is one class of product that meets all of our criteria, has a manufacturing lead time of less than a week in small quantities, and often permits not just an $8–10\times$ markup, but a $20–50\times$ markup.

No, not heroin or slave labor. Too much bribing and human interaction required.

Information.

Information products are low-cost, fast to manufacture, and time-consuming for competitors to duplicate. Consider that the top-selling non-information infomercial products—whether exercise equipment or supplements—have a useful life span of two to four months before imitators flood the market. I studied economics in Beijing for six months and observed firsthand how the latest Nike sneaker or Callaway golf club could be duplicated and on eBay within a week of first appearing on shelves in the U.S. This is not an exaggeration, and I am not talking about a look-alike product—I mean an exact duplicate for $1/20$ the cost.

Information, on the other hand, is too time-consuming for most knockoff artists to bother with when there are easier products to replicate. It's easier to circumvent a patent than to paraphrase an entire course to avoid copyright infringement. Three of the most successful television products of all time—all of which have spent more than 300 weeks on the infomercial top-10 bestseller lists—reflect the competitive and profit margin advantage of information products.

No Down Payment (Carlton Sheets)
Attacking Anxiety and Depression (Lucinda Bassett)
Personal Power (Tony Robbins)

I know from conversations with the principal owners of one of the above products that more than $65 million worth of information moved through their doors in 2002. Their infrastructure consisted of fewer than 25 in-house operators, and the rest of the infrastructure, ranging from media purchasing to shipping, was outsourced.

Their annual revenue-per-employee is more than $2.7 million. Incredible.

On the opposite end of the market size spectrum, I know a man who created a low-budget how-to DVD for less than $200 and sold it to owners of storage facilities who wanted to install security systems. It's hard to get more niche than that. In 2001, selling DVDs that cost $2 to duplicate for $95 apiece through trade magazines, he made several hundred thousand dollars with no employees.

But I'm Not an Expert!

If you aren't an expert, don't sweat it.

First, "expert" in the context of selling product means that you know more about the topic than the purchaser. No more. It is not necessary to be the best—just better than a small target number of your prospective customers. Let's suppose that your current dreamline—to compete in the 1,150-mile Iditarod dogsledding race in Alaska—requires $5,000 to realize. If there are 15,000 readers and even 50 (0.33%) can be convinced of your superior expertise in skill X and spend $100 for a program that teaches it, that is $5,000. Bring on the Huskies. Those 50 customers are what I call the "minimal customer base"—the minimum number of customers you need to convince of your expertise to fulfill a given dreamline.

Second, expert status can be created in less than four weeks if you understand basic credibility indicators. It's important to learn how the PR pros phrase resume points and position their clients. See the boxed text later in this chapter to learn how.

The degree to which you personally need expert status also depends on how you obtain your content. There are three main options.

1. Create the content yourself, often via paraphrasing and combining points from several books on a topic.
2. Repurpose content that is in the public domain and not subject to copyright protection, such as government documents and material that predates modern copyright law.
3. License content or compensate an expert to help create content. Fees can be one-time and paid up front or royalty-based (5–10% of net revenue, for example).

If you choose option 1 or 2, you need expert status within a limited market.

Let's assume you are a real estate broker and have determined that, like yourself, most brokers want a simple but good website to promote themselves and their businesses. If you read and understand the three top-selling books on home-page design, you will know more about that topic than 80% of the readership of a magazine for real estate brokers. If you can summarize the content and make recommendations specific to the needs of the real estate market, a 0.5–1.5% response from an ad you place in the magazine is not unreasonable to expect.

Use the following questions to brainstorm potential how-to or informational products that can be sold to your markets using your expertise or borrowed expertise. Aim for a combination of formats that will lend itself to $50–200 pricing, such as a combination of two CDs (30–90 minutes each), a 40-page transcription of the CDs, and a 10-page quickstart guide. Digital delivery is perfectly acceptable—in some cases, ideal—if you can create a high enough perceived value.

1. How can you tailor a general skill for your market—what I call "niching down"—or add to what is being sold successfully in your target magazines? Think narrow and deep rather than broad.

2. What skills are you interested in that you—and others in your markets—would pay to learn? Become an expert in this skill for yourself and then create a product to teach the same. If you need help or want to speed up the process, consider the next question.

3. What experts could you interview and record to create a sellable audio CD? These people do not need to be the best, but just better than most. Offer them a digital master copy of the interview to do with or sell as they like (this is often enough) and/or offer them a small up-front or ongoing royalty payment. Use Skype.com with HotRecorder (more on these and related tools in Tools and Tricks) to record these conversations directly to your PC and send the mp3 file to an online transcription service.

4. Do you have a failure-to-success story that could be turned into a how-to product for others? Consider problems you've overcome in the past, both professional and personal.

The Expert Builder: How to Become
a Top Expert in 4 Weeks

I t's time to obliterate the cult of the expert. Let the PR world scorn me. First and foremost, there is a difference between *being perceived* as an expert and *being* one. In the context of business, the former is what sells product and the latter, relative to your "minimal customer base," is what creates good products and prevents returns.

It is possible to know all there is to know about a subject— medicine, for example—but if you don't have M.D. at the end of your name, few will listen. The M.D. is what I term a "credibility indicator." The so-called expert with the most credibility indicators, whether acronyms or affiliations, is often the most successful in the market-place, even if other candidates have more in-depth knowledge. This is a matter of superior positioning, not deception.

How, then, do we go about acquiring credibility indicators in the least time possible? Emulating the client-grooming techniques of some of the best PR firms in New York City and Los Angeles isn't a bad place to start.

It took a friend of mine just three weeks to become a "top rela-tionship expert who, as featured in *Glamour* and other national media, has counseled executives at Fortune 500 companies on how to improve their relationships in 24 hours or less." How did she do it?

She followed a few simple steps that created a credibility snowball effect. Here's how you can do the same.

1. **Join two or three related trade organizations** with official-sounding names. In her case, she chose the Association for Conflict Resolution (www.acrnet.org) and The International Foun-dation for Gender Education (www.ifge.org). This can be done online in five minutes with a credit card.
2. **Read the three top-selling books** on your topic (search his-torical *New York Times* bestseller lists online) and summarize each on one page.
3. **Give one free one-to-three-hour seminar** at the closest well-known university, using posters to advertise. Then do the same at branches of two well-known big companies (AT&T, IBM, etc.) lo-

cated in the same area. Tell the company that you have given seminars at University X or X College and are a member of those groups from step 1. Emphasize that you are offering it to them for free to get additional speaking experience outside of academics and will not be selling products or services. Record the seminars from two angles for later potential use as a CD/DVD product.

4. Optional: Offer to write one or two articles for trade magazines related to your topics, citing what you have accomplished in steps 1 and 3 for credibility. If they decline, offer to interview a known expert and write the article—it still gets your name listed as a contributor.

5. Join ProfNet, which is a service that journalists use to find experts to quote for articles. Getting PR is simple if you stop shouting and start listening. Use steps 1, 3, and 4 to demonstrate credibility and online research to respond to journalist queries. Done properly, this will get you featured in media ranging from small local publications to the *New York Times* and ABC News.

Becoming a recognized expert isn't difficult, so I want to remove that barrier now.

I am not recommending pretending to be something you're not. I can't! "Expert" is nebulous media-speak and so overused as to be indefinable. In modern PR terms, proof of expertise in most fields is shown with group affiliations, client lists, writing credentials, and media mentions, not IQ points or Ph.D.s.

Presenting the truth in the best light, but not fabricating it, is the name of the game.

See you on CNN.

►Q&A: QUESTIONS AND ACTIONS

For this hands-on chapter, the Q&A is simple. In fact, it's more like a Q.

The question is, "Did you read the chapter and follow the directions?" If not, do it! Instead of the usual Q&A, the end of this chapter and the following two will feature more extensive resources for taking the action steps described in detail in the text.

►COMFORT CHALLENGE

Find Yoda (3 Days)

Call at least one potential superstar mentor per day for three days. E-mail only after attempting a phone call. I recommend calling before 8:30 A.M. or after 6:00 P.M. to reduce run-ins with secretaries and other gatekeepers. Have a single question in mind, one that you have researched but have been unable to answer yourself. Shoot for "A" players—CEOs, ultrasuccessful entrepreneurs, famous authors, etc.—and don't aim low to make it less frightening. Use www.contactanycelebrity.com if need be, and base your script on the following.

Unknown answerer: This is Acme Inc. [or "the office of Mentor X"].
You: Hi, this is Tim Ferriss calling for John Grisham, please.[31]
Answerer: May I ask what this is regarding?
You: Sure. I know this might sound a bit odd,[32] but I'm a first-time author and just read his interview in *Time Out New York*.[33] I'm a longtime[34] fan and have finally built up the courage to[35] call him for one specific piece of advice. It wouldn't take more than two minutes of his time. Is there any way you can help me

---

31. Said casually and with confidence, this alone will get you through surprisingly often. "I'd like to speak with Mr./Ms. X, please" is a dead giveaway that you don't know them. If you want to up the chances of getting though but risk looking foolish if they call the bluff, ask for the target mentor by first name only.

32. I use this type of lead-in whenever making off-the-wall requests. It softens it and makes the person curious enough to listen before spitting out an automatic "no."

33. This answers the questions they'll have in their head: "Who are you and why are you calling now?" I like to be a "first-time" something to play the sympathy card, and I find a recent media feature online to cite as the trigger for calling.

34. I call people I'm familiar with. If you can't call yourself a longtime fan, tell them that you have followed the mentor's career or business exploits for a certain number of years.

35. Don't pretend to be strong. Make it clear you're nervous and they'll lower their guard. I often do this even if I'm not nervous.

get through to him?[36] I really, really appreciate whatever you can do.

Answerer: Hmmm . . . Just a second. Let me see if he's available. [two minutes later] Here you go. Good luck. [rings to another line]

John Grisham: John Grisham here.

You: Hi, Mr. Grisham. My name is Tim Ferriss. I know this might sound a bit odd, but I'm a first-time author and a longtime fan. I just read your interview in *Time Out New York* and finally built up the courage to call. I have wanted to ask you for a specific piece of advice for a long time, and it shouldn't take more than two minutes of your time. May I?[37]

John Grisham: Uh . . . OK. Go ahead. I have to be on a call in a few minutes.

You (at the very end of the call): Thank you so much for being so generous with your time. If I have the occasional tough question—very occasional—is there any chance I could keep in touch via e-mail?[38]

►LIFESTYLE DESIGN IN ACTION

OVER THE MOON

My 13-year-old daughter would like to be an astronaut when she grows up. Last year she had an extreme challenge to deal with. The phrase from *Apollo 13* "Failure is not an option" sort of became our motto. I got the idea of contacting the commander of *Apollo 13,* Jim Lovell. It didn't take much to find him and he sent her a wonderful letter about his ordeal just to get into the *Apollo* program, not to mention dealing with a crippled spacecraft. His letter made a big

---

36. The wording here is critical. Ask them to "help" you do something.
37. Just rework the gatekeeper paragraph for this, and don't dillydally—get to the point quickly and ask for permission to pull the trigger.
38. End the conversation by opening the door for future contact. Start with e-mail and let the mentoring relationship develop from there.

difference to my daughter. A couple months later, we were able to take things a little further by getting her VIP access to a shuttle launch.
—ROB

►TOOLS AND TRICKS

Confirming Sufficient Market Size

►Compete (www.compete.com) and
  Quantcast (www.quantcast.com)
Find the number of monthly visitors for most websites, in addition to the search terms that generate the most traffic for them.

►Writer's Market (www.writersmarket.com)
Here you'll find a listing of thousands of specialty and niche magazines, including circulation and subscription numbers. I prefer the print version.

►Spyfu (www.spyfu.com)
Download competitors' online advertising spending, keywords, and adword details. Consistent and repeat spending generally indicates successful advertising ROI.

►Standard Rate and Data Services (www.srds.com)
Check out this resource for annual listings of magazine and company customer mailing lists available for rent. If you're considering creating a how-to video for duck hunting, check out the size of customer lists from hunting gun manufacturers and related magazines first. Use the print version in libraries instead of paying for the somewhat confusing online access.

Finding Products to Resell or Manufacturing

►Affiliate Networks: Clickbank (www.clickbank.com),
  Commission Junction (www.cj.com),
  Amazon Associates (www.amazon.com/associates)
No inventory, no invoices. Experimenting with products and categories through affiliate networks such as Clickbank and Commission Junction, which pay you 10–75% of each purchase, is a fast method for doing a proof-of-concept using similar products. It's often worth setting up ac-

counts at both just to observe how bestselling items are being sold and promoted.

Amazon Associates averages 7–10% commissions, but bestselling books are excellent for testing target markets for more elaborate informational products. For all of the above: Do not get into bidding wars against other affiliates using expensive general keywords or overexposed brand names. Go niche or go broke.

► Alibaba (www.alibaba.com)
Based in China, Alibaba is the world's largest business-to-business marketplace. From MP3 players for $9 each to red wine for $2 per bottle, this site is the source. If someone here doesn't make it, it probably can't be made.

► Worldwide Brands (www.fourhourblog.com/wwb)
Offers an extensive how-to guide for finding manufacturers willing to dropship product to your customers, which allows you to avoid pre-purchasing inventory. This is where Amazon and eBay power users find not just drop shippers, but also wholesalers and liquidators. Shopster (www.fourhourblog.com/shopster) is also a popular option, with more than 1,000,000 dropship products to choose from.

► Thomas's Register of Manufacturers (www.thomasnet.com)
  (800-699-9822)
Searchable database of contract manufacturers for every conceivable product, from underwear and food products to airplane parts.

► Electronics, DVDs, Books (www.ingrambook.com,
  www.techdata.com)

► Housewares and Hardware (www.housewares.org,
  www.nationalhardwareshow.com) (847-292-4200)
For these product categories and related talent (on-screen demonstrations), also consider attending local or state fairs.

► Consumables and Vitamin Products (www.expoeast.com,
  expowest.com)

Finding Public Domain Information to Repurpose
Be sure to speak with an intellectual property attorney before using apparent public domain material. If someone modifies 20% of a public domain

work (through abridging and footnotes, for example), their "new" complete work can be copyrighted. Using it without permission would then be a punishable infringement. The details can get confusing. Do the beginning research yourself, but get a pro to look over your findings before moving ahead with product development.

► Project Gutenberg (www.gutenberg.org)
Project Gutenberg is a digital library of more than 15,000 pieces of literature considered to be in the public domain.

► LibriVox (www.librivox.org)
LibriVox is a collection of audiobooks from the public domain that are available for free download.

Recording Seminars or Phone Interviews with Experts for CD Downloadable Products

► HotRecorder (www.hotrecorder.com) (PC),
  Call Recorder (http://ecamm.com/mac/callrecorder/) (Mac)
Use these programs to record any inbound or outbound phone call via computer using Skype (www.skype.com) and other VoIP programs.

► NoCost Conference (www.nocostconference.com)
Provides a free 800-number conference line, as well as free recording and file retrieval. Normal phones can be used for call-in, so no computer or web connection is required for participants. If you'll have a Q&A, I suggest soliciting attendee questions beforehand to avoid issues with muting/unmuting of lines.

► Jing Project (www.jingproject.com) and DimDim
  (www.dimdim.com)
If you'd like to record the actions on your screen for video tutorials, both of these free programs will get the job done. If you need advanced editing features, Jing's big brother Camtasia is the industry standard (www.camtasia.com).

Licensing Ideas to Others for Royalties

► InventRight (www.inventright.com) (800-701-7993)
Stephen Key is the most consistently successful inventor I've ever met, with millions in royalties from companies like Disney, Nestlé, and Coca-Cola.

He is not high-tech but specializes in creating simple products, or improving on existing products, and then licensing (renting) his ideas to large corporations. He comes up with the idea, files a provisional patent for less than $200, and then lets another company do the work while he collects checks. This site introduces his fail-proof process for doing the same. His techniques for cold-calling alone are invaluable. Highly recommended.

► **Guthy-Renker Corporation** (www.guthyrenker.com) (760-773-9022) GRC is the 800-pound infomercial gorilla. It brings in more than $1.3 billion per year in sales with mega-hits like Tony Robbins, Proactiv Solution, and Winsor Pilates. Don't expect more than a 2–4% royalty if you make the cut, but the numbers are huge enough to make it worth a look. Submit your product online.

Searching Patents for Unexploited Ideas to Turn into Products

► United States Patent and Trademark Office (www.uspto.gov) (800-786-9199)

► Licensable Technologies Developed at Universities (www.autm.net; see "view all listings" under "Technology Transfer Offices")

► Inventors Groups and Associations (call and ask if members have anything to license) (www.uiausa.org/Resources/ InventorGroups.htm

Becoming an Expert

► ProfNet via PR Leads (www.prleads.com) and HARO (www.helpareporterout.com) Receive daily leads from journalists and TV and radio producers looking for experts to cite and interview for media ranging from local outlets to CNN and the *New York Times*. Stop swimming upstream and start responding to stories people are already working on. HARO offers select leads at no cost, and you can mention my name with PR Leads to get two months for the price of one.

► PRWeb Press Releases (www.prwebdirect.com) The press release is dead for most purposes, but using this service has some serious search-engine benefits, such as appearing at the top of related Google News and Yahoo! News results.

►ExpertClick (www.expertclick.com)

This is another secret of the PR pros. Put up an expert profile for media to see, receive an up-to-date database of top media contacts, and send free press releases to 12,000 journalists, all on one website that gets more than 5 million hits per month. This is how I got on NBC and ended up developing a prime-time TV show. It works. Mention my name on the phone, or use "Tim Ferriss $100" online, to get a $100 discount.

►LIFESTYLE DESIGN IN ACTION

Bon Jour Tim,

I was in Barnes & Noble at the help desk this past Saturday, April 25, waiting for an employee to get a book for me (*Tropic of Cancer* if you must know). While I was waiting, I noticed a copy of *4-Hour Workweek* on the counter that someone else had ordered. Not one to be shy, I reached over the counter and started reading their copy. As you might guess, I had the employee go back and get me my own copy. Haven't finished *Tropic of Cancer* but finished your book . . .

. . . On Monday I got a yes when I asked my boss to work two days remotely per week. I start next week.

On Monday I also booked the most stunning apartment in Paris for the month of September, at a cost of half of the rent I pay in Southern California. I plan to increase my remote time now through August so that September will be an easy ask to leave for remote work. If the answer happens to be no (which I now doubt), I will be prepared to quit my job.

Now at work on my Income Autopilot project.

Tim: amazing. My life has changed in three days. (Plus, your book was funny as hell.) Thank you!!!   —*CINDY FRANKEY*

10

Income Autopilot II

►TESTING THE MUSE

Many of these theories have been killed off only when some decisive experiment exposed their incorrectness. . . . Thus the yeoman work in any science . . . is done by the experimentalist, who must keep the theoreticians honest.
—MICHIO KAKU, theoretical physicist and cocreator of String Field Theory, *Hyperspace*

Fewer than 5% of the 195,000 books published each year sell more than 5,000 copies. Teams of publishers and editors with decades of combined experience fail more times than not. The founder of Border's Books lost $375 million of investor funding with WebVan,[39] a nationwide grocery delivery service. The problem? No one wanted it.

The moral is that intuition and experience are poor predictors of which products and businesses will be profitable. Focus groups are equally misleading. Ask ten people if they would buy your product. Then tell those who said "yes" that you have ten units in your car and ask them to buy. The initial positive responses, given by people who want to be liked and aim to please, become polite refusals as soon as real money is at stake.

To get an accurate indicator of commercial viability, don't ask

---

39. http://news.com.com/2100-1017-269594.html?legacy=cnet.

people if they would buy—ask them to buy. The response to the second is the only one that matters.

The approach of the **NR** reflects this.

Step Three: Micro-Test Your Products

Micro-testing involves using inexpensive advertisements to test consumer response to a product prior to manufacturing.[40]

In the pre-Internet era, this was done using small classified ads in newspapers or magazines that led prospects to call a prerecorded sales message. Prospects would leave their contact information, and based on the number of callers or response to a follow-up sales letter, the product would be abandoned or manufactured.

In the Internet era, there are better tools that are both cheaper and faster. We'll test the product ideas from the last chapter on Google Adwords—the largest and most sophisticated Pay-Per-Click (PPC) engine—in five days for $500 or less. PPC here refers to the highlighted search results that are listed above and to the right of normal search results on Google. Advertisers pay to have these ads displayed when people search for a certain term related to the advertisers' product, such as "cognitive supplement," and are charged a small fee from $.05 to over $1 each time someone clicks through to their site. For a good introduction to Google Adwords and PPC, visit www.google.com/onlinebusiness. For expanded examples of the following PPC strategies, visit www.fourhourblog .com and search "PPC."

The basic test process consists of three parts, each of which is covered in this chapter.

---

40. It can be illegal to charge customers prior to shipment—so we will not charge customers—but it is still common practice. Why do so many commercials state "allow three to four weeks for delivery" if it only takes three to five days for a shipment to get from New York to California? It gives the companies time to manufacture product and use customers' credit card payments to finance it. Clever but often against the law.

Best: Look at the competition and create a more-compelling offer on a basic one-to-three-page website (one to three hours).

Test: Test the offer using short Google Adwords advertising campaigns (three hours to set up and five days of passive observation).

Divest or Invest: Cut losses with losers and manufacture the winner(s) for sales rollout.

Let's use two people, Sherwood and Johanna, and their two product ideas—French sailor shirts and a how-to yoga DVD for rock climbers—as case studies of what the testing steps look like and how you can do the same.

Sherwood bought a striped sailing shirt in France while traveling last summer, and upon returning to NYC has been continually approached by 20–30-year-old males on the street who want to know where to get their own. Sensing an opportunity, he requests back issues of NYC-based weekly magazines aimed at this demographic and calls the manufacturer in France for pricing. He learns that he can purchase shirts at a wholesale price of $20 that sell for $100 retail. He adds $5 per shirt to account for shipping to the U.S. and arrives at a per-shirt cost of $25. It's not quite our ideal markup (4× vs. 8–10×), but he wants to test the product regardless.

Johanna is a yoga instructor who has noticed her growing client base of rock climbers. She is also a rock climber and is considering creating a yoga instructional DVD tailored to that sport, which would include a 20-page spiral-bound manual and be priced at $80. She predicts that production of a low-budget first edition of the DVD would cost nothing more than a borrowed digital camera and a friend's iMac for simple editing. She can burn small quantities of this first-edition DVD—no menus, just straight footage and titles—on the laptop and create labels with freeware from www.download .com. She has contacted a duplication house and learned that more-professional DVDs will cost \$3–5 apiece to duplicate in small quantities (minimum of 250), including cases.

Now that they have ideas and estimates of start-up costs, what next?

Besting the Competition

First and foremost, each product must pass a competitive litmus test. How can Sherwood and Johanna beat the competition and offer a superior product or guarantee?

1. Sherwood and Johanna Google the top terms each would use to try and find their respective products. To come up with related terms and derivative terms, both use search term suggestion tools.

> **Google Adwords Keyword Tool** (https://adwords.google
> .com/select/KeywordToolExternal) Enter the potential
> search terms to find search volume and alternative terms
> with more search traffic. Click on the "Approx Avg
> Search Volume" column to sort results from most to
> least searched.
>
> **SEOBook Keyword Tool, SEO for Firefox Extension**
> (http://tools.seobook.com/) This is an outstanding
> resource page with searches powered by Wordtracker
> (www.wordtracker.com).

Both then visit the three websites that consistently appear in top search and PPC positions. How can Sherwood and Johanna differentiate themselves?

> ►Use more credibility indicators? (media, academia,
> associations, and testimonials)
> ►Create a better guarantee?

➤ Offer better selection?[41]

➤ Free or faster shipping?

Sherwood notices that the shirts are often hard to find on the competitive sites, all of which feature dozens of products, and the shirts are either made in the U.S. (inauthentic) or shipped from France (customers must wait two to four weeks). Johanna cannot find a "yoga for rock climbing" DVD, so she is starting from a blank slate.

2. Sherwood and Johanna now need to create a one-page (300–600 words) testimonial-rich advertisement that emphasizes their differentiators and product benefits using text and either personal photos or stock photos from stock photo websites. Both have spent two weeks collecting advertisements that have prompted them to make purchases or that have caught their attention in print or online—these will serve as models.[42] Johanna asks her clients for testimonials and Sherwood lets his friends try on the shirts to get several for his page. Sherwood also asks the manufacturer for photos and advertising samples.

See www.pxmethod.com for a good example of how I have created a test page using testimonials from seminar attendees. Please note that it's just a template for readers and not a live sales page. Free how-to seminars as recommended in the Expert Builder are ideal for identifying popular selling points and securing testimonials.

---

41. This applies to Sherwood and not Johanna.

42. How did I come up with the most successful BodyQUICK headline ("The Fastest Way to Increase Power and Speed Guaranteed")? I borrowed it from the longest-running, and thus most profitable, Rosetta Stone headline: "The Fastest Way to Learn a Language Guaranteed.™" Reinventing the wheel is expensive—become an astute observer of what is already working and adapt it. I keep a folder of all print and direct mail advertising that compels me to call a number or visit a website, and I use www.delicious.com to bookmark websites that convince me to provide my e-mail address or make a purchase.

Testing the Advertisement

Sherwood and Johanna now need to test actual customer response to their advertisements. Sherwood first tests his concept with a 72-hour eBay auction that includes his advertising text. He sets the "reserve" (the lowest price he'll accept) for one shirt at $50 and cancels the auction last minute to avoid legal issues since he doesn't have product to ship. He has received bids up to $75 and decides to move to the next phase of testing. Johanna doesn't feel comfortable with the apparent deception and skips this preliminary testing.

Sherwood's cost: <$5.

Both register domain names for their soon-to-be one-page sites using the cheap domain registrar www.domainsinseconds.com. Sherwood chooses www.shirtsfromfrance.com and Johanna chooses www.yogaclimber.com. For additional domain names, Johanna uses www.domainsinseconds.com.

Cost to both: <$20.

Sherwood uses www.fourhourblog.com/weebly to create his one-page site advertisement and then creates two additional pages using the form builder www.wufoo.com. If someone clicks on the "purchase" button at the bottom of the first page, it takes them to a second page with pricing, shipping and handling,[43] and basic contact fields to fill out (including e-mail and phone). If the visitor presses "continue with order," it takes them to a page that states, "Unfortunately, we are currently on back order but will contact you as soon as we have product in stock. Thank you for your patience." This structure allows him to test the first-page ad and his pricing separately. If someone gets to the last page, it is considered an order.

Johanna is not comfortable with "dry testing," as Sherwood's approach is known, even though it is legal if the billing data isn't

---

43. Sherwood includes shipping and handling prior to the final order page so that people don't finalize the order just to confirm total pricing. He wants his "orders" to reflect real orders and not price checkers.

captured. She instead uses the same two services to create a single webpage with the content of her one-page ad and an e-mail sign-up for a free "top 10 tips" list for using yoga for rock climbing. She will consider 60% of the sign-ups as hypothetical orders.

Cost to both: <$0.

Both set up simple Google Adwords campaigns with 50–100 search terms to simultaneously test headlines while driving traffic to their pages. Their daily budget limits are set at $50 per day. (At this segue into PPC testing, I recommend you first visit www.adwords/ google.com/onlinebusiness and then follow along by creating your own account, which should take about 10 minutes. It would be a waste of rain forests to use ten pages to explain terms that can be understood at a glance online.)

Sherwood and Johanna decide on the best search terms by using the search term suggestion tools mentioned earlier. Both aim for specific terms when possible ("french sailor shirts" vs. "french shirts"; "yoga for sports" vs. "yoga") for higher conversion rates (the percentage of visitors that purchase) and lower cost-per-click (CPC). They aim also for second through fourth positioning, but no more than $.20 CPC.

Sherwood will use Google's free analytical tools to track "orders" and page abandonment rates—what percentage of visitors leave the site from which pages. Johanna will use www.wufoo.com to track e-mail sign-ups on this small testing scale.[44]

Cost to both: $0.

Both Johanna and Sherwood design Adwords ads that focus on their differentiators. Each Google Adwords ad consists of a headline and then two lines of description, neither of which can exceed 35 characters. In Sherwood's case, he creates five groups of 10 search terms each. The following are two of his ads.

---

44. If you are rolling out after a successful test or building a large e-mail database, tools like www.fourhourblog.com/aweber in the resources are better at scaling.

SAILOR SHIRTS FROM FRANCE
French Quality, Shipped from U.S.
Lifetime Guarantee!
www.shirtsfromfrance.com

REAL FRENCH SAILOR SHIRTS
French Quality, Shipped from U.S.
Lifetime Guarantee!
www.shirtsfromfrance.com

Johanna creates the same five groups of 10 terms each and tests a number of ads, including these:

YOGA FOR ROCK CLIMBERS
DVD Used by 5.12 Climbers
Get Flexible Fast!
www.yogaclimber.com

YOGA FOR ROCK CLIMBERS
DVD Used by 5.12 Climbers
Get Flexible Fast!
www.yogaforsports.com

Notice that these ads can be used to test not just headlines but guarantees, product names, and domain names. It's as simple as creating several ads, rotated automatically by Google, that are identical except for the one variable to be tested. How do you think I determined the best title for this book?

<u>Both Sherwood and Johanna disable the feature on Google that serves only the best-performing ad.</u> This is necessary to later compare the click-through rates from each and combine the best elements (headline, domain name, and body text) into a final ad.

Last but not least, ensure that the ads don't trick prospects into visiting the site. The product offer should be clear. Our goal is qualified traffic, so we do not want to offer something "free" or otherwise attract window shoppers or the curious who are unlikely to buy.

Cost to both: $50 or less per day × 5 days = $250.[45]

---

45. Keeping in mind that 100 specific terms at $0.10 per click will perform better than 10 broad terms at $1.00 per click, the more you spend, and thus the more traffic you drive, the more statistically valid the results will be. If budget permits, increase the number of related terms and daily expenditure so that the entire PPC test costs $500–1,000.

Investing or Divesting

Five days later, it's time to tally the results.

What can we consider a "good" click-through and conversion rate? This is where the math can be deceiving. If we're selling a $10,000 abominable snowman suit with an 80% profit margin, we obviously need a much lower conversion rate than someone who is selling a $50 DVD with a 70% profit margin. For sophisticated tools and free spreadsheets that do all sorts of calculations for you, visit the reader-only resources at www.fourhourblog.com.

Johanna and Sherwood decide to keep it simple at this stage: How much did they spend on PPC ads and how much did they "sell"?

Johanna has done well. The traffic wasn't enough to make the test stand up to statistical scrutiny, but she spent about $200 on PPC and got 14 sign-ups for a free 10-tip report. If she assumes 60% would purchase, that means 8.4 people × $75 profit per DVD = $630 in hypothetical total profit. This is also not taking into account the potential lifetime value of each customer.

The results of her small test are no guarantee of future success, but the indications are positive enough that she decides to set up a Yahoo Store for $99 per month and a small per-transaction fee. Her credit isn't excellent, so she will opt to use www.paypal.com to accept credit cards online instead of approaching her bank for a merchant account.[46] She e-mails the 10-tip report to those who signed up and asks for their feedback and recommendations for content on the DVD. Ten days later, she has a first attempt at the DVD ready to ship and her store is online. Her sales to the original sign-ups cover costs of production and she is soon selling a respectable 10 DVDs per week ($750 profit) via Google Adwords. She plans to test advertising in niche magazines and blogs and now needs to create an automation architecture to remove herself from the equation.

Sherwood didn't fare as well but still sees potential. He spent

---

46. This is a checking account for receiving credit card payments.

$150 on PPC and "sold" three shirts for a hypothetical $225 in profit. He had more than enough traffic, but the bulk of visitors left the site on the pricing page. Rather than drop pricing, he decides to test a "2× money-back guarantee" on the pricing page, which will enable customers to get a $200 refund if the $100 shirts aren't the "most comfortable they've ever owned." He retests and "sells" seven shirts for $525 in profit. Based on these results, he sets up a merchant account through his bank and Authorize.net to process credit cards, orders a dozen shirts from France, and sells them all over the following ten days. This gives him enough profit to buy a small display ad at 50% off (asking for a "first-time advertiser discount" and then citing a competing magazine to get another 20% off) in a local weekly art magazine, in which he calls the shirt "Jackson Pollock Shirts." He orders two dozen more shirts with net-30 payment terms and puts a toll-free number[47] in the print ad that forwards to his cell phone. He does this instead of using a website for two reasons: (1) He wants to determine the most common questions for his FAQ online, and (2) he wants to test an offer of $100 for one shirt ($75 in profit) or "buy two, get one free" ($200 − $75 = $125 profit).

He sells all 24 shirts in the first five days the magazine runs, most through the special offer. Success. He redesigns the print ad, putting answers to common questions in the text to cut down on calls for information, and decides to negotiate a longer-term ad agreement with the magazine. He sends his sales rep a check for four issues at 30% of their published rates. He calls to confirm that they received his check via FedEx and, with check in hand and deadlines looming, they don't refuse.

Sherwood wants to go to Berlin during a two-week break from his job, which he is now considering quitting. How can he roll out his success and escape his own company? He needs to build the architecture and get his mobile M.B.A.

That's where the next chapter comes in.

---

47. Set this up using services detailed at the end of this chapter and the next.

New Rich Revisited: How Doug Did It

Remember Doug from ProSoundEffects.com? How did he test the idea and go from $0 to $10,000 per month in the process? He followed these steps.

1. Market Selection
He chose music and television producers as his market because he is a musician himself and has used these products.

2. Product Brainstorm
He chose the most popular products available for resale from the largest manufacturers of sound libraries and arranged a wholesale purchase and drop-ship agreement with them. Many of these libraries cost well above $300 (up to $7,500), and this is precisely why he needs to answer more customer-service questions than someone with a lower-priced product of $50–200.

3. Micro-Testing
He auctioned the products on eBay to test demand (and the highest possible pricing) before purchasing inventory. He ordered product only when people placed orders from him, and product shipped immediately from the manufacturers' warehouses. Based on this demand confirmed on eBay, Doug created a Yahoo Store with these products and began testing Google Adwords and other PPC search engines.

4. Rollout and Automation
Following this testing, and upon generating sufficient cash flow, Doug began experimenting with print advertising in trade magazines. Simultaneously, he streamlined and outsourced operations to reduce his time requirements from two hours per day to two hours per week.

►COMFORT CHALLENGE

Rejecting First Offers and Walking Away (3 Days)

Before performing this exercise, if possible, read the bonus chapter "How to Get $700,000 of Advertising for $10,000" on our companion site, and then set aside two hours on a consecutive Saturday, Sunday, and Monday.

On Saturday and Sunday, go to a farmers' market or other outdoor event where goods are sold. If this isn't possible, go to small independent retailers (not chains or mass retail).

Set a budget of $100 for your negotiating tuition and look for items to purchase that total at least $150. Your job is to get the sellers down to a total of $100 or less for the lot. It is better to practice on many cheap items rather than a few big items. Be sure to reply to their first offer with, "What type of discount can you offer?" to let them negotiate against themselves. Negotiate near closing time, choose your objective price, bracket, and make a firm offer with cash in hand for that amount.[48] Practice walking away if your objective price isn't met. On Monday, call two magazines (expect the first to be awkward) and use the script on the companion site to negotiate, minus the last firm offer. Get them as low as possible and then call them back later to indicate that your proposal was refused by upper management or otherwise vetoed.

This is the negotiating equivalent of paper trading.[49] Get used to refusing offers and countering in person and—most importantly—on the phone.

---

48. See the online bonus chapter on www.fourhourblog.com to understand all of these terms in context. Search "Jedi Mind Tricks."

49. "Paper trading" refers to setting an imaginary budget, "purchasing" stocks (writing their current values on a piece of paper), and then tracking their performance over time to see how your investment would have done had it been for real. It is a no-risk method for honing investment skills before putting skin in the game.

►TOOLS AND TRICKS

Sample Muse Test Page

►The PX Method (www.pxmethod.com)
This sales template was used to determine the viability of a speed-reading product, which tested successfully. Notice how testimonials, credibility indicators, and risk-reversal guarantees are used, as well as how the pricing is put on a separate page so it can be isolated as a testing variable. Use this as a reference—it is a simple and effective model that can be copied. Please do not input your credit card information, as it is just a mock-up for teaching purposes.

Fast and Simple Website Creation for Non-Techies (and Techies)

►Weebly (www.fourhourblog.com/weebly)
Weebly, which the BBC labeled "a must," allowed me to create www .timothyferriss.com in less than two hours and have it appear on the front page of Google for "timothy ferriss" searches within 48 hours. It is, like WordPress.com below, designed to be very SEO-friendly (search-engine optimization) without any knowledge or action on your part. No HTML or Internet expertise is required.

►WordPress.com (www.wordpress.com)
I used WordPress.com to set up www.litliberation.org from a coffee shop in Bratislava, Slovakia, when a U.S.-based designer flaked out and left me scrambling. It took me less than three hours to learn how to use it and build the site. The site, an experimental educational fundraiser, ended up raising 200%+ more than Stephen Colbert in the same period of time. I also use their free open-sourced version of WordPress (www.wordpress.org, which requires separate hosting) to manage everything for my top-1,000 blog at www.fourhourblog.com. This offers greater customization but requires more management and technical know-how.

Both Weebly and WordPress.com host your site for you, so additional hosting setup isn't required.

If you choose to use www.wordpress.org (not .com) for greater customizability, I suggest using a hosting service with one-click WordPress installation like www.fourhourblog.com/bluehost. The Shopp plug-in (http://shopplugin .net/) or Market Theme plug-in (www.fourhour blog.com/markettheme) can then be used to add e-commerce capabilities. Shopify.com (discussed later) is another good all-in-one alternative.

Create Forms in Seconds for Testing Checkout with or Without Payment

► Wufoo (www.wufoo.com)

Wufoo does not offer a full-featured shopping cart, but it provides the cleanest, easiest-to-use forms on the web. Create a checkout page that connects to PayPal and you can (1) link to this checkout page from your site on Weebly, WordPress.com, or elsewhere, or (2) drop the code into your own website and have it hosted there. Wufoo is appropriate for testing and selling single products, as people can't add multiple items to a shopping cart or otherwise customize the order à la Amazon. For those additional options, which are often desirable after successful testing, you will want to use an "end-to-end site solutions" listed later in these resources.

Cost-Effective Trademark Filing and Company Formation (LLC, C-Corp, etc.)

Though I also have a C-Corporation (often used to issue common and preferred stock to investors), created through the second option below, LLCs and S-Corps are generally favored by small businesses. Consult your accountant to determine the best entity form.

► LegalZoom (www.legalzoom.com)

Company formation, trademarks, and nearly all legal documents. I know one founder who used this service to incorporate his tech start-up, which is now worth more than $200 million.

► Corporate Creations (www.corporatecreations.com)

Domestic and overseas company formation.

Services for Selling Downloadable Products (e-books, videos, audio, etc., in descending order of reader preference)

► E-Junkie (www.e-junkie.com)

➤ **Lulu (www.lulu.com)**
Lulu will also do print-on-demand and other forms of manufacture and fulfillment. Like Lightning Source (www.lightningsource.com), it offers distribution through Amazon, Barnes & Noble online, and other major outlets.

➤ **CreateSpace (www.createspace.com)**
A subsidiary of Amazon.com that offers inventory-free, physical distribution of books, CD and DVDs on Demand, as well as video downloads through Amazon Video On Demand™.

➤ **Clickbank (www.clickbank.com)**
Provides integrated access to affiliates willing to sell your product for a percentage of sales.

Introduction to Pay-Per-Click (PPC) Advertising and Testing

➤ Google Adwords (www.google.com/adwords)

Market Sizing and Keyword Suggestion Tools
Brainstorm additional PPC search terms and determine the number of people who are searching for them.

➤ **Google Adwords Keyword Tool (https://adwords.google.com/ select/KeywordToolExternal)**
Enter the potential search terms to find search volume and alternative terms with more search traffic. Click on the "Approx Avg Search Volume" column to sort results from most to least searched.

➤ **SEOBook Keyword Tool, SEO for Firefox Extension (http://tools.seobook.com/)**
Outstanding resource page with searches powered by Wordtracker (www.wordtracker.com).

Low-Cost Domain Registration

➤ **Domains in Seconds (www.domainsinseconds.com)**
I have registered more than 100 domains through this service.

►Joker (www.joker.com)
►GoDaddy (www.fourhourblog.com/godaddy)

Inexpensive but Dependable Hosting Services

Shared hosting solutions, where your site is hosted alongside other sites on a single server, are so cheap that I recommend using two providers, one as a primary and one as a backup. Put your site pages on each host and sign up with www.no-ip.com, which can redirect traffic (DNS) to the backup in five minutes instead of the usual 24 to 48 hours.

►1and1 (www.1and1.com)
►BlueHost (www.fourhourblog.com/bluehost)
►RackSpace (www.fourhourblog.com/rackspace; known for dedicated and managed servers)
►Hosting.com (www.hosting.com; known for dedicated and managed servers)

Royalty-Free Photos and Materials

►iStockphoto (www.istockphoto.com)
iStockphoto is the Internet's original member-generated image and design site, which has more than 4 million photographs, vector illustrations, videos, audio tracks, and Flash files available for use.

►Getty Images (www.gettyimages.com)
This is where the pros go. Stock photos and film of anything for a price. I pay $150–400 for most images I use in national print campaigns and the quality is outstanding.

E-mail Sign-up Tracking and Scheduled Autoresponders

Both of these programs can be used to embed e-mail address sign-up forms on your site.

►AWeber (www.fourhourblog.com/aweber)
►MailChimp (www.mailchimp.com)

End-to-End Site Solutions with Payment Processing

►Shopify (www.fourhourblog.com/shopify)
This is a reader favorite that, in addition to beautiful design, offers full

SEO (search-engine optimization), drag-and-drop use, statistics, and product fulfillment through one of their certified partners such as Fulfillment by Amazon.com. Clients range from small-business owners to Tesla Motors. Unlike with Yahoo and eBay, however, you will need to set up a payment-processing service to accept payments from customers. (See below—PayPal is the easiest to integrate.)

►Yahoo! Store (http://smallbusiness.yahoo.com/ecommerce) (866-781-9246)
This is what Doug of Pro Sound Effects used. As little as $40 a month with 1.5% per transaction.

►eBay Store (http://pages.ebay.com/storefronts/start.html)
From $15–500 per month, plus eBay fees.

Simple Payment Processing for Testing Pages, from Least to Most Involved

►PayPal Cart (www.paypal.com; see "merchant")
Accept credit card payments in minutes. No monthly fees, 1.9–2.9% of each transaction (called "discount rate") and $0.30 per transaction.

►Google Checkout (http://checkout.google.com/sell)
Get $10 in free processing for each $1 spent on AdWords; 2% and $0.20 per transaction thereafter. Requires that customers have a Google ID, and is thus most useful as a supplement to one of the aforementioned payment solutions. Be sure to link your Checkout account to your AdWords account to receive credit. Important note: free transaction processing for nonprofits.

►Authorize.net (www.fourhourblog.com/authorize)
The Authorize.Net Payment Gateway can help you accept credit card and electronic check payments quickly and affordably. More than 230,000 merchants trust Authorize.net to manage their transactions, help prevent fraud, and grow their business. The fees per transaction are lower than PayPal or Google Checkout, but setup will require a merchant account, covered in the next chapter, and other time-consuming applications. I suggest setting up Authorize.net only after a product has tested successfully through one of the other two options above.

Software for Understanding Web Traffic (Web Analytics)

How are people finding, browsing, and leaving your site? How many prospective customers are being delivered by each PPC ad, and which pages are most popular? These programs tell you all this and more. Google is free for most low-volume sites—and better than a lot of paid software-and the others cost $30 and upward per month.

► Google Analytics (www.google.com/analytics)

► CrazyEgg (www.crazyegg.com)

I use CrazyEgg to see exactly where people are clicking most and least on homepages and landing pages. It is particularly helpful for repositioning the most important links or buttons to help prompt visitors to take specific next actions. Don't guess what's working or not—measure it.

► Clicktracks (www.clicktracks.com)
► WebTrends (www.webtrends.com)

A/B Testing Software

Testing is, as you know, the name of the game, but testing all the variables can be confusing. How do you know which combination of headlines, text, and images on your homepage results in the most sales? Instead of using one version for a bit, then alternating, which is time-consuming, use software that serves up different versions to prospects at random, then does the math for you.

► Google Website Optimizer (WO) (http://www.google.com/
   websiteoptimizer)

This is a free tool that, like Google Analytics, is better than most paid services. I used Google WO to test three potential homepages for www .dailyburn.com and increased sign-ups 19%, then again by more than 16%.

► Offermatica (www.offermatica.com)
► Vertster.com (www.vertster.com)
► Optimost (www.optimost.com)

Low-Cost Toll-free Numbers

► TollFreeMAX (www.tollfreemax.com) (877-888-8MAX) and
   Kall8 (www.kall8.com)

TollFreeMAX and Kall8 both allow you to set up toll-free numbers in 2–5 minutes. Calls can then be forwarded to any other numbers, and voicemail and statistics can be managed online or via e-mail.

Checking Competitive Site Traffic

Want to see how much traffic your competition is getting and who is linking to them?

► Compete (www.compete.com)
► Quantcast (www.quantcast.com)
► Alexa (www.alexa.com)

Freelance Designers and Programmers

► 99Designs (www.fourhourblog.com/99designs) and
  Crowdspring (www.fourhourblog.com/crowdspring)

I used 99Designs to get an excellent logo for www.litliberation.org in 24 hours for less than $150. I submitted the concept, more than 50 designers worldwide uploaded their best attempts, which I could browse, and I chose the best after suggesting a few improvements. From Crowdspring's site: "Name your price, name your deadline, see entries within hours and be done in just days. The average project gets a whopping 68 entries. 25 entries or your money back."

► eLance (www.fourhourblog.com/elance) (877-435-2623)
► Craigslist (www.craigslist.org)

►LIFESTYLE DESIGN IN ACTION

I'm a U.S. citizen and it was impossible for my friends and relatives to track me down by phone. Enter Skype In. It's not new but allows you to lease a fixed U.S. (or other country) phone number which then forwards to your Skype account. About $60/year. Within Skype you can then set up call forwarding to ring you at your local number. You pay the rate as if you were calling from the United States to wherever you are. I've used this in about 40 countries and it works like a treat. The call quality is usually great and the convenience is amazing. http://www.skype.com/allfeatures/onlinenumber/. A caveat is to always, ALWAYS get a local SIM card for your unlocked

GSM phone. Roaming is for amateurs. A local SIM also gets you GPRS, Edge, or 3G. Sometimes even free Wifi. Cheers,   —*TY KROLL*

• • •

Basically I try to keep all of my tools online so that if my laptop gets stolen, I can buy a new one and have everything up and running within 24 hours. Here are a few of the tools I use on a regular basis:

- RememberTheMilk.com has been really crucial to me keeping on top of my daily tasks.
- Freshbooks.com for online invoicing
- Highrise (http://www.highrisehq.com/) for online CRM
- Dropbox (getdropbox.com) for easy file sharing/automatic backup of critical files while on the road
- TrueCrypt (truecrypt.org) for keeping your laptop data secure while on the road. *[Tim comment: This can also be used with a USB flash drive, and another cool feature—it provides two levels of "plausible deniability" (hidden volumes, etc.) if someone forces you to reveal the password.]*
- PBwiki.com - Wiki site that helps me keep on top of the notes and ideas that I collect as I go through life.
- FogBugz on Demand: http://www.fogcreek.com/FogBUGZ/IntrotoOnDemand.html. It's a "bug tracker" aimed at software development companies, but I use it every day for both personal and business tasks. It's almost like a VA, as you can route your mail through it and it will help you sort it and keep track of it. It has great features to track e-mails, and there's a free version for two users (me + VA!).   —*RB CARTER*

• • •

A really useful service is Amazon's Mechanical Turk. With a small investment in time or money, a business that requires hundreds of people doing small bits of defined work becomes possible for extraordinarily low work-per-unit costs. Examples include the search for Steve Fosset (literally thousands of people looked at satellite photos that would have overwhelmed SAR agencies) and a trouble-ticket business that utilizes qualified labor all over the world (see Amazon.com/webservices). I am not an owner nor do I have any stake in Amazon—but I have used their services and some are transforming when it comes to muse creation. Cheers,   —*J MARYMEE*

• • •

FAST TO MARKET
The fastest way to market with a product idea is: Registera.com. Get hosting from dathorn.com [a cheap reseller account, like www .domainsinseconds.com]. With two clicks set up a wordpress blog. Apply a theme to it. Add your content and a buy now button. The buy now button links to an enter e-mail address, phone number, etc., page. The user then clicks a continue to PayPal button. This automatically e-mails me their details, but then shows the user a message stating that the link to PayPal is currently not working. I use this to determine how many sales I would have achieved. I use Google ads to drive traffic . . . I calculate theoretical ROI (ideally using Google analytics). If after a week or two I can see a positive ROI that's worth my effort I create or outsource the creation of the product (emag, PDF, whatever). I set it all up with a working link to PayPal, and then retrospectively send a message to the users who already tried to buy. Normally within hours I've got all my money back, and the cash starts to roll. An example is the DIY public relations pack at www.mybusinesspr.com.au. Great work of the 4HWW . . . looking forward to the next edition.   Regards, *MATT SCHMIDT*

11

Income Autopilot III

►MBA—MANAGEMENT BY ABSENCE

> The factory of the future will have only two employees, a man and a dog. The man will be there to feed the dog. The dog will be there to keep the man from touching the equipment.
> —WARREN G. BENNIS, University of Southern California Professor of Business Administration; adviser to Ronald Reagan and John F. Kennedy

Most entrepreneurs don't start out with automation as a goal. This leaves them open to mass confusion in a world where each business guru contradicts the next. Consider the following:

> A company is stronger if it is bound by love rather than by fear. . . . If the employees come first, then they're happy.
> —HERB KELLEHER, cofounder of Southwest Airlines

> Look, kiddie. I built this business by being a bastard. I run it by being a bastard. I'll always be a bastard, and don't you ever try to change me.[50]
> —CHARLES REVSON, founder of Revlon, to a senior executive within his company

Hmm . . . Whom to follow? If you are fast on your feet, you'll notice that I just offered you an either-or option. The good news is that, as usual, there is a third option.

---

50. Richard Tedlow, *Giants of Enterprise: Seven Business Innovators and the Empires They Built* (2001; reprint, HarperBusiness, 2003).

The contradictory advice you find in business books and elsewhere usually relates to managing employees—how to handle the human element. Herb tells you to give them a hug, Revson tells you to kick them in the balls, and I tell you to solve the problem by eliminating it altogether: Remove the human element.

Once you have a product that sells, it's time to design a self-correcting business architecture that runs itself.

The Remote-Control CEO

The power of hiding ourselves from one another is mercifully given, for men are wild beasts, and would devour one another but for this protection.

—HENRY WARD BEECHER, U.S. abolitionist and clergyman, "Proverbs from Plymouth Pulpit"

RURAL PENNSYLVANIA

In a 200-year-old stone farmhouse, a quiet "experiment in 21st-century leadership" is proceeding exactly as planned.[51]

Stephen McDonnell is upstairs in his flip-flops looking at a spreadsheet on his computer. His company has increased its annual revenue 30% per year since it all began, and he is able to spend more time with his three daughters than he ever thought possible.

The experiment? As CEO of Applegate Farms, he insists on spending just one day per week at the company headquarters in Bridgewater, New Jersey. He's not the only CEO who spends time at home, of course—there are hundreds who have heart attacks or nervous breakdowns and need time to recover—but there is a huge difference. McDonnell has been doing it for more than 17 years. Rarer still, he started doing it just six months after founding the company.

---

51. This is adapted from "The Remote Control CEO," *Inc.* magazine, October 2005.

This intentional absence has enabled him to create a process-driven instead of founder-driven business. Limiting contact with managers forces the entrepreneur to develop operational rules that enable others to deal with problems themselves instead of calling for help.

This isn't just for small operations. Applegate Farms sells more than 120 organic and natural meat products to high-end retailers and generates more than $35 million in revenue per year.

It is all possible because McDonnell started with the end in mind.

Behind the Scenes: The Muse Architecture

Orders are nobody can see the Great Oz! Not nobody, not nohow!

—GUARDIAN OF THE EMERALD CITY GATES, *The Wizard of Oz*

Starting with the end in mind—an organizational map of what the eventual business will look like—is not new.

Infamous deal-maker Wayne Huizenga copied the org chart of McDonald's to turn Blockbuster into a billion-dollar behemoth, and dozens of titans have done much the same. In our case, it's the "end in mind" that is different. Our goal isn't to create a business that is as large as possible, but rather a business that bothers us as little as possible. The architecture has to place us out of the information flow instead of putting us at the top of it.

I didn't get this right the first time I tried.

In 2003, I was interviewed in my home office for a documentary called *As Seen on TV*. We were interrupted every 20–30 seconds with beeping e-mail notifications, IM pings, and ringing phones. I couldn't leave them unanswered, because dozens of decisions depended on me. If I didn't ensure the trains were running on time and put out the fires, no one would.

The Anatomy of Automation

THE 4-HOUR WORKWEEK VIRTUAL ARCHITECTURE

1. This cost includes a webmaster/programmer.
2. Declined credit cards are also sent back to fulfillment for phone calls to customers.
3. Fulfillment house refunds customers through the processor.
4. Chargebacks are disputed credit card charges.

Splitting the Pie: Outsourcer Economics

Each outsourcer takes a piece of the revenue pie. Here is what the general profit-loss might look like for a hypothetical $80 product sold via phone and developed with the help of an expert, who is paid a royalty. I recommend calculating profit margins using higher-than-anticipated expenses. This will account for unforeseen costs (read: screwups) and miscellaneous fees such as monthly reports, etc.

REVENUE

Product cost	$80.00
Shipping/Handling	$12.95
Total Revenue	**$92.95**

EXPENSES

Product manufacturing	$10.00
Call center ($0.83 per minute × average call time of 4 minutes)	$3.32
Shipping	$5.80
Fulfillment ($1.85 per package + $0.50 for boxes/packing)	$2.35
Credit card processing (2.75% of $92.95)	$2.56
Returns + declined cards (6% of $92.95)	$5.58
Royalties (5% of wholesale price of $48 [$80 × .6])	$2.40
Total expenses	**$32.01**

PROFIT (revenue minus expenses)	**$60.94**

How do you factor in advertising cost? If a $1,000 ad or $1,000 in PPC produces 50 sales, my advertising cost per order (CPO) is $20. *This makes the actual per-unit profit $40.94.*

I set a new goal after that experience, and when I was interviewed six months later as a follow-up, one change was more pronounced than all others: silence. I had redesigned the business from the ground up so that I had no phone calls to answer and no e-mail to respond to.

I'm often asked how big my company is—how many people I

employ full-time. The answer is one. Most people lose interest at that point. If someone were to ask me how many people run Brain-QUICKEN LLC, on the other hand, the answer is different: between 200 and 300. I am the ghost in the machine.[52]

From advertisements—print in this example—to a cash deposit in my bank account, the diagram on page 203 is what a simplified version of my architecture looks like, including some sample costs. If you have developed a product based on the guidelines in the last two chapters, it will plug into this structure hand-in-glove.

Where am I in the diagram? Nowhere.

I am not a tollbooth through which anything needs to pass. I am more like a police officer on the side of the road who can step in if need be, and I use detailed reports from outsourcers to ensure the cogs are moving as intended. I check reports from fulfillment each Monday and monthly reports from the same the first of each month. The latter reports include orders received from the call center, which I can compare to the call center bills to gauge profit. Otherwise, I just check bank accounts online on the first and fifteenth of each month to look for odd deductions. If I find something, one e-mail will fix it, and if not, it's back to kendo, painting, hiking, or whatever I happen to be doing at the time.

Removing Yourself from the Equation: When and How

> The system is the solution.   —AT&T

The diagram on page 203 should be your rough blueprint for designing a self-sustaining virtual architecture. There could be differences—more or fewer elements—but the main principles are the same:

---

52. Actually, I'm the ghost in new machines now, as I sold BrainQUICKEN in 2009 to a private equity firm.

1. Contract outsourcing companies[53] that specialize in one function vs. freelancers whenever possible so that if someone is fired, quits, or doesn't perform, you can replace them without interrupting your business. Hire trained groups of people who can provide detailed reporting and replace one another as needed.

2. Ensure that all outsourcers are willing to communicate among themselves to solve problems, and *give them written permission to make most inexpensive decisions without consulting you first* (I started at less than $100 and moved to $400 after two months).

How do you get there? It helps to look at where entrepreneurs typically lose their momentum and stall permanently.

Most entrepreneurs begin with the cheapest tools available, bootstrapping and doing things themselves to get up and running with little cash. This isn't the problem. In fact, it's necessary so that the entrepreneurs can train outsourcers later. The problem is that these same entrepreneurs don't know when and how to replace themselves or their homemade infrastructure with something more **scalable.**

By "scalable," I mean a business architecture that can handle 10,000 orders per week as easily as it can handle 10 orders per week. Doing this requires minimizing your decision-making responsibilities, which achieves our goal of time freedom while setting the stage for doubling and tripling income with no change in hours worked.

Call the companies at the end of the chapter to research costs. Plan and budget accordingly to upgrade infrastructure at the following milestones, which I measure in units of product shipped:

Phase I: 0–50 Total Units of Product Shipped

Do it all yourself. Put your phone number on the site for both general questions and order-taking—this is important in the beginning—

---

53. "Contract outsourcing companies" can be as simple as dependable web-based services. Don't let the term intimidate you.

and take customer calls to determine common questions that you will answer later in an online FAQ. This FAQ will also be the main material for training phone operators and developing sales scripts.

Is PPC, an offline advertisement, or your website too vague or misleading, thus attracting unqualified and time-consuming consumers? If so, change them to answer common questions and make the product benefits (including what it isn't or doesn't do) clearer.

Answer all e-mail and save your responses in one folder called "customer service questions." CC yourself on responses and put the nature of the customers' questions in the subject lines for future indexing. Personally pack and ship all product to determine the cheapest options for both. Investigate opening a merchant account from your local small bank (easier to get than with a larger bank) for later outsourced credit card processing at higher roll-out volumes.

Phase II: >10 Units Shipped Per Week

Add the extensive FAQ to your website and continue to add answers to common questions as received. Find local fulfillment companies in the yellow pages under "fulfillment services" or "mailing services." If you cannot find one there or at www.mfsanet.org, call local printers and ask them for recommendations. Narrow the field to those (often the smallest) who will agree not to charge you setup fees and monthly minimums. If this isn't possible, ask for at least 50% off both and then request that the setup fee be applied as an advance against shipping or their other fees.

Limit the candidates further to those who can respond to order status e-mail (ideal) or phone calls from customers. The e-mail from your "customer service" folder will be provided as copy-and-paste responses, especially those related to order status and refund requests.[54]

To lower or eliminate miscellaneous fees, explain that you are a

---

54. Sample e-mail responses for fulfillment purposes can be found at www .fourhourblog.com.

start-up and that your budget is small. Tell them you need the cash for advertising that will drive more shipments. If needed, mention the competitive companies that you are considering and pit them against one another, using lower pricing or concessions from one to get larger discounts and bonuses from the others.

Before making your final selection, ask for at least three client references and use the following to elicit the negatives: "I understand they're good, but everyone has weaknesses. If you had to point out where you've had some issues and what they're not the best at, what would you say? Can you please describe an incident or a disagreement? I expect these with all companies, so it's no big deal, and it's confidential, of course."

Ask for "net-30 terms"—payment for services 30 days after they're rendered—after one month of prompt payment for their services. It is easier to negotiate all of the above points with smaller operations that need the business. Have your contract manufacturer ship product directly to the fulfillment house once you have decided on one and put the fulfillment house's e-mail (you can use an e-mail address at your domain and forward it) or phone number on the online "thank you" page for order status questions.

Phase III: >20 Units Shipped Per Week

Now you will have the cash flow to afford the setup fees and the monthly minimums that bigger, more sophisticated outsourcers will ask for. Call the end-to-end fulfillment houses that handle it all—from order status to returns and refunds. Interview them about costs and ask them for referrals to call centers and credit card processors they've collaborated with for file transfers and problem solving. Don't assemble an architecture of strangers—there will be programming costs and mistakes, both of which are expensive.

Set up an account with the credit card processor first, for which you will need your own merchant account. This is critical, as the fulfillment house can only handle refunds and declined cards for transactions they process themselves through an outsourced credit card processor.

Optionally, set up an account with one of the call centers your new fulfillment center recommends. These will often have toll-free numbers you can use instead of purchasing your own. Look at the percentage split of online to phone orders during testing and consider carefully if the extra revenue from the latter is worth the hassle. It often isn't. Those who call to order will generally order online if given no other option.

Before signing on with a call center, get several 800 numbers they answer for current clients and make test calls, asking difficult product-related questions and gauging sales abilities. Call each number at least three times (morning, afternoon, and evening) and note the make-or-break factor: wait time. The phone should be answered within three to four rings, and if you are put on hold, the shorter the wait the better. More than 15 seconds will result in too many abandoned calls and waste advertising dollars.

The Art of Undecision:
Fewer Options = More Revenue

> Companies go out of business when they make the wrong decisions or, just as important, make too many decisions. The latter creates complexity.
> —MIKE MAPLES, cofounder of Motive Communications (IPO to $260 million market cap), founding executive of Tivoli (sold to IBM for $750 million), and investor in companies such as Digg.com

Joseph Sugarman is the marketing genius behind dozens of direct-response and retail successes, including the BluBlocker sunglasses phenomenon. Prior to his string of home runs on television (he sold 20,000 pairs of BluBlockers within 15 minutes of his first QVC appearance), his domain was print media, where he made millions and built an empire called JS&A Group. He was once recruited to design an advertisement for a manufacturer's watch line. The manufacturer wanted to feature nine different watches in the ad, and Joe recommended featuring just one. The client insisted and Joe offered to do both and test them in the same issue of *The Wall Street Journal*. The result? The one-watch offer outsold the nine-watch offer 6-to-1.[55]

Henry Ford once said, referring to his Model-T, the bestselling car of all time,[56] "The customer can have any color he wants, so long as it's black." He understood something that businesspeople seem to have forgotten: Serving the customer ("customer service") is not becoming a personal concierge and catering to their every whim and want. Customer service is providing an excellent product at an acceptable price and solving legitimate problems (lost packages, replacements, refunds, etc.) in the fastest manner possible. That's it.

The more options you offer the customer, the more indecision you create and the fewer orders you receive—it is a disservice all around. Furthermore, the more options you offer the customer, the more manufacturing and customer service burden you create for yourself.

The art of "undecision" refers to minimizing the number of decisions your customers can or need to make. Here are a few methods that I and other **NR** have used to reduce service overhead 20–80%:

1. Offer one or two purchase options ("basic" and "premium," for example) and no more.

2. Do not offer multiple shipping options. Offer one fast method instead and charge a premium.

3. Do not offer overnight or expedited shipping *(it is possible to refer them to a reseller who does, as is true with all of these*

---

55. Joseph Sugarman, *Advertising Secrets of the Written Word* (DelStar Books, 1998).
56. Depending on whose math is used (number of cars vs. gross sales), some claim the original Volkswagen Beetle holds the record.

points), as these shipping methods will produce hundreds of anxious phone calls.

4. Eliminate phone orders completely and direct all prospects to online ordering. This seems outrageous until you realize that success stories like Amazon.com have depended on it as a fundamental cost-saver to survive and thrive.

5. Do not offer international shipments. Spending 10 minutes per order filling out customs forms and then dealing with customer complaints when the product costs 20–100% more with tariffs and duties is about as fun as headbutting a curb. It's about as profitable, too.

Some of these policies hint at what is perhaps the biggest time-saver of all: customer filtering.

Not All Customers Are Created Equal

Once you reach Phase III and have some cash flow, it's time to re-evaluate your customers and thin the herd. There are good and bad versions of all things: good food, bad food; good movies, bad movies; good sex, bad sex; and, yes, good customers and bad customers.

Decide now to do business with the former and avoid the latter. I recommend looking at the customer as an equal trading partner and not as an infallible blessing of a human being to be pleased at all costs. If you offer an excellent product at an acceptable price, it is an equal trade and not a begging session between subordinate (you) and superior (customer). Be professional but never kowtow to unreasonable people.

Instead of dealing with problem customers, I recommend you prevent them from ordering in the first place.

I know dozens of **NR** who don't accept Western Union or checks as payment. Some would respond to this with, "You're giving up 10–15% of your sales!" The **NR**, in turn, would say, "I am, but I'm also avoiding the 10–15% of the customers who create 40% of the expenses and eat 40% of my time." It's classic 80/20.

Those who spend the least and ask for the most before ordering will do the same after the sale. Cutting them out is both a good lifestyle decision and a good financial decision. Low-profit and high-maintenance customers like to call operators and spend up to 30 minutes on the phone asking questions that are unimportant or answered online, costing—in my case—$24.90 (30 × $0.83) per 30-minute incident, eliminating the minuscule profit they contribute in the first place.

Those who spend the most complain the least. In addition to our premium $50–200 pricing, here are a few additional policies that attract the high-profit and low-maintenance customers we want:

1. Do not accept payment via Western Union, checks, or money order.

2. Raise wholesale minimums to 12–100 units and require a tax ID number to qualify resellers who are real businesspeople and not time-intensive novices. Don't run a personal business school.

3. Refer all potential resellers to an online order form that must be printed, filled out, and faxed in. Never negotiate pricing or approve lower pricing for higher-volume orders. Cite "company policy" due to having had problems in the past.

4. Offer low-priced products (à la MRI's NO2 book) instead of free products to capture contact information for follow-up sales. Offering something for free is the best way to attract time-eaters and spend money on those unwilling to return the favor.

5. Offer a **lose-win guarantee** (see boxed text) instead of free trials.

6. Do not accept orders from common mail fraud countries such as Nigeria.

Make your customer base an exclusive club, and treat the members well once they've been accepted.

The Lose-Win Guarantee—
How to Sell Anything to Anyone

If you want a guarantee, buy a toaster. —CLINT EASTWOOD

The 30-day money-back guarantee is dead. It just doesn't have the pizzazz it once did. If a product doesn't work, I've been lied to and will have to spend an afternoon at the post office to return it. This costs me more than just the price I paid for the product, both in time and actual postage. Risk elimination just isn't enough.

This is where we enter the neglected realm of **lose-win** guarantees and risk reversal. The **NR** use what most consider an afterthought— the guarantee—as a cornerstone sales tool.

The **NR** aim to make it profitable for the customer even if the product fails. Lose-win guarantees not only remove risk for the consumer but put the company at financial risk.

Here are a few examples of putting your money where your mouth is.

Delivered in 30 minutes or less or it's free!
(Domino's Pizza built its business on this guarantee.)

We're so confident you'll like CIALIS, if you don't we'll pay for the brand of your choice.
(The "CIALIS® Promise Program" offers a free sample of CIALIS and then offers to pay for competing products if CIALIS doesn't live up to the hype.)

If your car is stolen, we'll pay $500 of your insurance deductible.
(This guarantee helped THE CLUB become the #1-selling mechanical automobile anti-theft device in the world.)

110% guaranteed to work within 60 minutes of the first dose.
(This was for BodyQUICK and a first among sports nutrition products. I offered to not only refund customers the price of

the product if it didn't work within 60 minutes of the *first dose*, but also to send them a check for 10% more.)

The lose-win guarantee might seem like a big risk, especially when someone can abuse it for profit like in the BodyQUICK example, but it isn't . . . *if* your product delivers. Most people are honest.

Let's look at some actual numbers.

Returns for BodyQUICK, even with a 60-day return period (and partially because of it[57]), are less than 3% in an industry in which the average is 12–15% for a normal 30-day 100% money-back guarantee. Sales increased more than 300% within four weeks of introducing the 110% guarantee, and returns decreased overall.

Johanna adopted this lose-win offer and came up with "Increase sport-specific flexibility 40% in two weeks or return it for a full refund (including shipping) and keep the 20-minute bonus DVD as our gift."

Sherwood found his guarantee as well: "If these shirts are not the most comfortable you've ever worn, return them and get 2-times your purchase price back. Each shirt is also guaranteed for life—if it gets threadbare, send it back and we'll replace it free of charge."

Both of them increased sales more than 200% in the first two months. Return percentage remained the same for Johanna and increased 50% for Sherwood, from 2 to 3%. Disaster? Far from it. Instead of selling 50 and getting one back with a 100% guarantee [(50 × $100) − $100 = $4,900 in revenue], he sold 200 and got six back with the 200% guarantee [(200 × $100) − (6 × $200) = $18,800 in revenue]. I'll take the latter.

Lose-win is the new win-win. Stand out and reap the rewards.

---

57. For the benefit of the customer and to capitalize on universal laziness (me included), provide as much time as possible to consider or forget the product. Ginsu knives offered a 50-year guarantee. Can you offer a 60-, 90-, or even 365-day guarantee? Gauge average return percentages with a 30- or 60-day guarantee first (for budgeting calculations and cash-flow projections) and then extend it.

Little Blue Chip: How to Look
Fortune 500 in 45 Minutes

Are you tired of sand being kicked in your face? I promise
you new muscles in days!
—CHARLES ATLAS, strongman who sold more than $30 million
worth of "dynamic-tension" muscle courses through comic books

I f approaching large resellers or potential partners, small company size will be an obstacle. This discrimination is often as
insurmountable as it is unfounded. Fortunately, a few simple steps
can dramatically upgrade your budding Fortune 500 image and take
your muse from coffee shop to boardroom in 45 minutes or less.

1. Don't be the CEO or founder.
Being the "CEO" or "Founder" screams start-up. Give yourself the
mid-level title of "vice president" (VP), "director," or something
similar that can be added to depending on the occasion (Director
of Sales, Director of Business Development, etc.). For negotiation
purposes as well, remember that it is best *not* to appear to be the
ultimate decision-maker.

2. Put multiple e-mail and phone contacts on the website.
Put various e-mail addresses on the "contact us" page for different departments, such as "human resources," "sales," "general
inquiries," "wholesale distribution," "media/PR," "investors," "web
comments," "order status," and so on. In the beginning, these will
all forward to your e-mail address. In Phase III, most will forward
to the appropriate outsourcers. Multiple toll-free numbers can be
used in the same fashion.

3. Set up an Interactive Voice Response (IVR) remote receptionist.
It is possible to sound like a blue chip for less than $30. In fewer
than ten minutes on a site such as www.angel.com, which boasts
clients such as Reebok and Kellog's, it is possible to set up an 800
number that greets callers with a voice prompt such as, "Thank

you for calling [business name]. Please say the name of the person or department you would like to reach or just hold on for a list of options."

Upon speaking your name or selecting the appropriate department, the caller is forwarded to your preferred phone or the appropriate outsourcer—with on-hold music and all.

4. Do not provide home addresses.
Do not use your home address or you will get visitors. Prior to securing an end-to-end fulfillment house that can handle checks and money orders—if you decide to accept them—use a post office box but leave out the "PO Box" and include the street address of the post office itself. Thus "PO Box 555, Nowhere, US 11936" becomes "Suite 555, 1234 Downtown Ave., US 11936."

Go forth and project professionalism with a well-designed image. *Perceived* size does matter.

►COMFORT CHALLENGE

Relax in Public (2 days)

This is the last Comfort Challenge, placed prior to the chapter that tackles the most uncomfortable turning point for most office dwellers: negotiating remote work agreements. This challenge is intended to be fun while showing—in no uncertain terms—that the rules most follow are nothing more than social conventions. There are no legal boundaries stopping you from creating an ideal life . . . or just being self-entertained and causing mass confusion.

So, relaxing in public. Sounds easy, right? I'm somewhat famous for relaxing in style to get a laugh out of friends. Here is the deal, and I don't care if you're male or female, 20 or 60, Mongolian or Martian. I call the following a "time-out."

Once per day for two days, simply lie down in the middle of a crowded public place at some point. Lunchtime is ideal. It can be a well-trafficked sidewalk, the middle of a popular Starbucks, or a popular bar. There is no real technique involved. Just lie down and remain silent on the ground for about ten seconds, and then get up and continue on with whatever you were doing before. I used to do this at nightclubs to clear space for break-dancing circles. No one responded to pleading, but going catatonic on the ground did the trick.

Don't explain it at all. If someone asks about it after the fact (he or she will be too confused to ask you while you're doing it for 10 seconds), just respond, "I just felt like lying down for a second." The less you say, the funnier and more gratifying this will be. Do it on solo missions for the first two days, and then feel free to do it when with a group of friends. It's a riot.

It isn't enough to think outside the box. Thinking is passive. Get used to acting outside the box.

►TOOLS AND TRICKS

Looking Huge—Virtual Receptionist and IVR

►Angel (www.angel.com)
Get an 800 number with professional voice menu (voice recognition departments, extensions, etc.) in five minutes. Incredible.

►Ring Central (www.fourhourblog.com/ringcentral)
Offers toll-free numbers, call screening and forwarding, voicemail, fax send and receive, and message alerts, all online.

CD/DVD Duplication, Printing, and Product Packaging

►AVC Corporation (www.avccorp.com)
►SF Video (www.sfvideo.com)

Local Fulfillment (fewer than 20 units shipped per week)

►Mailing Fulfillment Service Association (www.mfsanet.org)

End-to-End Fulfillment Companies (more than 20 units shipped per week, $500+ setup)

►Motivational Fulfillment (www.mfpsinc.com)
The secret backend to campaigns from HBO, PBS, Comic Relief, Body by Jake, and more.

►Innotrac (www.innotrac.com)
They are currently one of the largest DR marking companies.

►Moulton Fulfillment (www.moultonfulfillment.com)
200,000-square-foot facility with real-time online inventory reports.

Call Centers (per-minute and/or per-sale fees)

There are generally two classes of call centers: order takers and commissioned reps. Interview each provider you consider to understand the options and costs involved.

The former is a good option if you give the product price in an advertisement (hard offer), are offering free information (lead generation), or don't need trained salespeople who can overcome objections. In other words, your ad or website is pre-qualifying prospects.

The latter would more appropriately be called "sales centers." Operators are commissioned and trained "closers" whose sole goal is to convert callers to buyers. These calls are often in response to "call for information/trial/sample" ads that don't feature a price (soft offers). Expect higher costs per sale.

►LiveOps (www.liveops.com)
Pioneer in home-based reps, which often ensures more calls are answered. Provides comprehensive service with agents, IVR, and Spanish. Often used for one-step order taking instead of soft offers.

►West Teleservices (www.west.com)
29,000 employees worldwide, processes billions of minutes per year. All the high-volume and low-price players use them for lower-priced products or higher-end products with free trials and installment plans.

►NexRep (www.nexrep.com)
Highly skilled home-based sales agents that specialize in B2C and B2B, inbound and outbound programs. If performance, speed to respond, Inter-

net integration, and quality customer experience are your priorities, this is a strong option to consider.

► **Triton Technology (www.tritontechnology.com)**
Commission-only sales center know for incredible closing abilities (see the movie *Boiler Room* and Alec Baldwin's character in *Glengarry, Glen Ross*). Don't call unless your product sells for at least $100.

► **CenterPoint Teleservices (http://www.centerpointllc.com)**
This sales force has experience to convert sales from hard offers, soft offers, and multiple offers (upselling additional products after a caller agrees to purchase the advertised product) originating from radio, TV, print, or the web.

► **Stewart Response Group (www.stewartresponsegroup.com)**
Sales-driven call center leveraging the home-agent model for both inbound and outbound programs. Another high-touch boutique center.

Credit Card Processors (merchant account through your bank necessary)

These companies, unlike options in the last chapter, specialize in not only processing credit cards but interacting with fulfillment on your behalf, removing you from the flowchart.

► **TransFirst Payment Processing (www.transfirst.com)**
► **Chase Paymentech (www.paymentech.com)**
► **Trust Commerce (www.trustcommerce.com)**

► **PowerPay (www.fourhourblog.com/powerpay)**
One of the Inc. 500 Fastest-Growing Private Companies. Process credit cards from your iPhone and more.

Affiliate Program Software

► **My Affiliate Program (www.myaffiliateprogram.com)**
Also see the affiliate programs listed in the "Tools and Tricks" at the end of Chapter 9.

Discount Media Buying Agencies

If you go to a magazine, radio station, or TV channel and pay rate card—

the "retail" pricing first given—you will never make it big. To save a lot of headache and expense, consider using ad agencies that negotiate discounts of up to 90% in their chosen media.

►**Manhattan Media (Print) (www.manhmedia.com)**
Great agency with fast turnaround. I've used them since the beginning.

►**Novus Media (Print) (www.novusprintmedia.com)**
Relationships with 1,400+ magazine and newspaper publishers with an average of 80% of rate card. Clients include Sharper Image and Office Depot.

►**Mercury Media (TV) (www.mercurymedia.com)**
Largest private DR media agency in the U.S. Specialists in TV but can also handle radio and print. Offer full tracking and reporting to determine ROI.

►**Euro RSCG (Cross Media) (http://www.eurorscgedge.com/)**
One of the worldwide leaders in DRTV media across all platforms.

►**Canella Media Response Television (TV) (http://www.drtv.com)**
Uses the innovative P/I (per inquiry) model for compensation, where you split order profits instead of paying for time upfront. This is more expensive per order if you have a successful campaign, but it lowers upfront investment in media.

►**Marketing Architects (Radio) (www.marketingarchitects.com)**
The de facto leaders in radio DR but a bit on the expensive side. Almost all of the most successful DR products—Carlton Sheets No Money Down, Tony Robbins, etc.—have used them.

►**Radio Direct Response (Radio) (www.radiodirect.com)**
Mark Lipsky has put together a great firm, with clients ranging from small direct marketers to Travel Channel and Wells Fargo.

Online Marketing and Research Firms (PPC campaign management, etc.)

Starting Small—Find a Local Individual to Help

►**SEMPO (www.sempo.org;** see the member directory)

Excellent Mid-Size Firms

► Clicks 2 Customers (www.clicks2customers.com)
► Working Planet (www.workingplanet.com)

*The Hard-Hitting Pros—Small Campaigns Start at
Several Thousand Dollars*

► Marketing Experiments (www.marketingexperiments.com)
This is my team.

► Did It (www.did-it.com)

► ROIRevolution (www.roirevolution.com)
Cost is determined by a percentage above monthly PPC spend.

► iProspect (www.iprospect.com)

Full-Service Infomercial Producers
These are the companies that made Oreck Direct, Nutrisystem, Nordic-Track, and Hooked on Phonics household names. The first has an excellent DRTV glossary and both sites offer excellent resources. Don't call unless you can budget at least $15,000 for a short-form commercial or $50,000+ for a long-form infomercial.

► Cesari Direct (http://www.cesaridirect.com/)
► Hawthorne Direct (www.hawthornedirect.com)
► Script-to-Screen (www.scripttoscreen.com)

Retail and International Product Distribution
Want to get your product on the shelves of Wal-Mart, Costco, Nordstrom, or the leading department store in Japan? Sometimes it pays to have experts with relationships get you there.

► Tristar Products (http://www.tristarproductsinc.com)
Behind the PowerJuicer and other hits. Tristar also owns their own production studio and can therefore offer end-to-end services in addition to retail distribution.

► BJ Direct (International) (www.bjgd.com)

Celebrity Brokers

Want a celebrity to endorse your product or be a spokesperson? It can cost a lot less than you think, if you do it right. I know of one clothing endorsement deal with the best pitcher in Major League Baseball that cost just $20,000 per year. Here are the brokers who can make it happen:

► Celeb Brokers (www.celebbrokers.com)
President Jack King was the one who first turned me on to this fascinating world. He knows it all inside and out.

► Celebrity Endorsement Network (www.celebrityendorsement.com)

Celebrity Finding

► Contact Any Celebrity (www.fourhourblog.com/celebrity)
It is possible to do it yourself, as I have done many times. This online directory and its helpful staff will help you find any celebrity in the world.

►LIFESTYLE DESIGN IN ACTION

After I read the section on outsourcing, I thought it sounded like a novel idea but would never work for me. However, since the rest of the book was "spot on," I decided to try it. Rather than ship my money overseas, I opted to keep it in the U.S. and use my niece in college, with skills on computers I can't even fathom, to test the theory. Turns out it has been a great experience and timesaver for me, as well as moneymaker for her. It seems I have all of the positives of outsourcing but none of the hassles of language and such. . . . Being able to mold a young mind for the better ties in well with the rest of your book . . .   —*KEN D.*

• • •

Hey Tim, You mentioned www.weebly.com a few months ago, and I've been using that to build all my muse sites and think it's great! Also, Facebook groups has (almost) every niche imaginable. So what I have found success in doing is: (1) Finding a niche group that would buy my muse, (2) sending a message to each admin telling them how my muse will help their group members. Then politely asking them to put a blurb in the "Recent News" section of the group. This makes it more trustworthy than a wall post, and it stays up there (free advertising) until the admin removes it. One hundred times better than a wall post. In one case, the admin purchased my muse, posted my note for me on the groups' "Recent News" section, then e-mailed the entire group telling them they have to check out my site.

—*GAVIN*

Step IV:
L is for Liberation

It is far better for a man to go wrong in freedom than to go right in chains.

—THOMAS H. HUXLEY,
English biologist; known as "Darwin's Bulldog"

12

Disappearing Act

►HOW TO ESCAPE THE OFFICE

By working faithfully eight hours a day, you may eventually get to be a boss and work twelve hours a day.
—ROBERT FROST, American poet and winner of four Pulitzer Prizes

On this path, it is only the first step that counts.
—ST. JEAN–BAPTISTE–MARIE VIANNEY, Catholic saint, "Curé d'Ars"

PALO ALTO, CALIFORNIA

"We're not going to expense the phone."
"I'm not asking you to."
Silence. Then a nod, a laugh, and a crooked smile of resignation. "OK, then—it's fine."
And that was that, lickity-split. Forty-four-year old Dave Camarillo, lifelong employee, had cracked the code and started his second life.

He hadn't been fired; he hadn't been yelled at. His boss seemed to be handling the whole situation quite well. Granted, Dave delivered the goods on the job, and it wasn't like he was doing naked snow angels in client meetings, but still—he had just spent 30 days in China without telling anyone.

"It wasn't half as hard as I thought it would be."

Dave works among more than 10,000 employees at Hewlett-

Packard (HP), and—against all odds—he actually likes it. He has no desire to start his own company and has spent the last seven years doing tech support for customers in 45 states and 22 countries. Six months ago, however, he had a small problem.

She measured 5'2" and weighed 110 pounds.

Was he, like most men, afraid of commitment, unwilling to stop running around the house in Spider-Man underoos, or inseparable from the last refuge of any self-respecting man, the PlayStation? No, he was past all that. In fact, Dave was locked and loaded, ready to pop the big question, but he was short on vacation days and his girlfriend lived out of town. Waaaaay out of town—5,913 miles out of town.

He had met her on a client visit to Shenzhen, China, and it was now time to meet the parents, logistics be damned.

Dave had only recently begun to take tech calls at home, and, well, isn't home where the heart is? One plane ticket and one T-Mobile GSM tri-band phone later, he was somewhere over the Pacific en route to his first seven-day experiment. Twelve time zones hence, he proposed, she accepted, and no one was the wiser stateside.

The second field trip was a 30-day tour of Chinese family and food (pig face, anyone?), ending with Shumei Wu becoming Shumei Camarillo. Back in Palo Alto, HP continued its quest for world domination, neither knowing nor caring where Dave was. He had his calls forwarded to his newly begotten wife's cell phone and all was right in the world.

Now back in the U.S. after hoping for the best and preparing for the worst, Dave had earned his Eagle Scout mobility badge. The future looks flexible, indeed. He is going to start by spending two months in China every summer and then move to Australia and Europe to make up for lost time, all with the full support of his boss.

The key to cutting the leash was simple—he asked for forgiveness instead of permission.

"I didn't travel for 30 years of my life—so why not?"

. . .

THAT'S PRECISELY THE question everyone should be asking—why the hell not?

From Caste to Castaway

The old rich, the upper class of yore with castles and ascots and irritating little lapdogs, are characterized as being well-established in one place. The Schwarzes of Nantucket and the McDonnells of Charlottesville. Blech. Summers in the Hamptons is sooooo 1990s.

The guard is changing. Being bound to one place will be the new defining feature of middle class. The New Rich are defined by a more elusive power than simple cash—unrestricted mobility. This jet-setting is not limited to start-up owners or freelancers. Employees can pull it off, too.[58]

Not only can they pull it off, but more and more companies want them to pull it off. BestBuy, the consumer electronics giant, is now sending thousands of employees home from their HQ in Minnesota and claims not only lowered costs, but also a 10–20% increase in results. The new mantra is this: Work wherever and whenever you want, but get your work done.

In Japan, a three-piece zombie who joins the 9–5 grind each morning is called a *sarari-man*—salaryman—and, in the last few years, a new verb has emerged: *datsu-sara suru,* to escape (datsu) the salaryman (sara) lifestyle.

It's your turn to learn the datsu-sara dance.[59]

---

58. If you're an entrepreneur, don't skip this chapter. This introduction to remote working tools and tactics is integral to the international pieces of the puzzle that follow.

59. This verb is used by Japanese women as well, even though female workers are referred to as "OL"—office ladies.

Trading Bosses for Beer:
An Oktoberfest Case Study

To create the proper leverage to be unshackled, we'll do two things: demonstrate the business benefit of remote working and make it too expensive or excruciating to refuse a request for it.

Remember Sherwood?

His French shirts are beginning to move and he is itching to ditch the U.S. for a global walkabout. He has more than enough cash now but needs to escape constant supervision in the office before he can implement all the timesaving tools from **Elimination** and travel.

He is a mechanical engineer and is producing twice as many designs in half the time since erasing 90% of his time-wasters and interruptions. This quantum leap in performance has been noticed by his supervisors and his value to the company has increased, making it more expensive to lose him. More value means more leverage for negotiations. Sherwood has been sure to hold back some of his productivity and efficiency so that he can highlight a sudden jump in both during a remote work trial period.

Since eliminating most of his meetings and in-person discussions, he has naturally moved about 80% of all communication with his boss and colleagues to e-mail and the remaining 20% to phone. Not only this, but he has used tips from chapter 7, "Interrupting Interruption and the Art of Refusal," to cut unimportant and repetitive e-mail volume in half. This will make the move to remote less noticeable, if at all noticeable, from a managerial standpoint. Sherwood is running at full speed with less and less supervision.

Sherwood implements his escape in five steps, beginning on July 12 during the slow business season and lasting two months, ending with a trip to Oktoberfest in Munich, Germany, for two weeks as a final test before bigger and bolder vagabonding plans.

Step 1: Increase Investment

First, he speaks with his boss on **July 12** about additional training that might be available to employees. He proposes having the company pay for a four-week industrial design class to help him better interface with clients, being sure to mention the benefit to the boss and business (i.e., he'll decrease intradepartmental back-and-forth and increase both client results and billable time). Sherwood wants the company to invest as much as possible in him so that the loss is greater if he quits.

Step 2: Prove Increased Output Offsite

Second, he calls in sick the next Tuesday and Wednesday, **July 18 and 19,** to showcase his remote working productivity.[60] He decides to call in sick between Tuesday and Thursday for two reasons: It looks less like a lie for a three-day weekend and it also enables him to see how well he functions in social isolation without the imminent reprieve of the weekend. He ensures that he doubles his work output on both days, leaves an e-mail trail of some sort for his boss to notice, and keeps quantifiable records of what he accomplished for reference during later negotiations. Since he uses expensive CAD software that is only licensed on his office desktop, Sherwood installs a free trial of GoToMyPC remote access software so that he can pilot his office computer from home.

Step 3: Prepare the Quantifiable Business Benefit

Third, Sherwood creates a bullet-point list of how much more he achieved outside the office with explanations. He realizes that he needs to present remote working as a good business decision and

---

60. Any reason to be home will do (cable or phone installation, home repairs, etc.) or, if you prefer not to use a ruse, work a weekend or take two vacation days.

not a personal perk. The quantifiable end result was three more designs per day than his usual average and three total hours of additional billable client time. For explanations, he identifies removal of
commute and fewer distractions from office noise.

Step 4: Propose a Revocable Trial Period

Fourth, fresh off completing the comfort challenges from previous
chapters, Sherwood confidently proposes an innocent one-day-per-
week remote work trial period for two weeks. He plans a script in
advance but does not make it a PowerPoint presentation or otherwise give it the appearance of something serious or irreversible.[61]

Sherwood knocks on his boss's office door around 3 P.M. on a
relatively relaxed Thursday, **July 27,** the week after his absence, and
his script looks like the following. Stock phrases are underlined and
footnotes explain negotiating points.

Sherwood: Hi, Bill. <u>Do you have a quick second?</u>

Bill: Sure. What's up?

Sherwood: <u>I just wanted to bounce an idea off of you that's been on
my mind. Two minutes should be plenty.</u>

Bill: OK. Shoot.

Sherwood: Last week, as you know, I was sick. Long story short,
I decided to work at home despite feeling terrible. So here's the
funny part. I thought I would get nothing done, but ended up
finishing three more designs than usual on both days. Plus, I
put in three more billable hours than usual without the commute, office noise, distractions, etc. OK, so here's where I'm
going. <u>Just as a trial, I'd like to propose</u> working from home
Mondays and Tuesdays for just two weeks. <u>You can veto it
whenever you want,</u> and I'll come in if we need to do meetings,
but I'd like to try it for just two weeks and review the results.

---

61. Review the Puppy Dog Close from "Income Autopilot II: Testing the Muse."

I'm 100% confident that I'll get twice as much done. <u>Does that seem reasonable?</u>

Bill: Hmm . . . What if we need to share client designs?

Sherwood: There's a program called GoToMyPC that I used to access the office computer when I was sick. I can view everything remotely, and I'll have my cell phone on me 24/7. <u>Soooo . . . What do you think? Test it out starting next Monday and see how much more I get done?</u>[62]

Bill: Ummm . . . OK, fine. But it's just a test. I have a meeting in five and have to run, but let's talk soon.

Sherwood: Great. Thanks for the time. I'll keep you posted on it all. I'm sure you'll be pleasantly surprised.

Sherwood didn't expect to get two days per week approved. He asked for two so that, in the case his boss refused, he could ask for just one as a fallback position (bracketing). Why didn't Sherwood go for five days remote per week? Two reasons. First, it's a lot for management to accept off the bat. We need to ask for an inch and turn it into a foot without setting off panic alarms. Second, it is a good idea to hone your remote-working abilities—rehearse a bit—before shooting for the big time, as it decreases the likelihood of crises and screwups that will get remote rights revoked.

Step 5: Expand Remote Time

Sherwood ensures that his days outside of the office are his most productive to date, even minimally dropping in-office production to heighten the contrast. He sets a meeting to discuss the results with his boss on **August 15** and prepares a bullet-point page detailing increased results and items completed compared to in-office time. He suggests upping the ante to four days per week remote for a two-week trial, fully prepared to concede to three days if need be.

---

62. Do not digress from your goal. Once you've addressed an objection or concern, go for the close.

Sherwood: It really turned out even better than I expected. If you look at the numbers, it makes a lot of business sense, and I'm enjoying work a lot more now. So, here we are. <u>I'd like to suggest,</u> if you think it makes sense, that I try four days a week for another two-week trial. <u>I was thinking that</u> coming in Friday[63] would make sense to prepare for the coming week, but we could do whichever day you prefer.

Bill: Sherwood, I'm really not sure we can do that.

Sherwood: <u>What's your main concern?</u>[64]

Bill: It seems like you're on your way out. I mean, are you going to quit on us? Second, what if everyone wants to do the same?

Sherwood: <u>Fair enough. Good points.</u>[65] <u>First, to be honest, I was close to quitting before, with all the interruptions and commute and whatnot, but I'm actually feeling great now with the change in routine.</u>[66] I'm doing more and feel relaxed for a change. Second, no one should be allowed to work remotely unless they can show increased productivity, and I'm the perfect experiment. If they can show it, however, why not let them do it on a trial basis? It lowers costs for the office, increases productivity, and makes employees happier. <u>So, what do you say?</u> Can I test it out for two weeks and come in Fridays to take care of the office stuff? I'll still document everything, and <u>you, of course, have the right to change your mind at any point.</u>

---

63. Friday is the best day to be in the office. People are relaxed and tend to leave early.

64. Do not accept a vague refusal. Pinpointing the main concern in detail enables you to overcome it.

65. Don't jump to the defensive after an objection. Acknowledge the validity of a boss's concerns to prevent an ego-driven battle of wills.

66. Note this indirect threat dressed as a confession. It will make the boss think twice about refusing but prevents the win-lose outcome of an ultimatum.

Bill: Man, you are an insistent one. OK, we'll give it a shot, but don't go blabbing about it.

Sherwood: Of course. Thanks, Bill. I appreciate the trust. Talk to you soon.

Sherwood continues to be productive at home and maintains his lower in-office performance. He reviews the results with his boss after two weeks and continues with four remote days per week for an additional two weeks until Tuesday, **September 19,** when he requests a full-time remote trial of two weeks while he is visiting relatives out of state.[67] Sherwood's team is in the middle of a project that requires his expertise, and he is prepared to quit if his boss refuses. He realizes that, just as you want to negotiate ad pricing close to deadlines, getting what you want often depends more on *when* you ask for it than *how* you ask for it. Though he would prefer not to quit, his income from shirts is more than enough to fund his dreamlines of Oktoberfest and beyond.

His boss acquiesces and Sherwood doesn't have to use his threat of quitting. He goes home that evening and buys a $524 round-trip ticket, less than one week's shirt sales, to Munich for Oktoberfest.

Now he can implement all the time-savers possible and hack out the inessentials. Somewhere between drinking wheat beer and dancing in lederhosen, Sherwood will get his work done in fine form, leaving his company better off than prior to 80/20 and leaving himself all the time in the world.

But hold on a second . . . What if your boss still refuses? Hmm . . . Then they force your hand. If upper management won't see the light, you'll just have to use the next chapter to fire their asses.

---

67. This removes the boss's ability to call you to the office. This is critical for making the first jump overseas.

An Alternative: The Hourglass Approach

It can be effective to take a longer period of absence up front in what some **NR** have termed the "hourglass" approach, so named because you use a long proof-of-concept up front to get a short remote agreement and then negotiate back up to full-time out of the office. Here's what it looks like.

1. Use a preplanned project or emergency (family issue, personal issue, relocation, home repairs, whatever) that requires you to take one or two weeks out of the office.
2. Say that you recognize you can't just stop working and that you would prefer to work instead of taking vacation days.
3. Propose how you can work remotely and offer, if necessary, to take a pay cut for that period (and that period only) if performance isn't up to par upon returning.
4. Allow the boss to collaborate on how to do it so that he or she is invested in the process.
5. Make the two weeks "off" the most productive period you've ever had at work.
6. Show your boss the quantifiable results upon returning, and tell him or her that—without all the distractions, commute, etc.—you can get twice as much done. Suggest two or three days at home per week as a trial for two weeks.
7. Make those remote days ultraproductive.
8. Suggest only one or two days in the office per week.
9. Make those days the least productive of the week.
10. Suggest complete mobility—the boss will go for it.

►Q&A: QUESTIONS AND ACTIONS

Recently, I was asked if I was going to fire an employee who made a mistake that cost the company $600,000. No, I replied, I just spent $600,000 training him.

—THOMAS J. WATSON, founder of IBM

Liberty means responsibility. That is why most men dread it.
—GEORGE BERNARD SHAW

While entrepreneurs have the most trouble with **Automation,** since they fear giving up control, employees get stuck on **Liberation** because they fear taking control. Resolve to grab the reins—the rest of your life depends on it.

The following questions and actions will help you to replace presence-based work with performance-based freedom.

1. **If you had a heart attack, and assuming your boss were sympathetic, how could you work remotely for four weeks?**
   If you hit a brick wall with a task that doesn't seem remote-compatible or if you predict resistance from your boss, ask the following:

   - ►What are you accomplishing with this task—what is the purpose?
   - ►If you *had to* find other ways to accomplish the same—if your life depended on it—how would you do it? Remote conferencing? Video conferencing? GoToMeeting, GoToMyPC, DimDim.com (Mac), or related services?
   - ►Why would your boss resist remote work? What is the immediate negative effect it would have on the company and what could you do to prevent or minimize it?

2. **Put yourself in your boss's shoes. Based on your work history, would you trust yourself to work outside of the office?**
   If you wouldn't, reread **Elimination** to improve production and consider the hourglass option.

3. **Practice environment-free productivity.**
   Attempt to work for two to three hours in a café for two Saturdays prior to proposing a remote trial. If you exercise in a gym, attempt to exercise for those two weeks at home or otherwise

outside of the gym environment. The purpose here is to separate your activities from a single environment and ensure that you have the discipline to work solo.

4. **Quantify current productivity.**

   If you have applied the 80/20 Principle, set the rules of interrupting interruption, and completed related groundwork, your performance should be at an all-time high in quantifiable terms, whether customers served, revenue generated, pages produced, speed of accounts receivable, or otherwise. Document this.

5. **Create an opportunity to demonstrate remote work productivity before asking for it as a policy.**

   This is to test your ability to work outside of an office environment and rack up some proof that you can kick ass without constant supervision.

6. **Practice the art of getting past "no" before proposing.**

   Go to farmers' markets to negotiate prices, ask for free first-class upgrades, ask for compensation if you encounter poor service in restaurants, and otherwise ask for the world and practice using the following magic questions when people refuse to give it to you.

   > "What would I need to do to [desired outcome]?"
   > "Under what circumstances would you [desired outcome]?"
   > "Have you ever made an exception?"
   > "I'm sure you've made an exception before, haven't you?"
   > (If no for either of the last two, ask, "Why not?" If yes, ask, "Why?")

7. **Put your employer on remote training wheels—propose Monday or Friday at home.**

   Consider doing this, or the following step, during a period when it would be too disruptive to fire you, even if you were marginally less productive while remote.

If your employer refuses, it's time to get a new boss or become an entrepreneur. The job will never give you the requisite time freedom. If you decide to jump ship, consider letting them make you walk the plank—quitting is often less appealing than tactfully getting fired and using severance or unemployment to take a long vacation.

8. **Extend each successful trial period until you reach full-time or your desired level of mobility.**
   Don't underestimate how much your company needs you. Perform well and ask for what you want. If you don't get it over time, leave. It's too big a world to spend most of life in a cubicle.

►LIFESTYLE DESIGN IN ACTION

Consider trying Earth Class Mail, a service that you can reroute all your mail to, at which point they scan and e-mail you everything that comes in, giving you the option of recycling/shredding junk, getting a scan of the contents, or having specific items forwarded to you or someone you designate. I have not personally used it yet (will be testing it out this month in preparation for an upcoming trip in May), but a friend and author in Portland swears by them and knows the CEO. Seems they've gotten good press and the idea seems far better than relying on friends/family who, if they're anything like my friends/family . . . will surely drop the ball at some point :-).

—NATHALIE

• • •

I also use GreenByPhone.com to process checks electronically that come in through my Earth Class Mail account—they charge $5 a check, but I live in San Diego, my Earth Class Mail office address is in Seattle, and I bank in Ohio. It works great!   *—ANDREW*

• • •

To add to your excellent list (we've traveled just like that for several years SWEET!), I'd like to add my modifications as a female traveler and a new mom (16-month-old baby). Personal favorites:

(1) Athleta carries excellent, light, quick-dry clothing that hold up well to sports but still look very fashionable. Skorts are a must for looking feminine but being fully covered for hiking and steep pyramid steps—you know what I mean, ladies! Just a note, a slightly longer length will serve you well in a lot of countries, as well as tankini tops and swim skirts for swimming. (2) Fresh & Go toothbrush is simple to use. (3) Marsona sound machine for drowning out unfamiliar noises is a must (regularly use with baby at home too so when they hear the sound they know it's sleep time!). This has been a lifesaver for us on many trips, and we now use it regularly at home for better sleep. No more changing hotels midtrip to avoid noise. AND, I know we have to travel light, but with baby a lot of things are nonnego-tiable. These make for smoother sailing: (1) Peanut shell sling in black fleece—it's more comfy than the cotton and you can pop baby in and out wherever you are, from birth to 35 lbs. I never take mine off, it's part of my outfit; (2) Peapod plus portable tent—this is baby's main bed at home and travel so baby has the same sleep place everywhere we go, and the flaps give all travel parties privacy—great from small babies to five-year-olds. I can still jam this onto a little wheeled carry-on and pack mine and baby's minimal clothing around it; (3) Go Go Kidz TravelMate (great for wheeling car seat up to the gate for gate check or use on plane); (4) Britax Diplomat car seat is small but kids can use it from birth to approx. four years old.

Make sure the wheeled carry-on bag you get is one size smaller than the allowed carry-on size so you don't get bumped to check the bag in if the plane is full. You can always nicely argue/reason/bat your eyelashes that you will put the bag in your foot space. Also, very helpful to give baby something to sip or munch on during take-off and landing so yours isn't the baby screaming from ear pain. Happy travels!   **—KARYL**

. . .

PRE-EMPTING THE BOSS: COMMON CONCERNS ABOUT REMOTE WORK
In the linked article, Cisco acknowledges that remote work arrangements are "here to stay" yet lists a set of security issues. It makes sense to preemptively research solutions so that you are armed and ready if your employer raises these concerns. http://newsroom.cisco.com/dlls/2008/prod_020508.html.

—Contributed by RAINA

Beyond Repair

►KILLING YOUR JOB

All courses of action are risky, so prudence is not in avoiding danger (it's impossible), but calculating risk and acting decisively. Make mistakes of ambition and not mistakes of sloth. Develop the strength to do bold things, not the strength to suffer. —NICCOLÒ MACHIAVELLI, *The Prince*

Existential Pleas and Resignations Mad Libs
BY ED MURRAY

Dear _____,
          preferred deity of choice
    I realized something very _____ today as I was washing my
                                          adjective
_____, and that something is this: You are a/an _____
          animal   adverb
cruel _____.
          personal expletive pronoun
    Last night, after drinking seven shots of _____ and
                                                least favorite hard liquor
snorting enough _____ to make _____ blush,
                      drug   politician
it became clear: It really is them, and not me.

    I am the one who is completely _____ when it
                                              helpless state of being
comes to the _____ personal relationships in my life, and yet,
                  favorite color
I share my innermost _____ with no one else on this _____
                          type of candy   adjective
planet . . . because they are all _____ _____.
                                        insulting adjective   extinct animals

I _____ them all, and I hope they meet a _____ demise
    emotion   adjective

choking on a platter of their own _____.
                                     (Applebee's appetizer)

   This _____ catharsis made me feel _____
                 adjective   smiley emotion

and strangely alone, simultaneously. How can I connect with these

_____ I am surrounded by on a daily basis? I am just so sick of
  herd animals

_____ in the _____ every day . . . Maybe it would
synonym for "crying"   part of your house

help if I shoved a fistful of _____ into my _____. It
                           vegetables   bodily orifice

makes my heart _____ when I see the defeat in my parents'
                       verb

_____, and it becomes _____ clear that they love the
  body parts   adverb

_____ more than _____ . . . Maybe I should
  type of car   sibling's name

stab my _____ with a _____.
         genitalia   sharp object

   Today I have decided to buy a _____, which will serve as a
                                  noun

_____, and as a _____ symbol for the _____-
  metaphor   timeless adjective   expletive

faced servitude I am bound to in this life . . . no more in control than

the most _____-minded of _____. I am trying
              adjective   farm animals

desperately to _____ myself from _____ all of my
              "st__p"   active violent act

co-workers . . . except _____. I've always wanted to
                       person in the room

_____ him/her/it. I didn't ask to be _____.
  forceful sexual act   verb

   If reincarnation does exist, please leave me out of it.

Some jobs are simply beyond repair.

   Improvements would be like adding a set of designer curtains to a jail cell: better but far from good. In the context of this chapter, "job" will refer to both a company if you run one and a normal job if you have one. Some recommendations are limited to one of the two but most are relevant to both. So we begin.

I have quit three jobs and been fired from most of the rest. Getting fired, despite sometimes coming as a surprise and leaving you scrambling to recover, is often a godsend: Someone else makes the decision for you, and it's impossible to sit in the wrong job for the rest of your life. Most people aren't lucky enough to get fired and die a slow spiritual death over 30–40 years of tolerating the mediocre.

Pride and Punishment

> If you must play, decide on three things at the start: the
> rules of the game, the stakes, and the quitting time.
> —CHINESE PROVERB

Just because something has been a lot of work or consumed a lot of time doesn't make it productive or worthwhile.

Just because you are embarrassed to admit that you're still living the consequences of bad decisions made 5, 10, or 20 years ago shouldn't stop you from making good decisions now. If you let pride stop you, you will hate life 5, 10, and 20 years from now for the same reasons. I hate to be wrong and sat in a dead-end trajectory with my own company until I was forced to change directions or face total breakdown—I know how hard it is.

Now that we're all on a level playing field: Pride is stupid.

Being able to quit things that don't work is integral to being a winner. Going into a project or job without defining when worthwhile becomes wasteful is like going into a casino without a cap on what you will gamble: dangerous and foolish.

"But, you don't understand my situation. It's complicated!" But is it really? Don't confuse the complex with the difficult. Most situations are simple—many are just emotionally difficult to act upon.

The problem and the solution are usually obvious and simple. It's not that you don't know what to do. Of course you do. You are just terrified that you might end up worse off than you are now.

I'll tell you right now: If you're at this point, you won't be worse off. Revisit fear-setting and cut the cord.

Like Pulling Off a Band-Aid: It's Easier and Less Painful Than You Think

> The average man is a conformist, accepting miseries and disasters with the stoicism of a cow standing in the rain.
> —COLIN WILSON, British author of *The Outsider;*
> New Existentialist

There are several principal phobias that keep people on sinking ships, and there are simple rebuttals for all of them.

1. Quitting is permanent.
Far from it. Use the Q&A questions in this chapter and chapter 3 (Fear-setting) to examine how you could pick up your chosen career track or start another company at a later point. I have never seen an example where a change of direction wasn't somehow reversible.

2. I won't be able to pay the bills.
Sure you will. First of all, the objective will be to have a new job or source of cash flow before quitting your current job. Problem solved.

If you jump ship or get fired, it isn't hard to eliminate most expenses temporarily and live on savings for a brief period. From renting out your home to refinancing or selling it, there are options. There are always options.

It might be emotionally difficult, but you won't starve. Park your car in the garage and cancel insurance for a few months. Carpool or take the bus until you find the next gig. Rack up some more credit card debt and cook instead of eating out. Sell all the crap that you spent hundreds or thousands on and never use.

Take a full inventory of your assets, cash reserves, debts, and monthly expenses. How long could you survive with your current resources or if you sold some assets?

Go through all expenses and ask yourself, If I *had to* eliminate this because I needed an extra kidney, how would I do it? Don't be melodramatic when there is no need—few things are fatal, particularly for smart people. If you've made it this far in life, losing or dropping a job will often be little more than a few weeks of vacation (unless you want more) prior to something better.

3. Health insurance and retirement accounts disappear if I quit.
Untrue.

I was scared of both when I was eliminated from TrueSAN. I had visions of rotting teeth and working at Wal-Mart to survive.

Upon looking at the facts and exploring options, I realized that I could have identical medical and dental coverage—the same provider and network—for $300–500 per month. To transfer my 401(k) to another company (I chose Fidelity Investments) was even easier: It took less than 30 minutes via phone and cost nothing.

Covering both of these bases takes less time than getting a customer service rep on the phone to fix your electric bill.

4. It will ruin my resume.
I love creative nonfiction.

It is not at all difficult to sweep gaps under the rug and make uncommon items the very things that get job interviews. How? Do something interesting and make them jealous. If you quit and then sit on your ass, I wouldn't hire you either.

On the other hand, if you have a one-to-two-year world circumnavigation on your resume or training with professional soccer teams in Europe to your credit, two interesting things happen upon returning to the working world. First, you will get more interviews because you will stand out. Second, interviewers bored in their own jobs will spend the entire meeting asking how you did it!

If there is any question of why you took a break or left your previous job, there is one answer that cannot be countered: "I had a once-in-a-lifetime chance to do [exotic and envy-producing experience] and couldn't turn it down. I figured that, with [20–40] years of work to go, what's the rush?"

The Cheesecake Factor

Would you like me to give you a formula for success? It's quite simple, really. Double your rate of failure.
—THOMAS J. WATSON, founder of IBM

SUMMER 1999

Even before I tasted it, I knew something wasn't quite right. After eight hours in the refrigerator, this cheesecake still hadn't set at all. It swished in the gallon bowl like a viscous soup, chunks shifting and bobbing as I tilted it under close inspection. Somewhere a mistake had been made. It could have been any number of things:

Three 1 lb. sticks of Philly Cream Cheese
Eggs
Stevia
Unflavored gelatin
Vanilla
Sour cream

In this case, it was probably a combination of things and the lack of a few simple ingredients that generally make cheesecake a form of cake.

I was on a no-carbohydrate diet, and I had used this recipe before. It had been so delicious that my roommates wanted their fair share and insisted on an attempt at bulk production. Hence began the mathematical shenanigans and problems.

Before Splenda® and other miracles of sugar imitation came on the scene, the hard core used stevia, an herb 300 times sweeter than sugar. One drop was like 300 packets of sugar. It was a delicate tool and I wasn't a delicate cook. I had once made a small handful of cookies using baking soda instead of baking powder, and that was bad enough to drive my roommates to puke on the lawn. This new masterpiece made the cookies look like fine dining: It tasted like liquid cream cheese mixed with cold water and about 600 packets of sugar.

I then did what any normal and rational person would do: I grabbed the largest soup ladle with a sigh and sat down in front of the TV to face my punishment. I had wasted an entire Sunday and a boatload of ingredients—it was time to reap what I had sown.

One hour and 20 large spoonfuls later, I hadn't made a dent in the enormous batch of soup, but I was down for the count. Not only could I not eat anything but soup for two days, I couldn't bring myself to even look at cheesecake, previously my favorite dessert, for more than four years.

Stupid? Of course. It's about as stupid as one can get. This is a ridiculous and micro example of what people do on a larger scale with jobs all the time: self-imposed suffering that can be avoided. Sure, I learned a lesson and paid for the mistake. The real question is—for what?

There are two types of mistakes: mistakes of ambition and mistakes of sloth.

The first is the result of a decision to act—to do something. This type of mistake is made with incomplete information, as it's impossible to have all the facts beforehand. This is to be encouraged. Fortune favors the bold.

The second is the result of a decision of sloth—to not do something—wherein we refuse to change a bad situation out of fear despite having all the facts. This is how learning experiences become terminal punishments, bad relationships become bad marriages, and poor job choices become lifelong prison sentences.

"Yeah, but what if I'm in an industry where jumping around is looked down upon? I've been here barely a year, and prospective employers would think . . ."

Would they? Test assumptions before condemning yourself to more misery. I've seen one determinant of sex appeal to good employers: performance. If you are a rock star when it comes to results, it doesn't matter if you jump ship from a bad company after three weeks. On the other hand, if tolerating a punishing work environment for years at a time is a prerequisite for promotion in your field, could it be that you're in a game not worth winning?

The consequences of bad decisions do not get better with age.

What cheesecake are you eating?

►Q&A: QUESTIONS AND ACTIONS

Only those who are asleep make no mistakes.

—INGVAR KAMPRAD, founder of IKEA, world's largest furniture brand

Tens of thousands of people, most of them less capable than you, leave their jobs every day. It's neither uncommon nor fatal. Here are a few exercises to help you realize just how natural job changes are and how simple the transition can be.

1. First, a familiar reality check: Are you more likely to find what you want in your current job or somewhere else?

2. If you were fired from your job today, what would you do to get things under financial control?

3. Take a sick day and post your resume on the major job sites. Even

if you have no immediate plans to leave your job, post your resume on sites such as www.monster.com and www.career-builder.com, using a pseudonym if you prefer. This will show you that there are options besides your current place of work. Call headhunters if your level makes such a step appropriate, and send a brief e-mail such as the one below to friends and non-work contacts.

> Dear All,
>   I am considering making a career move and am interested in all opportunities that might come to mind. Nothing is too outrageous or out of left field. [If you know what you want or don't want on some level, feel free to add, "I am particularly interested in . . ." or "I would like to avoid . . ."]
>   Please let me know if anything comes to mind!
> Tim

Call in sick or take a vacation day to complete all of these exercises during a normal 9–5 workday. This will simulate unemployment and lessen the fear factor of non-office limbo.

In the world of action and negotiation, there is one principle that governs all others: The person who has more options has more power. Don't wait until you need options to search for them. Take a sneak peek at the future now and it will make both action and being assertive easier.

4. If you run or own a company, imagine that you have just been sued and must declare bankruptcy. The company is now insolvent and you must close up shop. This is something you *must* legally do, and there are no finances to entertain other options. How would you survive?

►TOOLS AND TRICKS

Considering Options and Pulling the Trigger

►I-Resign (www.i-resign.com)
This site provides everything from non-quitting options (work-leave, vacations) to sample resignation letters and second-life job-hunting advice. Don't miss the helpful discussion forums and hysterical "web consultant from London" letter.

Opening Retirement Accounts

If you want an adviser and don't mind some fees:

►Franklin-Templeton (www.franklintempleton.com) (800-527-2020)
►American Funds (www.americanfunds.com) (800-421-0180)

If you will do your own investing and want no-load funds:

►Fidelity Investments (www.fidelity.com) (800-343-3548)
►Vanguard (www.vanguard.com) (800-414-1321)

Health Insurance for Self-employed or Unemployed (in descending order of reader endorsement)

►Ehealthinsurance (www.fourhourblog.com/health) (800-977-8860)
►AETNA (www.aetna.com) (800-MY-HEALTH)
►Kaiser Permanente (www.kaiserpermanente.com) (866-352-0290)
►American Community Mutual (www.american-community.com) (800-991-2642)

14

Mini-Retirements

►EMBRACING THE MOBILE LIFESTYLE

Before the development of tourism, travel was conceived to be like study, and its fruits were considered to be the adornment of the mind and the formation of the judgment.
—PAUL FUSSELL, *Abroad*

The simple willingness to improvise is more vital, in the long run, than research.   —ROLF POTTS, *Vagabonding*

Upon Sherwood's return from Oktoberfest, dazed from killing neurons but the happiest he's been in four years, the remote trial is made policy and Sherwood is inducted into the world of the New Rich. All he needs now is an idea of how to exploit this freedom and the tools to give his finite cash near-infinite lifestyle output.

If you've gone through the previous steps, eliminating, automating, and severing the leashes that bind you to one location, it's time to indulge in some fantasies and explore the world.

Even if you have no ache for extended travel or think it's impossible—whether due to marriage or mortgage or those little things known as children—this chapter is still the next step. There are fundamental changes I and most others put off until absence (or preparation for it) forces them. This chapter is your final exam in muse design.

The transformation begins in a small Mexican village, in a parable that's been shared in various forms around the world.

Fables and Fortune Hunters

An American businessman took a vacation to a small coastal Mexican village on doctor's orders. Unable to sleep after an urgent phone call from the office the first morning, he walked out to the pier to clear his head. A small boat with just one fisherman had docked, and inside the boat were several large yellowfin tuna. The American complimented the Mexican on the quality of his fish.

"How long did it take you to catch them?" the American asked.

"Only a little while," the Mexican replied in surprisingly good English.

"Why don't you stay out longer and catch more fish?" the American then asked.

"I have enough to support my family and give a few to friends," the Mexican said as he unloaded them into a basket.

"But ... What do you do with the rest of your time?"

The Mexican looked up and smiled. "I sleep late, fish a little, play with my children, take a siesta with my wife, Julia, and stroll into the village each evening, where I sip wine and play guitar with my amigos. I have a full and busy life, señor."

The American laughed and stood tall. "Sir, I'm a Harvard M.B.A. and can help you. You should spend more time fishing, and with the proceeds, buy a bigger boat. In no time, you could buy several boats with the increased haul. Eventually, you would have a fleet of fishing boats."

He continued, "Instead of selling your catch to a middleman, you would sell directly to the consumers, eventually opening your own cannery. You would control the product, processing, and distribution. You would need to leave this small coastal fishing village, of course, and move to Mexico City, then to Los Angeles, and eventually New York City, where you could run your expanding enterprise with proper management."

The Mexican fisherman asked, "But, señor, how long will all this take?"

To which the American replied, "15–20 years. 25 tops."

"But what then, señor?"

The American laughed and said, "That's the best part. When the time is right, you would announce an IPO and sell your company stock to the public and become very rich. You would make millions."

"Millions, señor? Then what?"

"Then you would retire and move to a small coastal fishing village, where you would sleep late, fish a little, play with your kids, take a siesta with your wife, and stroll to the village in the evenings where you could sip wine and play your guitar with your amigos . . ."

I RECENTLY HAD lunch in San Francisco with a good friend and former college roommate. He will soon graduate from a top business school and return to investment banking. He hates coming home from the office at midnight but explained to me that, if he works 80-hour weeks for nine years, he could become a managing director and make a cool $3–10 million per year. Then he would be successful.

"Dude, what on earth would you do with $3–10 million per year?" I asked.

His answer? "I would take a long trip to Thailand."

That just about sums up one of the biggest self-deceptions of our modern age: extended world travel as the domain of the ultrarich. I've also heard the following:

"I'll just work in the firm for 15 years. Then I'll be partner and I can cut back on hours. Once I have a million or two in the bank, I'll put it in something safe like bonds, take $80,000 a year in interest, and retire to sail in the Caribbean."

"I'll only work in consulting until I'm 35, then retire and ride a motorcycle across China."

If your dream, the pot of gold at the end of the career rainbow, is to live large in Thailand, sail around the Caribbean, or ride a motor-cycle across China, guess what? All of them can be done for less than $3,000. I've done all three. Here are just two examples of how far a little can go.[68]

$250 U.S. Five days on a private Smithsonian tropical
   research island with three local fishermen who caught and
   cooked all my food and also took me on tours of the best
   hidden dive spots in Panamá.

$150 U.S. Three days of chartering a private plane in
   Mendoza wine country in Argentina and flying over the
   most beautiful vineyards around the snowcapped Andes
   with a personal guide.

Question: What did you spend your last $400 on? It's two or three weekends of nonsense and throwaway forget-the-workweek behavior in most U.S. cities. $400 is nothing for a full eight days of life-changing experiences. But eight days isn't what I'm recommending at all. Those were just interludes in a much larger production. I'm proposing much, much more.

The Birth of Mini-Retirements and the Death of Vacations

There is more to life than increasing its speed.
—MOHANDAS GANDHI

In February of 2004, I was miserable and overworked.
   My travel fantasy began as a plan to visit Costa Rica in March 2004 for four weeks of Spanish and relaxation. I needed a recharge

---

68. The dollar figures in this chapter are all from a period immediately following President Bush's reelection in 2004, which correlated to the worst dollar exchange rates of the last 20 years.

and four weeks seemed "reasonable" by whatever made-up bench-mark you can use for such a thing.

A friend familiar with Central America dutifully pointed out that it would never work, as Costa Rica was about to enter its rainy season. Torrential downpours weren't the uplifting jolt I needed, so I shifted my focus to four weeks in Spain. It's a long trip over the Atlantic, though, and Spain was close to other countries I'd always wanted to visit. I lost "reasonable" somewhere shortly thereafter and decided that I deserved a full three months to explore my roots in Scandinavia after four weeks in Spain.

If there were any real-time bombs or pending disasters, they would certainly crop up in the first four weeks, so *there really wasn't any additional risk in extending my trip to three months.* Three months would be great.

Those three months turned into 15, and I started to ask myself, "Why not take the usual 20–30-year retirement and redistribute it throughout life instead of saving it all for the end?"

The Alternative to Binge Traveling

Thanks to the Interstate Highway System, it is now pos-sible to travel from coast to coast without seeing anything.
—CHARLES KURALT, CBS news reporter

If you are accustomed to working 50 weeks per year, the tendency, even after creating the mobility to take extended trips, will be to go nuts and see 10 countries in 14 days and end up a wreck. It's like taking a starving dog to an all-you-can-eat buffet. It will eat itself to death.

I did this three months into my 15-month vision quest, visiting seven countries and going through at least 20 check-ins and check-outs with a friend who had negotiated three weeks off. The trip was an adrenaline-packed blast but like watching life on fast-forward.

It was hard for us to remember what had happened in which countries (except Amsterdam),[69] we were both sick most of the time, and we were upset to have to leave some places simply because our prepurchased flights made it so.

I recommend doing the exact opposite.

The alternative to binge travel—the mini-retirement—entails relocating to one place for one to six months before going home or moving to another locale. It is the anti-vacation in the most positive sense. Though it can be relaxing, the mini-retirement is not an escape from your life but a reexamination of it—the creation of a blank slate. Following elimination and automation, what would you be escaping from? Rather than seeking to *see* the world through photo ops between foreign-but-familiar hotels, we aim to *experience* it at a speed that lets it change us.

This is also different from a sabbatical. Sabbaticals are often viewed much like retirement: as a one-time event. Savor it now while you can. The mini-retirement is defined as recurring—it is a *lifestyle.* I currently take three or four mini-retirements per year and know dozens who do the same. Sometimes these sojourns take me around the world; oftentimes they take me around the corner— Yosemite, Tahoe, Carmel—but to a different world psychologically, where meetings, e-mail, and phone calls don't exist for a set period of time.

Purging the Demons: Emotional Freedom

> This is the very perfection of a man, to find out his own imperfection.   —SAINT AUGUSTINE (354 A.D.–430 A.D.)

True freedom is much more than having enough income and time to do what you want. It is quite possible—actually the rule rather than the exception—to have financial and time freedom but

---

69. I refer, of course, to the amazing bike-riding opportunities and famous pastries.

still be caught in the throes of the rat race. One cannot be free from the stresses of a speed- and size-obsessed culture until you are free from the materialistic addictions, time-famine mind-set, and comparative impulses that created it in the first place.

This takes time. The effect is not cumulative, and no number of two-week (also called "too weak")[70] sightseeing trips can replace one good walkabout.[71]

In the experience of those I've interviewed, it takes two to three months just to unplug from obsolete routines and become aware of just how much we distract ourselves with constant motion. Can you have a two-hour dinner with Spanish friends without getting anxious? Can you get accustomed to a small town where all businesses take a siesta for two hours in the afternoon and then close at 4:00 P.M.? If not, you need to ask, Why?

Learn to slow down. Get lost intentionally. Observe how you judge both yourself and those around you. Chances are that it's been a while. Take at least two months to disincorporate old habits and rediscover yourself without the reminder of a looming return flight.

The Financial Realities: It Just Gets Better

The economic argument for mini-retirements is the icing on the cake.

Four days in a decent hotel or a week for two at a nice hostel costs the same as a month in a nice posh apartment. If you relocate, the expenses abroad also begin to replace—often at much lower cost—bills you can then cancel stateside.

Here are some actual monthly figures from recent travels.

---

70. Coined by Joel Stein of the *LA Times*.
71. By all means, go ahead and take a post-office celebratory trip and go nuts for a few weeks. I know I did. Rock on. Ibiza and glow sticks here I come. Have some absinthe and drink lots of water. Following that, sit down and plan an introspective mini-retirement.

Highlights from both South America and Europe are shown side by side to prove that luxury is limited by your creativity and familiarity with the locale, not gross currency devaluation in third-world countries. It will be obvious that I did not survive on bread and begging—I lived like a rock star—and both experiences could be done for less than 50% of what I spent. My goal was enjoyment and not austere survival.

Airfare

- ►Free, courtesy of AMEX gold card and Chase Continental Airlines Mastercard[72]

Housing

- ►Penthouse apartment on the equivalent of New York's Fifth Avenue in Buenos Aires, including house cleaners, personal security guards, phone, energy, and high-speed Internet: $550 U.S. per month
- ►Enormous apartment in the trendy SoHo-like Prenz-lauerberg district of Berlin, including phone and energy: $300 U.S. per month

Meals

- ►Four- or five-star restaurant meals twice daily in Buenos Aires: $10 U.S. ($300 U.S. per month)
- ►Berlin: $18 U.S. ($540 U.S. per month)

---

72. Muses are low maintenance but often expensive in one or both of two tactical areas: manufacturing and advertising. Shop for providers of both that are willing to accept credit cards as payment, and negotiate this up front if necessary by saying, "Rather than trying to negotiate you down on pricing, I just ask that you accept payment by credit card. If you can do that, we'll choose you over Competitor X." This is yet another example of a "firm offer," and not a question, that puts you in a stronger negotiating position. For a detailed explanation of how I multiply points for travel using concepts like "piggybacking" and "recycling," search for both terms on www.fourhourblog.com.

Entertainment

- ►VIP table and unlimited champagne for eight people at the hottest club, Opera Bay, in Buenos Aires: $150 U.S. ($18.75 U.S. per person × four visits per month = $75 U.S. per month per person)
- ►Cover, drinks, and dancing at the hottest clubs in West Berlin: $20 U.S. per person per night × 4 = $80 U.S. per month

Education

- ►Two hours daily of private Spanish lessons in Buenos Aires, fives times per week: $5 U.S. per hour × 40 hours per month = $200 U.S. per month
- ►Two hours daily of private tango lessons with two world-class professional dancers: $8.33 U.S. per hour × 40 hours per month = $333.20 U.S. per month
- ►Four hours daily of top-tier German-language instruction in Nollendorfplatz, Berlin: $175 U.S. per month, which would have paid for itself even if I had not attended classes, as the student ID card entitled me to over 40% discounts on all transportation
- ►Six hours per week of mixed martial arts (MMA) training at the top Berlin academy: free in exchange for tutoring in English two hours per week

Transportation

- ►Monthly subway pass and daily cab rides to and from tango lessons in Buenos Aires: $75 U.S. per month
- ►Monthly subway, tram, and bus pass in Berlin with student discount: $85 U.S. per month

Four-Week Total for Luxury Living

- ►**Buenos Aires: $1533.20,** including round-trip airfare from JFK, with a one-month stopover in Panamá. Nearly one-third of this total is from the daily one-on-one instruction from world-class teachers in Spanish and Tango.

► **Berlin: $1180,** including round-trip airfare from JFK and a one-week stopover in London.

How do these numbers compare to your current domestic monthly expenses, including rent, car insurance, utilities, weekend expenditures, partying, public transportation, gas, memberships, subscriptions, food, and all the rest? Add it all up and you may well realize, like I did, that traveling around the world and having the time of your life can save you serious money.

Fear Factors: Overcoming Excuses Not to Travel

Travelling is the ruin of all happiness! There's no looking at a building here after seeing Italy.
—FANNY BURNEY (1752–1840), English novelist

But I have a house and kids. I can't travel!
What about health insurance? What if something happens?
Isn't travel dangerous? What if I get kidnapped or mugged?
But I'm a woman—traveling alone would be dangerous.

Most excuses not to travel are exactly that—excuses. I've been there, so this isn't a holier-than-thou sermon. I know too well that it's easier to live with ourselves if we cite an external reason for inaction.

I've since met paraplegics and the deaf, senior citizens and single mothers, home owners and the poor, all of whom have sought and found excellent life-changing reasons for extended travel instead of dwelling on the million small reasons *against it*.

Most of the concerns above are addressed in the Q&A, but one in particular requires a bit of preemptive nerve calming.

It's 10:00 P.M. Do You Know Where Your Children Are?

The prime fear of all parents prior to their first international trip is somehow losing a child in the shuffle.

The good news is that if you are comfortable taking your kids to New York, San Francisco, Washington, D.C., or London, you will have even less to worry about in the starting cities I recommend in the Q&A. There are fewer guns and violent crimes in all of them compared to most large U.S. cities. The likelihood of problems is decreased further when travel is less airport and hotel-hopping among strangers and more relocation to a second home: a mini-retirement.

But still, what if?

Jen Errico, a single mother who took her two children on a five-month world tour, had a more acute fear than most, one that often woke her at 2:00 A.M. in a cold sweat: What if something happens to me?

She wanted to prime her kids for worst-case scenario but didn't want to scare them to death, so—like all good mothers—she made it a game: Who can best memorize the itineraries, hotel addresses, and Mom's phone number? She had emergency contacts in each country whose numbers were loaded into the speed dial of her cell phone, which had global roaming. In the end, nothing happened. Now she's planning to move to a ski chalet in Europe and send her kids to school in multilingual France. Success begets success.

She was most afraid in Singapore, and in retrospect, it was where she had the least reason to be worried (she took her kids to South Africa, among other places). She was scared because it was the first stop and she was unaccustomed to traveling with her kids. It was perception, not reality.

Robin Malinsky-Rummell, who spent a year traveling through South America with her husband and seven-year-old son, was warned by friends and family not to visit Argentina after their devaluation riots in 2001. She did her homework, decided that the fear was unfounded, and proceeded to have the time of her life in Patagonia. When she told locals that she was originally from New York, their eyes widened and jaws dropped: "I saw those buildings blow up on TV! I would never go to such a dangerous place!" Don't assume that places abroad are more dangerous than your hometown. Most aren't.

Robin is convinced, as are other **NR** parents, that people use children as an excuse to stay in their comfort zones. It's an easy excuse not to do something adventurous. How to overcome the fear? Robin recommends two things:

1. Before embarking on a long international trip with your children for the first time, take a trial run for a few weeks.
2. For each stop, arrange a week of language classes that begin upon arrival and take advantage of transportation from the airport if available. The school staff will often handle apartment rentals for you, and you will be able to make friends and learn the area before setting off on your own.

But what if your concern isn't so much losing your children but losing your mind because of your children?

Several families interviewed for this book recommended the oldest persuasive tool known to man: bribery. Each child is given some amount of virtual cash, 25–50 cents, for each hour of good behavior. The same amount is subtracted from their accounts for breaking the rules. All purchases for fun—whether souvenirs, ice cream, or otherwise—come out of their own individual accounts. No balance, no goodies. This often requires more self-control on the part of the parents than the children.

How to Get Airfare at 50–80% Off

This is not a book on budget travel.

Most of the cost-cutting recommendations found in such guides are designed with the binge traveler in mind. For someone embarking on a mini-retirement, an extra $150 for hassle-free airfare amortized over two months is a better deal than 20 hours of manipulating frequent-flier points on an unknown airline or chasing questionable deals.

Following two weeks of research, I once bought a one-way standby ticket to Europe for $120. I arrived at JFK brimming with enthusiasm and confidence—look at all these schmucks paying retail!—and 90% of the "participating" airlines refused my ticket. Those that didn't were booked for weeks solid. I ended up staying in a hotel for two nights for a $300 tab, filing a complaint with AMEX, and eventually calling 1-800-FLY-EUROPE from the JFK terminal in frustration. I bought a round-trip ticket to London on Virgin Atlantic for $300 and left an hour later. The same ticket cost more than $700 a week earlier.

After 25 countries, I've found a few simple strategies that get you 90% of the possible savings without wasting time or producing migraines.

1. Use credit cards with reward points for large muse-related advertising and manufacturing expenses.

   I am not spending more money to get pennies on the dollar—these costs are inevitable, so I capitalize on them. This alone gets me a free round-trip international ticket each three months.

2. Purchase tickets far in advance (three months or more) or last minute, and aim for both departure and return between Tuesday and Thursday.

   Long-term travel planning turns me off and can be expensive if plans change, so I opt for purchasing all tickets in the last four or five days prior to target departure. The value of empty seats is $0 as soon as the flight takes off, so true last-minute seats are cheap.

Use Orbitz (www.orbitz.com) and www.kayak.com first. Fix the departure and return dates between Tuesday and Thursday. Then look at prices for alternative departure dates each of three days into the past and each of three days into the future. Using the cheapest departure date, do the same with the return dates to find the cheapest combination. Check this price against the fares on the website of the airline itself. Then begin bidding on www.priceline.com at 50% of the better of the two, working up in $50 increments until you get a better price or realize it's not possible.

3. Consider buying one ticket to an international hub and then an ongoing ticket with a cheap local airline.

If going to Europe on a tight budget, you could get three tickets. One free Southwest ticket (from transferring AMEX points) from CA to JFK, the cheapest ticket to Heathrow in London, and then an übercheap ticket on either Ryanair or EasyJet to a final destination. I have paid as little as $10 to go from London to Berlin or London to Spain. That is not a typo. Local airlines will often offer seats on flights for just the cost of taxes and gasoline. To Central or South American destinations, I'll often look at local flights from Panama or international flights from Miami.

When More Is Less: Cutting the Clutter

Human beings have the capacity to learn to want almost any conceivable material object. Given, then, the emergence of a modern industrial culture capable of producing almost anything, the time is ripe for opening the storehouse of infinite need! . . . It is the modern Pandora's box, and its plagues are loose upon the world.   —JULES HENRY

To be free, to be happy and fruitful, can only be attained through sacrifice of many common but overestimated things.   —ROBERT HENRI

I know the son of one deca-millionaire, a personal friend of Bill Gates, who now manages private investments and ranches. He has accumulated an assortment of beautiful homes over the last decade, each with full-time cooks, servants, cleaners, and support staff. How does he feel about having a home in each time zone? It's a pain in the ass! He feels like he's working for his staff, who spend more time in his homes than he does.

Extended travel is the perfect excuse to reverse the damage of years of consuming as much as you can afford. It's time to get rid of clutter disguised as necessities before you drag a five-piece Samsonite set around the world. That is hell on earth.

I'm not going to tell you to walk around in a robe and sandals scowling at people who have televisions. I hate that kashi-crunching holier-than-thou stuff. Turning you into a possession-less scribe is not my intention. Let's face it, though: There are tons of things in your home and life that you don't use, need, or even particularly want. They just came into your life as impulsive flotsam and jetsam and never found a good exit. Whether you're aware of it or not, this clutter creates indecision and distractions, consuming attention and making unfettered happiness a real chore. It is impossible to realize how distracting all the crap is—whether porcelain dolls, sports cars, or ragged T-shirts—until you get rid of it.

Prior to my 15-month trip, I was stressed about how to fit all of my belongings into a 14 × 10-foot rental storage space. Then I realized a few things: I would never reread the business magazines I'd saved, I wore the same five shirts and four pairs of pants 90% of the time, it was about time for new furniture, and I never used the outdoor grill or lawn furniture.

Even getting rid of things I *never* used proved to be like a capitalist short-circuit. It was hard to toss things I had once thought were valuable enough to spend money on. The first ten minutes of sorting through clothing was like choosing which child of mine should live or die. I hadn't exercised my throwing-out muscles in some time. It was a struggle to put nice Christmas clothing I'd never worn into the "go" pile and just as hard to separate myself from worn and ragged clothing I had for sentimental reasons. Once I'd passed through the first few tough decisions, though, the momentum had been built and it was a breeze. I donated all of the seldom-worn clothing to Goodwill. The furniture took less than 10 hours to off-load using Craigslist, and though I was paid less than 50% of the retail prices for some and nothing for others, who cared? I'd used and abused them for five years and would get a new set when I landed back in the U.S. I gave the grill and lawn furniture to my friend, who lit up like a kid at Christmas. I had made his month. It felt wonderful and I had an extra $300 in pocket change to cover at least a few weeks of rent abroad.

I created 40% more space in my apartment and hadn't even grazed the surface. It wasn't the extra physical space that I felt most. It was the extra mental space. It was as if I had 20 mental applications running simultaneously before, and now I had just one or two. My thinking was clearer and I was much, much happier.

I asked every vagabond interviewee in this book what their one recommendation would be for first-time extended travelers. The answer was unanimous: Take less with you.

The overpacking impulse is hard to resist. The solution is to set what I call a "settling fund." Rather than pack for all contingencies, I bring the absolute minimum and allocate $100–300 for purchasing things after I arrive and as I travel. I no longer take toiletries or more than a week's worth of clothing. It's a blast. Finding shaving cream or a dress shirt overseas can produce an adventure in and of itself.

Pack as if you were coming back in one week. Here are the bare essentials, listed in order of importance:

1. *One week* of clothing appropriate to the season, including *one* semiformal shirt and pair of pants or skirt for customs. Think T-shirts, one pair of shorts, and a multipurpose pair of jeans.
2. Backup photocopies or scanned copies of all important docu-

ments: health insurance, passport/visa, credit cards, debit cards, etc.

3. Debit cards, credit cards, and $200 worth of small bills in local currency (traveler's checks are not accepted in most places and are a hassle)

4. Small cable bike lock for securing luggage while in transit or in hostels; a small padlock for lockers if needed

5. Electronic dictionaries for target languages (book versions are too slow to be of use in conversation) and small grammar guides or texts

6. One broad-strokes travel guide

That's it.[73] To laptop or not to laptop? Unless you are a writer, I vote no. It's far too cumbersome and distracting. Using GoToMyPC to access your home computer from Internet cafés encourages the habit we want to develop: making the best use of time instead of killing it.

---

73. To see a video of how I pack to travel the world with less than 10 pounds, click on "travel" at www.fourhourblog.com.

The Bora-Bora Dealmaker

BAFFIN ISLAND, NUNAVUT

Josh Steinitz[74] stood at the edge of the world and stared in amazement. He dug his boots into the six feet of sea ice and the unicorns danced.

Ten narwhals—rare cousins of the beluga—came to the surface and pointed their six-foot-plus spiral tusks toward the heavens. The pod of 3,000-pound whales then fell into the depths once again. The narwhals are deep divers—more than 3,000 feet in some cases—so Josh had at least 20 minutes until their reappearance.

It seemed appropriate that he was with the narwhals. Their name came from Old Norse and referred to their mottled white and blue skin.

---

74. Founder of www.nileproject.com.

Náhvalr—corpse man.

He smiled as he had done often in the last few years. Josh himself was a dead man walking.

One year after graduating from college, Josh found out that he had oral squamous carcinoma—cancer. He had plans to be a management consultant. He had plans to be lots of things. Suddenly none of it mattered. Less than half of those who suffered from this particular type of cancer survived.[75] The reaper didn't discriminate and came without warning.

It became clear that the biggest risk in life wasn't making mistakes but regret: missing out on things. He could never go back and recapture years spent doing something he disliked.

Two years later and cancer-free, Josh set off on an indefinite global walkabout, covering expenses as a freelance writer. He later became the cofounder of a website that provides customized itineraries to would-be vagabonds. His executive status didn't lessen his mobile addiction. He was as comfortable cutting deals from the overwater bungalows of Bora-Bora as he was in the log cabins of the Swiss Alps.

He once took a call from a client while at Camp Muir on Mt. Rainier. The client needed to confirm some sales numbers and asked Josh about all the wind in the background. Josh's answer: "I'm standing at 10,000 feet on a glacier and this afternoon the wind is whipping us down the mountain." The client said he'd let Josh get back to what he was doing.

Another client called Josh while he was leaving a Balinese temple and heard the gongs in the background. The client asked Josh if he was in church. Josh wasn't quite sure what to say. All that came out was, "Yes?"

Back among the narwhals, Josh had a few minutes before heading to base camp to avoid polar bears. Twenty-four-hour daylight meant that he had much to share with his friends back in the land of cubicles. He sat down on the ice and produced his satellite phone and laptop from a waterproof bag. He began his e-mail in the usual way:

"I know you're all sick of seeing me have so much fun, but guess where I am?"

75. http://www.usc.edu/hsc/dental/opfs/SC/indexSC.html.

►Q&A: QUESTIONS AND ACTIONS

> It is fatal to know too much at the outcome: boredom
> comes as quickly to the traveler who knows his route as to
> the novelist who is overcertain of his plot.
> —PAUL THEROUX, *To the Ends of the Earth*

If this is your first time considering a commitment to the mobile lifestyle and long-term adventuring, I envy you! Making the jump and entering the new worlds that await is like upgrading your role in life from passenger to pilot.

The bulk of this Q&A will focus on the precise steps that you should take—and the countdown timeline you can use—when preparing for your first mini-retirement. Most steps can be eliminated or condensed once you get one trip under your belt. Some of the steps are one-time events, after which subsequent mini-retirements will require a maximum of two to three weeks of preparation. It now takes me three afternoons.

Grab a pencil and paper—this will be fun.

1. **Take an asset and cash-flow snapshot.**

   Set two sheets of paper on a table. Use one to record all assets and corresponding values, including bank accounts, retirement accounts, stocks, bonds, home, and so forth. On the second, draw a line down the middle and write down all incoming cash flow (salary, muse income, investment income, etc.) and outgoing expenses (mortgage, rent, car payments, etc.). What can you eliminate that is either seldom used or that creates stress or distraction without adding a lot of value?

2. **Fear-set a one-year mini-retirement in a dream location in Europe.**

   Use the questions from chapter 3 to evaluate your worst-case-scenario fears and evaluate the real potential consequences.

Except in rare cases, most will be avoidable and the rest will be reversible.

3. **Choose a location for your actual mini-retirement. Where to start?**
   This is the big question. There are two options that I advocate:

   a. Choose a starting point and then wander until you find your second home. This is what I did with a one-way ticket to London, vagabonding throughout Europe until I fell in love with Berlin, where I remained for three months.
   b. Scout a region and then settle in your favorite spot. This is what I did with a tour of Central and South America, where I spent one to four weeks in each of several cities, after which I returned to my favorite—Buenos Aires—for six months.

It is possible to take a mini-retirement in your own country, but the transformative effect is hampered if you are surrounded by people who carry the same socially reinforced baggage.

I recommend choosing an overseas location that will seem foreign but that isn't dangerous. I box, race motorcycles, and do all sorts of macho things, but I draw the line at *favelas*,[76] civilians with machine guns, pedestrians with machetes, and social strife. Cheap is good, but bullet holes are bad. Check the U.S. Department of State for travel warnings before booking tickets (http://travel.state.gov).

Here are just a few of my favorite starting points. Feel free to choose other locations. The most lifestyle for the dollar is underlined: <u>Argentina</u> (Buenos Aires, Córdoba), China (Shanghai, Hong Kong, Taipei), Japan (Tokyo, Osaka), England (London),

---

76. Brazilian shantytowns. See the movie *City of God (Cidade de Deus)* to get a taste of how fun these are.

Ireland (Galway), <u>Thailand</u> (Bangkok, Chiang Mai), Germany (<u>Berlin</u>, Munich), Norway (Oslo), Australia (Sydney), New Zealand (Queenstown), Italy (Rome, Milan, Florence), Spain (Madrid, Valencia, Sevilla), and Holland (Amsterdam). In all of these places, it is possible to live well while spending little. I spend less in Tokyo than in California because I know it well. Hip, recently gentrified artist areas, not unlike the Brooklyn of 10 years ago, can be found in almost all cities. The one place I can't seem to find a decent lunch for less than $20 U.S.? London.

Here are a few exotic places I don't recommend for vagabonding virgins, though veterans can make them all work: all countries in Africa, the Middle East, or Central and South America (excepting Costa Rica and Argentina). Mexico City and Mexican border areas are also a bit too kidnap-happy to make it onto my favorites list.

4. **Prepare for your trip. Here's the countdown.**

   ▶**Three months out—Eliminate**

   Get used to minimalism before the departure. Here are the questions to ask and act upon, even if you never plan to leave:

   What is the 20% of my belongings that I use 80% of the time? Eliminate the other 80% in clothing, magazines, books, and all else. Be ruthless—you can always repurchase things you can't live without.

   Which belongings create stress in my life? This could relate to maintenance costs (money and energy), insurance, monthly expenses, time consumption, or simple distraction. Eliminate, eliminate, eliminate. If you sell even a few expensive items, it could finance a good portion of your mini-retirement. Don't rule out the car and home. It's always possible to purchase either upon your return, often losing no money in the process.

Check current health insurance coverage for extended overseas travel. Get the wheels in motion to rent, swap, or sell your home—renting out is most recommended by serial vagabonds—or end your apartment lease and move all belongings into storage.

In all cases where doubts crop up, ask yourself, "If I had a gun to my head and had to do it, how would I do it?" It's not as hard as you think.

►Two months out—Automate

After eliminating the excess, contact companies (including suppliers) that bill you regularly and set up autopayment with credit cards that have reward points. Telling them that you will be traveling the world for a year often persuades them to accept credit cards rather than chase you around the planet like Carmen Sandiego.

For the credit card companies themselves and others that refuse, arrange automatic debit from your checking account. Set up online banking and bill payment. Set up all companies that won't take credit cards or automatic debit as online payees. Set these scheduled checks for $15–20 more than expected when dealing with utilities and other variable expenses. This will cover miscellaneous fees, prevent time-consuming billing problems, and accrue as a credit. Cancel paper bank and credit card statement delivery. Get bank-issued *credit* cards for all checking accounts—generally one for business and one for personal—and set the cash advances to $0 to minimize abuse potential. Leave these cards at home, as they are just for emergency overdraft protection.

Give a trusted member of your family and/or your accountant power of attorney,[77] which gives that person authority to

---

77. This is a serious step and should not be taken with those you do not trust. In this case, it helps because your accountant can then sign tax documents or checks in your name instead of consuming hours and days of your time with faxes, scanners, and expensive international FedEx'ing of documents.

sign documents (tax filings and checks, for example) in your name. Nothing screws up foreign fun faster than having to sign original documents when faxes are unacceptable.

►One month out—

Speak to the manager of your local post office and have all mail forwarded to a friend, family member, or personal assistant,[78] who will be paid $100–200 per month to e-mail you brief descriptions of all nonjunk mail each Monday.

Get all required and recommended immunizations and vaccinations for your target region. Check the Centers for Disease Control and Prevention (www.cdc.gov/travel/). Note that proof of immunizations is sometimes required to pass through foreign customs.

Set up a trial account with GoToMyPC or similar remote-access software and take a dry run to ensure that there are no technological glitches.[79]

If resellers (or distributors) still send you checks—the fulfillment house should handle customer checks at this point—do one of three things: give the resellers direct bank deposit information (ideal), have the fulfillment house handle these checks (second choice), or have the resellers pay via PayPal or mail checks to one of the people you are trusting with power of attorney (far third). In the last case, give the person with power of attorney deposit slips so he or she can sign or stamp and mail in the checks. It is convenient to become a member of a large bank (Bank of America, Wells Fargo, Washington Mutual, Citibank, etc.) with branches near the person assisting you so that they can

---

78. There are also services like www.fourhourblog.com/earthclass, which will receive, scan and e-mail all of your non–junk mail to you as PDFs.

79. This would be used if you leave your computer at home or in someone else's home while traveling. This step can be skipped if you bring your computer, but that is like a recovering heroin addict bringing a bag of opium to rehab. Don't tempt yourself to kill time instead of rediscovering it.

drop off the deposits while running other errands. No need to move all accounts to this bank if you don't want to; just open a single new account that is used solely for these deposits.

►Two weeks out—

Scan all identification, health insurance, and credit/debit cards into a computer from which you can print multiple copies, several to be left with family members and several to be taken with you in separate bags. E-mail the scanned file to yourself so that you can access it while abroad if you lose the paper copies.

If you are an entrepreneur, downgrade your cell phone to the cheapest plan and set up a voicemail greeting that states, "I am currently overseas on business. Please do not leave a voicemail, as I will not be checking it while gone. Please send me an e-mail at ___@___.com if the matter is important. Thank you for your understanding." Then set up e-mail autoresponders that indicate responses could take up to seven days (or whatever you decide for frequency) due to international business travel.

If you are an employee, consider getting a quad-band or GSM-compatible cell phone so that the boss can contact you. Get a BlackBerry only if your boss will be checking to see if you are working via e-mail. Be sure to disable the dead giveaway "Sent from a BlackBerry" signature on outgoing e-mail! Other options include using a SkypeIn account that forwards to your foreign cell phone (my preference) or a Vonage IP box that allows you to receive landline calls anywhere in the world via a phone number that begins with your home area code.

Find an apartment for your ultimate mini-retirement destination or reserve a hostel or hotel at your starting point for three to four days. Reserving an apartment before you arrive is riskier and will be much more expensive than using the latter three to four days to find an apartment. I recommend hostels for the starting point if possible—not for cost considerations but because the staff and fellow travelers are more knowledge-able and helpful with relocations.

Get foreign medical evacuation insurance if needed for peace of mind. This tends to be redundant if you are in a first-world country and can buy local insurance to augment your own, which I do, and it is useless if you are a 10-hour flight from civilization. I had evacuation insurance in Panama, as it's a 2-hour flight from Miami, but I didn't bother elsewhere. Don't freak out about this; it's just as true if you're in the middle of nowhere in the middle of the U.S.

►One week out—

Decide on a schedule for routine batched tasks such as e-mail, online banking, etc. to eliminate excuses for senseless pseudo-work procrasterbating. I suggest Monday mornings for checking e-mail and online banking. The first and third Mondays of the month can be used for checking credit cards and making other online payments such as affiliates. These promises to yourself will be the hardest to keep, so make a commitment now and expect serious withdrawal cravings.

Save important documents—including the scan of your identification, insurance, and credit/debit cards—to a small hand-held storage device that plugs into a computer USB port.

Move all things out of your home or apartment into storage, pack a single small backpack and carry-on bag for the adventure, and move in briefly with a family member or friend.

►Two days out—

Put remaining automobiles into storage or a friend's garage. Put fuel stabilizer like Sta-Bil® in the gas tanks, disconnect the negative leads from batteries to prevent drain, and put the vehicles on jack stands to prevent tire and shock damage. Cancel all auto insurance except for theft coverage.

►Upon arrival (assuming you have not booked an apartment in advance)—

First morning and afternoon after check-in Take a hop-on-hop-off bus tour of the city followed by a bike tour of potential apartment neighborhoods.

First late afternoon or evening Purchase an unlocked[80] cell phone with a SIM card that can be recharged with simple prepaid cards. E-mail apartment owners or brokers on Craigslist.com and online versions of local newspapers for viewings over the next two days.

Second and third days Find and book an apartment for one month. Don't commit to more than one month until you've slept there. I once prepaid two months only to find that the busiest bus stop downtown was on the other side of my bedroom wall.

Move-in day Get settled and purchase local health insurance. Ask hostel owners and other locals what insurance they use. Resolve not to buy souvenirs or other take-home items until two weeks prior to departure.

One week later Eliminate all the extra crap you brought but won't use often. Either give it to someone who needs it more, mail it back to the U.S., or throw it out.

---

80. "Unlocked" means that it is recharged with prepaid cards instead of being on a monthly payment plan with a single carrier such as O2 or Vodafone. This also means that the same phone can be used with carriers in other countries (assuming the frequency is the same) with a simple switch of the SIM memory card for $10–30 U.S. in most cases. Some U.S.-compatible quad-band phones can use SIM cards.

►TOOLS AND TRICKS

Brainstorming Mini-Retirement Locations

►Virtual Tourist (www.virtualtourist.com)
The single largest source of unbiased, user-generated travel content in the world. More than 1,000,000 members contribute tips and warnings for more than 25,000 locations. Each location is covered in 13 separate categories, including Things to Do, Local Customs, Shopping, and Tourist Traps. This is one-stop shopping for most mini-retirements.

►Escape Artist (www.escapeartist.com)
Interested in second passports, starting your own country, Swiss banking, and all the other things I wouldn't dare put in this book? This site is a fantastic resource. Drop me a note from the Caymans or jail, whichever comes first. Also search "How to Be Jason Bourne" at www.fourhourblog.com.

►Outside Magazine Online Free Archives (http://outside.away.com)
The entire archive of *Outside* magazine available online for free. From meditation camps to worldwide adrenaline hotspots, dream jobs to Patagonia winter highlights, there are hundreds of articles with beautiful photos to give you the walkabout itch.

►GridSkipper: The Urban Travel Guide (www.gridskipper.com)
For those who love *Blade Runner*–like settings and exploring the cool nooks and crannies of cities worldwide, this is the site. It is one of *Forbes*'s Top 13 Travel sites and is "high-falootin' and low-brow all in the same breath" *(Frommer's)*. Translation: Much of the content is not G-rated. If four-letter words or a "world's sluttiest city" poll bother you, don't bother visiting this site (or Rio de Janeiro, for that matter). Otherwise, check out the hysterical writing and "$100 a day" info for cities worldwide.

►Lonely Planet: The Thorn Tree (http://thorntree.lonelyplanet.com)
Discussion forum for global travelers with threads separated by region.

►Family Travel Forum (www.familytravelforum.com)
A comprehensive forum on, you guessed it, family travel. Want to sell your kids for top dollar in the Eastern Bloc? Or save a few dollars and cremate Grannie in Thailand? Then this isn't the site. But if you have kids and are planning a big trip, this is the place.

► U.S. Department of State Country Profiles
  (www.state.gov/r/pa/ei/bgn/)

► World Travel Watch (www.worldtravelwatch.com)
Larry Habegger and James O'Reilly's weekly online report of global events
and odd happenings relevant to travel safety, sorted by topic and geographic region. Concise and a must-see prior to finalizing plans.

► U.S. Department of State Worldwide Travel Warnings
  (http://travel.state.gov)

Mini-Retirement Planning and Preparation—Fundamentals

► Round-the-World FAQ (includes travel insurance)
  (www.perpetualtravel.com/rtw)
This FAQ is a lifesaver. Originally written by Marc Brosius, it has been
added to by newsgroup participants for years and now covers nuts and
bolts from financial planning to return culture shock and all in between.
How long can you afford to be away? Do you need travel insurance? Leave
of absence or resignation? This is an around-the-world almanac.

► Removing Clutter: 1-800-GOT-JUNK (www.1800gotjunk.com),
  Freecycle (www.freecycle.org), and Craigslist (www.craigslist.org)
I used Craigslist's "Free" category to get rid of four years of accumulated
possessions in less than three hours on a Saturday evening. There were
some for-sale items that I also cleared out at 30–40% of original retail. I
then hauled off the last remaining items using the überfast 1-800-GOT-
JUNK paid service. Freecycle is comparable to Craigslist for giving away,
and getting, things for free when you're short on time. Get unattached and
you'll make it a habit. I purge every 6–9 months, often including donations
to Goodwill (www.goodwill.org), which can do pickups for free with advanced notice.

► One-Bag: The Art and Science of Packing Light (www.onebag.com)
One of PC magazine's "Top 100 [Can't Live Without] Sites." Pack light
and experience lightness of being.

► U.S. Centers for Disease Control and Prevention
  (www.cdc.gov/travel)
Recommended vaccinations and health planning for every nation in the

world. Certain countries require proof of inoculations to pass through customs. Get the shots well ahead of time, as some take weeks to order.

►Tax Planning (www.irs.gov/publications/p54/index.html)
More good news. Even if you permanently relocate to another country, you will have to pay U.S. taxes as long as you have a U.S. passport! Not to fret—there are some creative legal sidesteps, such as form 2555-EZ, which can provide up to an $85,700 income exemption if you spend at least 330 days of a consecutive 365 days off U.S. soil. This means you have 35 days in a given 12-month period to spend in the U.S. as you like, but no more. That's part of the reason my 2004 trip extended to 15 months. Get a good accountant and let them do the detail work to keep yourself out of trouble.

►U.S.-Sponsored Overseas Schools (www.state.gov/m/a/os)
If the idea of pulling your children out of school for a year or two isn't appealing, stick them in one of more than 190 elementary and secondary schools sponsored by the U.S. Department of State in 135 countries. Kids love home work.

►Homeschooling 101 and Quickstart Guide
  (http://bit.ly/homeschooling101)
This subsection of http://homeschooling.about.com/ provides a step-by-step process for considering homeschooling options that can be applied to education during extended travel. Children can often return to traditional public or private schools ahead of their classmates.

►*Home Education* Magazine (www.homeedmag.com)
Rich collection of resources for homeschoolers, traveling families, and unschoolers. Links include curriculum, virtual support groups, legal resources, and archives. Good reasons to learn the law: Some U.S. states offer up to $1,600 of funding per year for qualified homeschooling expenditures, as it saves the state money to not educate your child in the public school system.

►Universal Currency Converter (www.xe.com)
Before you get caught up in the excitement and forget that five British pounds does not equal five U.S. dollars, use this to translate local costs into numbers you understand. Try not to have too many "Those coins are each worth four dollars?" moments.

►Universal Plug Adapter (www.fourhourblog.com/franzus)
Carrying bulky cables and connectors is irritating—get a Travel Smart all-in-one adapter with surge protection. The size of a pack of cards folded in half, it is the only adapter that I've used everywhere without problems. Note that it is an adapter (helps you plug things in), but it is *not a transformer*. If the foreign wall outlet has twice as much voltage as in the U.S., your gadgets will self-destruct. Yet another reason to purchase necessities abroad instead of taking them all with you.

►World Electric Guide (www.kropla.com)
Figure out outlets, voltage, mobile phones, international dialing codes, and all sorts of things related to electric mismatching worldwide.

Cheap and Round-the-World Airfare

►Orbitz (www.orbitz.com), Kayak (www.kayak.com), and
  Sidestep (www.sidestep.com)
Search 400+ airlines worldwide for each service. Orbitz is my starting point for pricing comparisons, after which I check both Kayak and Sidestep. Sidestep has proven most effective when searching for flights that start and end outside of the U.S.

►TravelZoo Top 20 (http://top20.travelzoo.com/)
Moscow for $129 one-way? These last-minute weekly travel specials might be the push you need to pull the trigger.

►Priceline (www.priceline.com)
Start bidding at 50% of the lowest Orbitz fare and move up in $50 increments.

►CFares (www.cfares.com)
Consolidator fares with free and low-cost memberships. I found a round-trip ticket from California to Japan for $500.

►1-800-FLY-EUROPE (www.1800flyeurope.com)
I used this to get the $300 roundtrip from JFK to London that left two hours later.

►Discount Airlines for Flights within Europe (www.ryanair.com,
  www.easyjet.com)

Free Worldwide Housing—Short Term

►Global Freeloaders (www.globalfreeloaders.com)
This online community brings people together to offer you free accommodation all over the world. Save money and make new friends while seeing the world from a local's perspective.

►The Couchsurfing Project (www.couchsurfing.com)
Similar to the above but tends to attract a younger, more party-hearty crowd.

►Hospitality Club (www.hospitalityclub.org)
Meet locals worldwide who can provide free tours or housing through this well-run network of more than 200,000 members in 200+ countries.

Free Worldwide Housing—Long Term

►Home Exchange International (www.homeexchange.com)
This is a home exchange listing and search service with more than 12,000 listings in more than 85 countries. E-mail directly owners of potential homes, put your own home/apartment on the site, and have unlimited access to view listings for one year for a small membership fee.

Paid Housing—from Arrival to the Long Haul

►Otalo (www.otalo.com)
Otalo is a search engine for vacation rentals that searches across the Internet's many different vacation rentals sites and 200,000+ homes. Otalo is like a Kayak.com for vacation rentals. The site scours a variety of other rental search sites and aggregates the results in one easy-to-use search tool.

►Hostels.com (www.hostels.com)
This site isn't just for youth hostels. I found a nice hotel in downtown Tokyo for $20 per night and have used this site for similar housing in eight countries. Think location and reviews (see HotelChatter next) instead of amenities. Four-star hotels are for binge travelers; this site can offer a real local flavor before you find an apartment or other longer-term housing.

►HotelChatter (www.hotelchatter.com)
Get the real scoop on this daily web journal with detailed and honest

reviews of housing worldwide. Updated several times daily, this site offers the stories of frustrated guests and those who have found hidden gems. Online booking is available.

► Craigslist (www.craigslist.org)
Besides local weekly magazines with housing listings, such as *Bild* or *Zitty* (no joke) in Berlin, I have found Craigslist to be the single best starting point for long-term overseas furnished apartments. As of this writing, there are more than 50 countries represented. That said, prices will be 30–70% less in the local magazines—if you have a tight budget, get a hostel employee or other local to help you make a few calls and strike a deal. Ask the local helper not to mention you're a foreigner until pricing is agreed upon.

► Interhome International (www.interhome.com)
Based in Zurich, more than 20,000 homes for rent in Europe.

► Rentvillas.com (www.rentvillas.com)
Provides unique renting experiences—from cottages and farmhouses to castles—throughout Europe, including France, Italy, Greece, Spain, and Portugal.

Computer Remote Access and Backup Tools

► GoToMyPC (www.gotomypc.com)
This software facilitates quick and easy remote access to your computer's files, programs, e-mail, and network. It can be used from any web browser or wireless device and works in real time. I have used GoToMyPC religiously for more than five years to access my U.S.-based computers from countries and islands worldwide. This gives me the freedom to leave all computers at home.

► WebExPCNow (http://pcnow.webex.com)
WebEx, the leader in corporate remote access, now offers software that does most of what GoToMyPC offers, including cut and paste between remote computers, local printing from remote computers, file transfers, and more.

► DropBox (www.getdropbox.com) and SugarSync
(www.fourhourblog.com/sugarsync); then JungleDisk
(www.jungledisk.com) and Mozy (www.mozy.com)

Both DropBox and SugarSync perform backups and synching of files between multiple computers (home and travel computers, for example). JungleDisk and Mozy—I use the latter—have fewer features and are more specifically designed for automatic backups to their online storage.

Free and Low-Cost Internet (IP) Telephones

►Skype (www.skype.com)

Skype is my default for all phone calls. It allows you to call landlines and mobile phones across the globe for an average of 2–5 cents per minute, or connect with other Skype users worldwide for free. For about 40 euros per year, you can get a U.S. number with your home area code and receive calls that forward to a foreign cell phone. This makes your travel invisible. Lounge on the beach in Rio and answer calls to your "office" in California. Nice. Skype Chat, which comes with the service, is also perfect for sharing sensitive log-in and password information with others, as it's encrypted.

►Vonage (www.vonage.com) and Ooma (www.ooma.com)

Vonage offers a small adapter for a monthly fee that connects your broadband modem to a normal phone. Take it on your travels and set it up in your apartment to receive calls to a U.S. number. Ooma has no monthly fees and doesn't require a landline, but it offers similar hardware you can connect to broadband for a local U.S. number anywhere in the world.

►VoIPBuster (www.voipbuster.com) and RebTel (www.fourhourblog.com/rebtel)

Both VoIPBuster and RebTel can provide "alias" numbers. Enter a friend's overseas number on their sites, and both will give you a local number in your area code that will forward to your friend. VoIPBuster also acts as a cheaper Skype with free calls to more than 20 countries.

International Multi-Band and GSM-Compatible Phones

►My World Phone (www.myworldphone.com)

I'm partial to Nokia phones. Ensure whichever phone you purchase is "unlocked"—that the SIM card can be swapped out in different countries with different providers.

►World Electronics USA (www.worldelectronicsusa.com)
Good explanation of which GSM frequencies and "bands" function in which countries, which will determine which phone you purchase for travel (and perhaps home).

Tools for Off-the-Beaten Path

►Satellite Phones (www.satphonestore.com)
If you will be in the mountains of Nepal or on a remote island and want the peace of mind (or headache) of having a phone nearby, these phones work via satellite instead of towers. Iridium has been recommended for widest reception (pole to pole), with GlobalStar in second place (three continents). Rent or purchase.

►Pocket-size Solar Panels (www.solio.com)
Satellite phones and other small electronics are of little use (skipping stones, perhaps?) if their batteries die. Solio is about the size of two packs of cards and fans out into small solar panels. I was surprised to find that it charged my cell phone in less than 15 minutes—more than twice as fast as a wall outlet. Adapters are available for almost anything.

What to Do Once You Get There—Career Experiments and More

►*Verge Magazine* (see Restricted Reading appendix)

►Meet Up (www.meetup.com)
Search by city and activity to find people who share similar interests all over the world.

►Become a Travel Writer (www.writtenroad.com)
Get paid to travel the world and record your thoughts? This is a dream job for millions. Get the inside scoop on the travel publishing world from veteran Jen Leo, author of *Sand in My Bra and Other Misadventures: Funny Women Write from the Road*. This blog was a *Frommer's Budget Travel* Top Choice and also features great practical articles about low-tech travel and going gadgetless.

►Teach Engrish (www.eslcafe.com)
Dave's ESL Café is one of the oldest and most useful resources for teach-

ers, would-be teachers, and learners of English. Features discussion boards and "teachers wanted" job postings worldwide.

► **Turn Your Brain into Play-Doh (www.jiwire.com)**
Travel the world so you can instant message (IM) with your friends in the U.S. This site lists more than 150,000 hotspots where you can feed your information OCD. Be ashamed if this becomes your default activity. If you're bored, just remember—it's your fault. I've been there, so I'm not preaching. It happens to the best of us from time to time, but get more creative.

► **Test a New Career Part- or Full-Time: Working Overseas (www.workingoverseas.com)**
This encyclopedia is an exhaustive menu of options for the globally minded, compiled and updated by Jean-Marc Hachey, former international careers editor of *Transitions Abroad* magazine.

► **World Wide Opportunities on Organic Farms (www.wwoof.org)**
Learn and then teach sustainable organic farming techniques in dozens of countries, including Turkey, New Zealand, Norway, and French Polynesia.

Chat and E-mail in a Language You Don't Know

► **Google Chat Bots (http://bit.ly/imbot)**
Use this to chat in real time using almost any language. Instant message (IM) directly from your Gmail e-mail account with anyone in the world.

► **Nice Translator (www.nicetranslator.com) and Free Translation (www.freetranslation.com)**
Translate text from English into a dozen languages and vice versa. Surprisingly accurate, though the lost-in-translation 10–20% can get you in trouble. Nice Translator is faster and can be used on the iPhone.

Become Fluent in Record Time

Language Addicts and Accelerated Learning
For all things language related, from detailed how-to articles (how to reactivate forgotten languages, memorize 1,000 words per week, master tones, etc.) to mnemonics and the best electronic shortcuts, click on "language" at www.fourhourblog.com. Learning languages is an addiction of mine and a

skill I have taken apart and reassembled to be faster. It is possible to become conversationally fluent in any language in 3–6 months.

Find Language Exchange Partners and Materials

► LiveMocha (www.livemocha.com),
  EduFire (www.edufire.com), and
  Smart.fm (http://smart.fm/)
I particularly like their BrainSpeed learning game.

► About.com (www.about.com)
Some of the more popular languages have excellent tutorials on About
.com:

  http://italian.about.com
  http://spanish.about.com
  http://german.about.com
  http://french.about.com

15

Filling the Void

▶ADDING LIFE AFTER SUBTRACTING WORK

To be engrossed by something outside ourselves is a power-ful antidote for the rational mind, the mind that so frequently has its head up its own ass.
—ANNE LAMOTT, *Bird by Bird*

There is not enough time to do all the nothing we want to do.
—BILL WATTERSON, creator of the Calvin and Hobbes cartoon strip

KING'S CROSS, LONDON

I stumbled into the deli across the cobblestone street and ordered a prosciutto sandwich. It was 10:33 A.M. now, the fifth time I'd checked the time, and the twentieth time I'd asked myself, "What the &%$# am I going to do today?"

The best answer I had come up with so far was: get a sandwich.

Thirty minutes earlier, I had woken up without an alarm clock for the first time in four years, fresh off arriving from JFK the night before. I had soooo been looking forward to it: awakening to musical birdsong outside, sitting up in bed with a smile, smelling the aroma of freshly brewed coffee, and stretching out overhead like a cat in the shade of a Spanish villa. Magnificent. It turned out more like this: bolt upright as if blasted with a foghorn, grab clock, curse, jump out of bed in underwear to check e-mail, remember that I was forbidden to do so, curse again, look for my host and former class-mate, realize that he was off to work like the rest of the world, and proceed to have a panic attack.

I spent the rest of the day in a haze, wandering from museum to botanical garden to museum as if on rinse and repeat, avoiding In-ternet cafés with some vague sense of guilt. I needed a to-do list to feel productive and so put down things like "eat dinner."

This was going to be a lot harder than I had thought.

Postpartum Depression: It's Normal

> Man is so made that he can only find relaxation from one kind of labor by taking up another.
> —ANATOLE FRANCE, author of *The Crime of Sylvestre Bonnard*

I've Got More Money and Time Than I Ever Dreamed Possible . . . Why Am I Depressed?

It's a good question with a good answer. Just be glad you're figuring this out now and not at the end of life! The retired and ultrarich are often unfulfilled and neurotic for the same reason: too much idle time.

But wait a second . . . Isn't more time what we're after? Isn't that what this book is all about? No, not at all. Too much free time is no more than fertilizer for self-doubt and assorted mental tail-chasing. Subtracting the bad does not create the good. It leaves a vacuum. Decreasing income-driven work isn't the end goal. Living more—and becoming more—is.

In the beginning, the external fantasies will be enough, and there is nothing wrong with this. I cannot overemphasize the importance of this period. Go nuts and live your dreams. This is not superficial or selfish. It is critical to stop repressing yourself and get out of the postponement habit.

Let's suppose you decide to dip your toe in dreams like relocating to the Caribbean for island-hopping or taking a safari in the Serengeti. It will be wonderful and unforgettable, and you should do it. There will come a time, however—be it three weeks or three years later—when you won't be able to drink another piña colada or photograph another damn red-assed baboon. Self-criticism and existential panic attacks start around this time.

But This Is What I Always Wanted! How Can I Be Bored?!

Don't freak out and fuel the fire. This is normal among all high-performers who downshift after working hard for a long time. The smarter and more goal-oriented you are, the tougher these growing pains will be. Learning to replace the perception of time famine with appreciation of time abundance is like going from triple espressos to decaf.

But there's more! Retirees get depressed for a second reason, and you will too: social isolation.

Offices are good for some things: free bad coffee and complaining thereof, gossip and commiserating, stupid video clips via e-mail with even stupider comments, and meetings that accomplish nothing but kill a few hours with a few laughs. The job itself might be a dead end, but it's the web of human interactions—the social environment—that keeps us there. Once liberated, this automatic tribal unit disappears, which makes the voices in your head louder.

Don't be afraid of the existential or social challenges. Freedom is like a new sport. In the beginning, the sheer newness of it is exciting enough to keep things interesting at all times. Once you have learned the basics, though, it becomes clear that to be even a half-decent player requires some serious practice.

Don't fret. The greatest rewards are to come, and you're 10 feet from the finish line.

Frustrations and Doubts:
You're Not Alone

People say that what we are seeking is a meaning for life.
I don't think this is what we're really seeking. I think what
we're seeking is an experience of being alive.

—JOSEPH CAMPBELL, *The Power of Myth*

Once you eliminate the 9–5 and the rubber hits the road, it's not all roses and white-sand bliss, though much of it can be. Without the distraction of deadlines and co-workers, the big questions (such as "What does it all mean?") become harder to fend off for a later time. In a sea of infinite options, decisions also become harder—What the hell should I do with my life? It's like senior year in college all over again.

Like all innovators ahead of the curve, you will have frightening moments of doubt. Once past the kid-in-a-candy-store phase, the comparative impulse will creep in. The rest of the world will continue with its 9–5 grind, and you'll begin to question your decision to step off the treadmill. Common doubts and self-flagellation include the following:

1. Am I really doing this to be more free and lead a better life, or am I just lazy?
2. Did I quit the rat race because it's bad, or just because I couldn't hack it? Did I just cop out?
3. Is this as good as it gets? Perhaps I was better off when I was following orders and ignorant of the possibilities. It was easier at least.
4. Am I really successful or just kidding myself?
5. Have I lowered my standards to make myself a winner? Are my friends, who are now making twice as much as three years ago, really on the right track?

6. Why am I not happy? I can do anything and I'm still not happy. Do I even deserve it?

Most of this can be overcome as soon as we recognize it for what it is: outdated comparisons using the more-is-better and money-as-success mind-sets that got us into trouble to begin with. Even so, there is a more profound observation to be made.

These doubts invade the mind when nothing else fills it. Think of a time when you felt 100% alive and undistracted—in the zone. Chances are that it was when you were completely focused in the moment on something external: someone or something else. Sports and sex are two great examples. Lacking an external focus, the mind turns inward on itself and creates problems to solve, even if the problems are undefined or unimportant. If you find a focus, an ambitious goal that seems impossible and forces you to grow,[81] these doubts disappear.

In the process of searching for a new focus, it is almost inevitable that the "big" questions will creep in. There is pressure from pseudo-philosophers everywhere to cast aside the impertinent and answer the eternal. Two popular examples are "What is the meaning of life?" and "What is the point of it all?"

There are many more, ranging from the introspective to the ontological, but I have one answer for almost all of them—I don't answer them at all.

I'm no nihilist. In fact, I've spent more than a decade investigating the mind and concept of meaning, a quest that has taken me from the neuroscience laboratories of top universities to the halls of religious institutions worldwide. The conclusion after it all is surprising.

I am 100% convinced that most big questions we feel compelled

---

81. Abraham Maslow, the American psychologist famous for proposing "Maslow's Hierarchy of Needs," would term this goal a "peak experience."

to face—handed down through centuries of overthinking and mis-translation—use terms so undefined as to make attempting to answer them a complete waste of time.[82] This isn't depressing. It's liberating.

Consider the question of questions: What is the meaning of life?

If pressed, I have but one response: It is the characteristic state or condition of a living organism. "But that's just a definition," the questioner will retort, "that's not what I mean at all." What do you mean, then? Until the question is clear—each term in it defined—there is no point in answering it. The "meaning" of "life" question is unanswerable without further elaboration.

Before spending time on a stress-inducing question, big or other-wise, ensure that the answer is "yes" to the following two questions:

1. Have I decided on a single meaning for each term in this question?
2. Can an answer to this question be acted upon to improve things?

"What is the meaning of life?" fails the first and thus the second. Questions about things beyond your sphere of influence like "What if the train is late tomorrow?" fail the second and should thus be ignored. These are not worthwhile questions. **If you can't define it or act upon it, forget it.** If you take just this point from this book, it will put you in the top 1% of performers in the world and keep most philosophical distress out of your life.

Sharpening your logical and practical mental toolbox is *not* being an atheist or unspiritual. It's not being crass and it's not being superficial. It's being smart and putting your effort where it can make the biggest difference for yourself and others.

---

82. There is a place for koans and rhetorical meditative questions, but these tools are optional and outside the scope of this book. Most questions without answers are just poorly worded.

The Point of It All: Drumroll, Please

What man actually needs is not a tensionless state but rather the striving and struggling for a worthwhile goal, a freely chosen task.

—VIKTOR E. FRANKL, Holocaust survivor; author of *Man's Search for Meaning*

I believe that life exists to be enjoyed and that the most important thing is to feel good about yourself.

Each person will have his or her own vehicles for both, and those vehicles will change over time. For some, the answer will be working with orphans, and for others, it will be composing music. I have a personal answer to both—to love, be loved, and never stop learning—but I don't expect that to be universal.

Some criticize a focus on self-love and enjoyment as selfish or hedonistic, but it's neither. Enjoying life and helping others—or feeling good about yourself and increasing the greater good—are no more mutually exclusive than being agnostic and leading a moral life. One does not preclude the other. Let's assume we agree on this. It still leaves the question, "What can I do with my time to enjoy life and feel good about myself?"

I can't offer a single answer that will fit all people, but, based on the dozens of fulfilled **NR** I've interviewed, there are two components that are fundamental: continual learning and service.

Learning Unlimited: Sharpening the Saw

Americans who travel abroad for the first time are often shocked to discover that, despite all the progress that has been made in the last 30 years, many foreign people still speak in foreign languages.   —DAVE BARRY

To live is to learn. I see no other option. This is why I've felt compelled to quit or be fired from jobs within the first six months or so. The learning curve flattens out and I get bored.

Though you can upgrade your brain domestically, traveling and relocating provides unique conditions that make progress much faster. The different surroundings act as a counterpoint and mirror for your own prejudices, making weaknesses that much easier to fix. I rarely travel somewhere without deciding first how I'll obsess on a specific skill. Here are a few examples:

- **Connemara, Ireland:** Gaelic Irish, Irish flute, and hurling, the fastest field sport in the world (imagine a mix of lacrosse and rugby played with axe handles)
- **Rio de Janeiro, Brazil:** Brazilian Portuguese and Brazilian jujitsu
- **Berlin, Germany:** German and locking (a form of upright break-dancing)

I tend to focus on language acquisition and one kinesthetic skill, sometimes finding the latter after landing overseas. The most successful serial vagabonds tend to blend the mental and the physical. Notice that I often transport a skill I practice domestically—martial arts—to other countries where they are also practiced. Instant social life and camaraderie. It need not be a competitive sport—it could be hiking, chess, or almost anything that keeps your nose out of a textbook and you out of your apartment. Sports just happen to be excellent for avoiding foreign-language stage fright and developing lasting friendships while still sounding like Tarzan.

Language learning deserves special mention. It is, bar none, the best thing you can do to hone clear thinking.

Quite aside from the fact that it is impossible to understand a culture without understanding its language, acquiring a new language makes you aware of your own language: your own thoughts. The benefits of becoming fluent in a foreign tongue are as underestimated as the difficulty is overestimated. Thousands of theoretical linguists will disagree, but I *know* from research and personal experimentation with more than a dozen languages that (1) adults can learn languages much faster than children[83] when constant 9–5 work is removed and that (2) it is possible to become conversationally fluent in any language in six months or less. At four hours per day, six months can be whittled down to less than three months. It is beyond the scope of this book to explain applied linguistics and the 80/20 of language learning, but resources and complete how-to guides can be found under "language" at www.fourhourblog.com. I learned six languages after failing Spanish in high school, and you can do the same with the right tools.

Gain a language and you gain a second lens through which to question and understand the world. Cursing at people when you go home is fun, too.

Don't miss the chance to double your life experience.

Service for the Right Reasons: To Save the Whales, or Kill Them and Feed the Children?

> Morality is simply the attitude we adopt toward people we personally dislike. —OSCAR WILDE

One would expect me to mention service in this chapter, and here it is. Like all before it, the twist is a bit different.

Service to me is simple: doing something that improves life besides your own. This is not the same as philanthropy. Philanthropy is the altruistic concern for the well-being of mankind— human life. Human life has long been focused on the exclusion of the environment and the rest of the food chain, hence our current

---

83. Ellen Bialystok and Kenji Hakuta, *In Other Words: The Science and Psychology of Second-Language Acquisition* (Basic Books, 1995).

race to imminent extinction. Serves us right. The world does not exist solely for the betterment and multiplication of mankind.

Before I start chaining myself to trees and saving the dart frogs, though, I should take my own advice: Do not become a cause snob.

How can you help starving children in Africa when there are starving children in Los Angeles? How can you save the whales when homeless people are freezing to death? How does doing volunteer research on coral destruction help those people who need help now?

Children, please. Everything out there needs help, so don't get baited into "my cause can beat up your cause" arguments with no right answer. There are no qualitative or quantitative comparisons that make sense. The truth is this: Those thousands of lives you save could contribute to a famine that kills millions, or that one bush in Bolivia that you protect could hold the cure for cancer. The downstream effects are unknown. Do your best and hope for the best. If you're improving the world—however you define that—consider your job well done.

Service isn't limited to saving lives or the environment either. It can also improve life. If you are a musician and put a smile on the faces of thousands or millions, I view that as service. If you are a mentor and change the life of one child for the better, the world has been improved. Improving the quality of life in the world is in no fashion inferior to adding more lives.

Service is an attitude.

Find the cause or vehicle that interests you most and make no apologies.

►Q&A: QUESTIONS AND ACTIONS

> Adults are always asking kids what they want to be when they grow up because they are looking for ideas.
>
> —PAULA POUNDSTONE

The miracle is not to walk on water. The miracle is to walk on the green earth, dwelling deeply in the present moment and feeling truly alive.

—THICH NHAT HANH

But I can't just travel, learn languages, or fight for one cause for the rest of my life! Of course you can't. That's not my suggestion at all. These are just good "life hubs"—starting points that lead to opportunities and experiences that otherwise wouldn't be found.

There is no right answer to the question "What should I do with my life?" Forget "should" altogether. The next step—and that's all it is—is pursuing something, it matters little what, that seems fun or rewarding. Don't be in a rush to jump into a full-time long-term commitment. Take time to find something that calls to you, not just the first acceptable form of surrogate work. That calling will, in turn, lead you to something else.

Here is a good sequence for getting started that dozens of **NR** have used with success.

1. **Revisit ground zero: Do nothing.**

   Before we can escape the goblins of the mind, we need to face them. Principal among them is speed addiction. It is hard to recalibrate your internal clock without taking a break from constant overstimulation. Travel and the impulse to see a million things can exacerbate this.

   Slowing down doesn't mean accomplishing less; it means cutting out counterproductive distractions and the *perception* of being rushed. Consider attending a short silence retreat of 3–7 days during which all media and speaking is prohibited.

   Learn to turn down the static of the mind so you can appreciate more before doing more:

   ►The Art of Living Foundation (Course II)—International—
   (www.artofliving.org)

► Spirit Rock Meditation Center in California
(http://www.spiritrock.org)

► Kripalu Center for Yoga and Health in Massachusetts
(http://www.kripalu.org)

► Sky Lake Lodge in New York (http://www.sky-lake.org)

2. **Make an anonymous donation to the service organization of your choice.**

This helps to get the juices flowing and disassociate feeling good about service with getting credit for it. It feels even better when it's pure. Here are some good sites to get started:

► Charity Navigator (www.charitynavigator.org)
This independent service ranks more than 5,000 charities using criteria you select. Create a personalized page of favorites and compare them side by side, all free of charge.

► Firstgiving (www.firstgiving.com)
Firstgiving.com allows you to create an online fund-raising page. Donations can be made through your personal URL. I have used Firstgiving in coordination with a nonprofit called Room to Read to build schools in both Nepal and Vietnam, with more countries pending: www.firstgiving.com/timferriss and www .firstgiving.com/timferriss2. If you specifically want to help animals, for example, you can click on a related link and access websites for hundreds of different animal charities, and then decide which one you want to donate to. The UK version of the website is http://www.justgiving.com.

► Network for Good (www.networkforgood.org)
Visitors to this website will find links to charities in need of donations as well as opportunities to do volunteer work. They can also set up an automated credit card donation online.

3. **Take a learning mini-retirement in combination with local volunteering.**

Take a mini-retirement—six months or more if possible—to focus on learning and serving. The longer duration will permit a language focus, which in turn enables more meaningful interaction and contribution through volunteering.

For the duration of this trip, note self-criticisms and negative self-talk in a journal. Whenever upset or anxious, ask "why" at least three times and put the answers down on paper. Describing these doubts in writing reduces their impact twofold. First, it's often the ambiguous nature of self-doubt that hurts most. Defining and exploring it in writing—just as with forcing colleagues to e-mail—demands clarity of thought, after which most concerns are found to be baseless. Second, recording these concerns seems to somehow remove them from your head.

But where to go and what to do? There is no one right answer to either. Use the following questions and resources to brainstorm:

> What makes you most angry about the state of the world?
> What are you most afraid of for the next generation, whether you have children or not?
> What makes you happiest in your life? How can you help others have the same?

There is no need to limit yourself to one location. Remember Robin, who traveled through South America for a year with her husband and seven-year-old son? The three of them spent one to two months doing volunteer work in each location, including building wheelchairs in Banos, Ecuador, rehabilitating exotic animals in the Bolivian rain forest, and shepherding leather-back sea turtles in Suriname.

How about doing archaeological excavation in Jordan or

tsunami relief on the islands of Thailand? These are just two of the dozens of foreign relocation and volunteering case studies in each issue of *Verge Magazine* (www.fourhourblog.com/verge). Reader-tested resources include:

> Hands on Disaster Response: www.hodr.org
> Project Hope: www.projecthope.org
> Relief International: www.ri.org
> International Relief Teams: www.irteams.org
> Airline Ambassadors International: www.airlineamb.org
> Ambassadors for Children:
>   www.ambassadorsforchildren.org
> Relief Riders International:
>   www.reliefridersinternational.com
> Habitat for Humanity Global Village Program:
>   www.habitat.org
> Planeta: Global Listings for Practical Ecotourism:
>   www.planeta.com

4. **Revisit and reset dreamlines.**
   Following the mini-retirement, revisit the dreamlines set in **Definition** and reset them as needed. The following questions will help:

> What are you good at?
> What could you be the best at?
> What makes you happy?
> What excites you?
> What makes you feel accomplished and good about
>   yourself?
> What are you most proud of having accomplished in your
>   life? Can you repeat this or further develop it?
> What do you enjoy sharing or experiencing with other
>   people?

5. **Based on the outcomes of steps 1–4, consider testing new part- or full-time vocations.**

Full-time work isn't bad if it's what you'd rather be doing. This is where we distinguish "work" from a "vocation."

If you have created a muse or cut your hours down to next to nothing, consider testing a part-time or full-time vocation: a true calling or dream occupation. This is what I did with this book. I can now tell people I'm a writer rather than giving them the two-hour drug dealer explanation. What did you dream of being when you were a kid? Perhaps it's time to sign up for Space Camp or intern as an assistant to a marine biologist.

Recapturing the excitement of childhood isn't impossible. In fact, it's required. There are no more chains—or excuses—to hold you back.

16

The Top 13 New Rich Mistakes

If you don't make mistakes, you're not working on hard enough problems. And that's a big mistake.
—FRANK WILCZEK, 2004 Nobel Prize winner in physics

Ho imparato che niente e impossibile, e anche che quasi niente e facile . . . (I've learned that nothing is impossible, and that almost nothing is easy . . .)
—ARTICOLO 31 (Italian rap group), "Un Urlo"

Mistakes are the name of the game in lifestyle design. It requires fighting impulse after impulse from the old world of retirement-based life deferral. Here are the slipups you will make. Don't get frustrated. It's all part of the process.

1. **Losing sight of dreams and falling into work for work's sake (W4W)** Please reread the introduction and next chapter of this book whenever you feel yourself falling into this trap. Everyone does it, but many get stuck and never get out.

2. **Micromanaging and e-mailing to fill time** Set the responsibilities, problem scenarios and rules, and limits of autonomous decision-making—then stop, for the sanity of everyone involved.

3. **Handling problems your outsourcers or co-workers can handle**

4. **Helping outsourcers or co-workers with the same problem more than once, or with noncrisis problems** Give them if-then

rules for solving all but the largest problems. Give them the free-dom to act without your input, set the limits in writing, and then emphasize in writing that you will not respond to help with problems that are covered by these rules. In my particular case, all outsourcers have at their discretion the ability to fix any prob-lem that will cost less than $400. At the end of each month or quarter, depending on the outsourcer, I review how their decisions have affected profit and adjust the rules accordingly, often adding new rules based on their good decisions and creative solutions.

5. Chasing customers, particularly unqualified or interna-tional prospects, when you have sufficient cash flow to finance your nonfinancial pursuits

6. Answering e-mail that will not result in a sale or that can be answered by a FAQ or auto-responder For a good example of an auto-responder that directs people to the appropriate infor-mation and outsourcers, e-mail info@fourhourworkweek.com.

7. Working where you live, sleep, or should relax Separate your environments—designate a single space for work and solely work—or you will never be able to escape it.[84]

8. Not performing a thorough 80/20 analysis every two to four weeks for your business and personal life

9. Striving for endless perfection rather than great or sim-ply good enough, whether in your personal or professional life Recognize that this is often just another W4W excuse. Most en-deavors are like learning to speak a foreign language: to be correct 95% of the time requires six months of concentrated ef-fort, whereas to be correct 98% of the time requires 20–30 years. Focus on great for a few things and good enough for the rest. Perfection is a good ideal and direction to have, but recognize it for what it is: an impossible destination.

---

84. To avoid the living room and coffee shop as offices, consider using a social "co-working" space on occasion: http://coworking.pbwiki.com.

10.   Blowing minutiae and small problems out of proportion as an excuse to work

11.   Making non-time-sensitive issues urgent in order to justify work How many times do I have to say it? Focus on life outside of your bank accounts, as scary as that void can be in the initial stages. If you cannot find meaning in your life, it is your responsibility as a human being to create it, whether that is fulfilling dreams or finding work that gives you purpose and self-worth—ideally a combination of both.

12.   Viewing one product, job, or project as the end-all and be-all of your existence Life is too short to waste, but it is also too long to be a pessimist or nihilist. Whatever you're doing now is just a stepping-stone to the next project or adventure. Any rut you get into is one you can get yourself out of. Doubts are no more than a signal for action of some type. When in doubt or overwhelmed, take a break and 80/20 both business and personal activities and relationships.

13.   Ignoring the social rewards of life Surround yourself with smiling, positive people who have absolutely nothing to do with work. Create your muses alone if you must, but do not live your life alone. Happiness shared in the form of friendships and love is happiness multiplied.

The Last Chapter

►AN E-MAIL YOU NEED TO READ

There is nothing the busy man is less busied with than living; there is nothing harder to learn.
—SENECA

For the past 33 years, I have looked in the mirror every morning and asked myself: "If today were the last day of my life, would I want to do what I am about to do today?" And whenever the answer has been "No" for too many days in a row, I know I need to change something . . . almost everything—all external expectations, all pride, all fear of embarrassment or failure—these things just fall away in the face of death, leaving only what is truly important. Remembering that you are going to die is the best way I know to avoid the trap of thinking you have something to lose.

—STEVE JOBS, college dropout and CEO of Apple Computer, Stanford University Commencement, 2005[85]

If you're confused about life, you're not alone. There are almost seven billion of us. This isn't a problem, of course, once you realize that life is neither a problem to be solved nor a game to be won.

If you are too intent on making the pieces of a nonexistent puzzle fit, you miss out on all the real fun. The heaviness of success-chasing can be replaced with a serendipitous lightness when you recognize that the only rules and limits are those we set for ourselves.

---

85. http://news-service.stanford.edu/news/2005/june15/jobs-061505.html.

So be bold and don't worry about what people think. They don't do it that often anyway.

Two years ago, I was forwarded the following poem—originally written by child psychologist David L. Weatherford—by a close friend. He quit his own deferred-life plan after reading it, and I hope you will do the same. Here it is.

SLOW DANCE

Have you ever watched kids
On a merry-go-round?

Or listened to the rain
Slapping on the ground?

Ever followed a butterfly's erratic flight?
Or gazed at the sun into the fading night?

You better slow down.
Don't dance so fast.

Time is short.
The music won't last.

Do you run through each day
On the fly?

When you ask: How are you?
Do you hear the reply?

When the day is done,
do you lie in your bed

With the next hundred chores
Running through your head?

You'd better slow down.
Don't dance so fast.

Time is short.
The music won't last.

Ever told your child,
We'll do it tomorrow?

And in your haste,
Not see his sorrow?

Ever lost touch,
Let a good friendship die

Cause you never had time
To call and say, "Hi"?

You'd better slow down.
Don't dance so fast.

Time is short.
The music won't last.

When you run so fast to get somewhere
You miss half the fun of getting there.

When you worry and hurry through your day,
It is like an unopened gift thrown away.

Life is not a race.
Do take it slower.

Hear the music
Before the song is over.

Last but Not Least

The Art of Letting Bad Things Happen

[AFTER 3 WEEKS OFF OF THE BLOG]

Long time no see! I just landed back in California from a long overdue mini-retirement through London, Scotland, Sardinia, the Slovak Republic, Austria, Amsterdam, and Japan. Some unpleasant surprises awaited me when I checked in on the evil e-mail inbox. Why? I let them happen.

I always do.

Here are just a few of the goodies that awaited me this time:

► One of our fulfillment companies had been shut down due to the CEO's death, causing a 20%+ loss in monthly orders and requiring an emergency shift of all web design and order processing
► Missed radio and magazine appearances and upset would-be interviewers
► More than a dozen lost joint-venture partnership opportunities

It's not that I go out of my way to irritate people—not at all— but I recognize one critical fact: Oftentimes, in order to do the big things, you have to let the small bad things happen. This is a skill we want to cultivate.

What did I get in exchange for temporarily putting on blinders and taking a few glancing blows?

- ►I followed the Rugby World Cup in Europe and watched the New Zealand All Blacks live, a dream I've had for the last five years.
- ►I shot every gun I've ever dreamed of firing since brainwashing myself with *Commando*. Bless the Slovak Republic and their paramilitaries.
- ►I filmed a television series pilot in Japan, a lifelong dream and the most fun I've had in months, if not years.
- ►I met with my Japanese publisher, Seishisha, and had media interviews in Tokyo, where the 4HWW is now #1 in several of the largest chains.
- ►I took a complete 10-day media fast and felt like I'd had a two-year vacation from computers.
- ►I attended the Tokyo International Film Festival and hung out with one of my heroes, the producer of the *Planet Earth* television series.

Once you realize that you can turn off the noise without the world ending, you're liberated in a way that few people ever know.

Just remember: If you don't have attention, you don't have time. Did I have time to check e-mail and voicemail? Sure. It might take 10 minutes. Did I have the attention to risk fishing for crises in those 10 minutes? Not at all.

As tempting as it is to "just check e-mail for one minute," I didn't do it. I know from experience that any problem found in the inbox will linger in the brain for hours or days after you shut down the computer, rendering "free time" useless with preoccupation. It's the worst of states, where you experience neither relaxation nor productivity. Be focused on work or focused on something else, never in-between.

Time without attention is worthless, so value attention over time.

Here are a few questions that can help you pop on the productivity blinders and put things in perspective. Even when you're not traveling the world, develop the habit of letting small bad things happen. If you don't, you'll never find time for the life-changing big things, whether important tasks or true peak experiences. If you do force the time but puncture it with distractions, you won't have the attention to appreciate it.

- ►What is the one goal, if completed, that could change everything?
- ►What is the most urgent thing right now that you feel you "must" or "should" do?
- ►Can you let the urgent "fail"—even for a day—to get to the next milestone for your potential life-changing tasks?
- ►What's been on your to-do list the longest? Start it first thing in the morning and don't allow interruptions or lunch until you finish.

Will "bad" things happen? Small problems will crop up, yes. A few people will complain and quickly get over it. BUT, the bigger picture items you complete will let you see these for what they are—minutiae and repairable hiccups.

Make this trade a habit. Let the small bad things happen and make the big good things happen. —*OCTOBER 25, 2007*

Things I've Loved and Learned in 2008

2008 was one of the most exciting years of my life. I did more dealmaking and met more people than in the last five years combined. This produced many surprise insights about business and human nature, especially as I uncovered dozens of my own false assumptions.

Here are some of the things I learned and loved in 2008.

Favorite reads of 2008: *Zorba the Greek* and *Seneca: Letters from a Stoic.* These are two of the most readable books of practical philosophies I've ever had the fortune to encounter. If you have to choose one, get *Zorba,* but *Lucius Seneca* will take you further. Both are fast reads of 2–3 evenings.

Don't accept large or costly favors from strangers. This karmic debt will come back to haunt you. If you can't pass it up, immediately return to karmic neutrality with a gift of your choosing. Repay it before they set the terms for you. Exceptions: über-successful mentors who are making introductions and not laboring on your behalf.

You don't have to recoup losses the same way you lose them. I own a home in San Jose but moved almost 12 months ago. It's been empty since, and I'm paying a large mortgage each month. The best part? I don't care. But this wasn't always the case. For many months, I felt demoralized as others pressured me to rent it, emphasizing how I was just flushing money away otherwise. Then I realized: You don't have to make money back the same way you lose it. If you lose $1,000 at the blackjack table, should you try and recoup it there? Of course not. I don't want to deal with renters, even with a property management company. The solution: Leave the house alone, use it on occasion, and just create incoming revenue elsewhere that would cover the cost of the mortgage through consulting, publishing, etc.

One of the most universal causes of self-doubt and depression: trying to impress people you don't like. Stressing to impress is fine, but do it for the right people—those you want to emulate.

Slow meals = life. From Daniel Gilbert of Harvard to Martin Seligman of Princeton, the "happiness" (self-reported well-being) researchers seem to agree on one thing: Mealtime with friends and loved ones is a direct predictor of well-being. Have at least one 2-to-3-hour dinner and/or drinks per week—yes, 2–3 hours—with those who make you smile and feel good. I find the afterglow effect to be greatest and longest with groups of five or more. Two times that are conducive to this: Thursday dinners or after-dinner drinks and Sunday brunches.

Adversity doesn't build character; it reveals it.

Related: Money doesn't change you; it reveals who you are when you no longer have to be nice.

It doesn't matter how many people don't get it. What matters is how many people do. If you have a strong informed opinion, don't keep it to yourself. Try to help people and make the world a better place. If you strive to do anything remotely interesting, just expect a small percentage of the population to always find a way to take it personally. F*ck 'em. There are no statues erected to critics.

Related: **You're never as bad as they say you are.** My agent used to send me every blog or media hit for *The 4-Hour Workweek*. Eight weeks after publication, I asked him to only forward me positive mentions in major media or factual inaccuracies I needed to respond to. An important correlate: You're never as good as they say you are, either. It's not helpful to get a big head or get depressed. The former makes you careless and the latter makes you lethargic. I wanted to have untainted optimism but remain hungry. Speaking of hungry . . .

Eat a high-protein breakfast within 30 minutes of waking and go for a 10-to-20-minute walk outside afterward, ideally bouncing a handball or tennis ball. This one habit is better than a handful of Prozac in the morning. (Suggested reading: The 3-Minute Slow-Carb Breakfast, How to "Peel" Hardboiled Eggs Without Peeling on www.fourhourblog.com.)

I dislike losing money about 50× more than I like making it. Why 50×? Logging time as an experiment, I concluded that I often spend at least 50× more time to prevent a hypothetical unit of $100 from being lost vs. earned. The hysterical part is that, even after becoming aware of this bias, it's hard to prevent the latter response. Therefore, I manipulate the environmental causes of poor responses instead of depending on error-prone self-discipline.

I should not invest in public stocks where I cannot influence outcomes. Once realizing that almost no one can predict risk tolerance and response to losses, I moved all of my investments into fixed-income and cashlike instruments in July 2008 for this reason, setting aside 10% of pretax income for angel investments where I can contribute significant UI/design, PR, and corporate partnership help. (Suggested reading: Rethinking Investing—Part 1, Rethinking Investing—Part 2 on www.fourhourblog.com.)

A good question to revisit whenever overwhelmed: Are you having a breakdown or a breakthrough?

Rehearse poverty regularly—restrict even moderate expenses for 1–2 weeks and give away 20%+ of minimally used clothing— so you can think big and take "risks" without fear (Seneca).

A mindset of scarcity (which breeds jealousy and unethical behavior) is due to a disdain for those things easily obtained (Seneca).

A small cup of black Kenyan AA coffee with cinnamon on top, no milk or sweeteners.

It's usually better to keep old resolutions than to make new ones.

To BRING IN a wonderful 2009, I'd like to quote an e-mail I received from a mentor of more than a decade:

> While many are wringing their hands, I recall the 1970s when we were suffering from an oil shock causing long lines at gas stations, rationing, and 55 MPH speed limits on

federal highways, a recession, very little venture capital ($50 million per year into VC firms), and what President Jimmy Carter (wearing a sweater while addressing the nation on TV because he had turned down the heat in the White House) called a "malaise." It was during those times that two kids without any real college education, Bill Gates and Steve Jobs, started companies that did pretty well. Opportunities abound in bad times as well as good times. In fact, the opportunities are often greater when the conventional wisdom is that everything is going into the toilet.

Well . . . we're nearing the end of another great year, and despite what we read about the outlook for 2009, we can look forward to a New Year filled with opportunities as well as stimulating challenges.

Happy New Year, everyone.

How to Travel the World with 10 Pounds or Less

Hauling a five-piece Samsonite set around the planet is hell on earth. I watched a friend do this up and down dozens of subway and hotel staircases in Europe for three weeks, and—while I laughed a lot, especially when he resorted to just dragging or throwing his bags down stairs—I'd like to save you the breakdown. Trip enjoyment is inversely proportionate to the amount of crap (read: distractions) you bring with you.

Practice in 30-plus countries has taught me that minimalist packing can be an art.

I returned from Costa Rica last Wednesday and have since landed in Maui, where I'll stay for one week. **What did I pack and why?** (See the companion video at www.fourhourblog.com.[86])

_____

86. This video explains how and why I pack the items in the list that follows. Links for all items are also included.

I practice what I'll label the **BIT method of travel: Buy It There.** If you pack for every possible contingency—better bring the hiking books in case we go hiking, better bring an umbrella in case it rains, better bring dress shoes and slacks in case we go to a nice restaurant, etc.—carrying a mule-worthy load is inevitable. I've learned to instead allocate $50–200 per trip to a "settling fund," which I use to buy needed items once they're 100% needed. This includes cumbersome and hassle items like umbrellas and bottles of sunscreen that love to explode. Also, never buy if you can borrow. If you're going on a bird-watching trip in Costa Rica, you don't need to bring binoculars—someone else will have them.

Here's the Maui list.

- ► 1 featherweight Marmot Ion jacket (3 oz.!)
- ► 1 breathable Coolibar long-sleeve shirt to prevent sunburn. This saved me in Panama.
- ► 1 pair of polyester pants. Polyester is light, wrinkle-resistant, and dries quickly. Disco dancers and flashpackers dig it.
- ► 1 Kensington laptop lock, also used to secure all bags to stationary objects
- ► 1 single Under Armour sock, used to store sunglasses
- ► 2 nylon tanktops
- ► 1 large MSR quick-dry microfiber towel, absorbs up to seven times its weight in water
- ► 1 Ziploc bag containing toothbrush, travel toothpaste, and disposable razor
- ► 1 Fly Clear biometric travel card (www.flyclear.com),[87] which cuts down my airport wait time about 95%
- ► 2 pairs of ExOfficio lightweight underwear. Their tagline is "17 countries. 6 weeks. And one pair of underwear." I think I'll opt for two, considering they weigh about as much as a

---

87. This company filed for Chapter 11 in June 2009.

handful of Kleenex. One other nice side effect of their weight: They're much more comfortable than normal cotton underwear.

- ► 2 pairs of shorts/swimsuits
- ► 2 books: *Lonely Planet Hawaii* and *The Entrepreneurial Imperative.* (The latter comes highly recommended. Check it out.)
- ► 1 sleeping mask and earplugs
- ► 1 pair of Reef sandals. Best to get a pair with removable straps that go around the heel.
- ► 1 Canon PowerShot SD300 digital camera with extra 2GB SD memory card. God, I love this camera more than words can describe. It is the best designed piece of electronics I have ever owned. I now use it not only for all of my photos and videos, but also as a replacement for my scanner. I'm considering testing the newer and cheaper SD1000.
- ► 1 coffee-harvesting hat to prevent my pale skin from burning off
- ► 1 Kiva keychain expandable duffel bag
- ► 1 Chapstick, 1 Mag-Lite Solitaire flashlight, and 1 roll of athletic tape. The last is a lifesaver. It's as useful as duct tape for repairing objects but gentle enough to use on injuries, which I am fond of inflicting on myself.
- ► 1 Lewis and Clark flex lock (for luggage, lockers, zippers, or whatever I need to lock down/shut together). Standard mini-padlocks are often too cumbersome to thread through holes on lockers, etc.
- ► 1 Radio Shack kitchen timer, which I've been using to wake up for about four years. The problem with using a cell phone alarm to wake up is simple: The phone often needs to be on, and even if you use vibrate, people can call and wake you up before you want to wake up. The second benefit to using a kitchen timer is that you know exactly how much sleep you

are—or aren't—getting, and you can experiment with things
like caffeine power naps of different durations . . . but that's
another post ;)　　　　　　　　　　　　　　—*JULY 11, 2007*

The Choice-Minimal Lifestyle: 6 Formulas for More Output and Less Overwhelm

I was stressed out . . . over dog cartoons.

　　It was 9:47 P.M. at Barnes and Noble on a recent Saturday
night, and I had 13 minutes to find a suitable exchange for *The
New Yorker Dog Cartoons*, $22 of expensive paper. Bestsellers?
Staff recommends? New arrivals or classics? I'd already been there
30 minutes.

　　Beginning to feel overwhelmed with a ridiculous errand I'd
expected to take five minutes, I stumbled across the psychology section. One tome jumped out at me as all too appropriate—*The Para-
dox of Choice: Why More Is Less*. It wasn't the first time I'd seen or
read Barry Schwartz's 2004 classic, but it seemed like a good time to
revisit the principles, among them, that:

- The more options you consider, the more buyer's regret
  you'll have.
- The more options you encounter, the less fulfilling your
  ultimate outcome will be.

This raises a difficult question: Is it better to have the best outcome but be less satisfied, or have an acceptable outcome and be
satisfied?

　　For example, would you rather deliberate for months and get the
1 of 20 houses that's the best investment but second-guess yourself
until you sell it five years later, or would you rather get a house that is
80% of the investment potential of the former (still to be sold at a
profit) but never second-guess it?

Tough call.

Schwartz also recommends making nonreturnable purchases. I decided to keep the stupid pooch cartoons. Why? Because it's not just about being satisfied, it's about being practical.

Income is renewable, but some other resources—like attention—are not. I've talked before about attention as a currency and how it determines the value of time.

For example: Is your weekend really free if you find a crisis in the inbox Saturday morning that you can't address until Monday morning?

Even if the inbox scan lasts 30 seconds, the preoccupation and forward projection for the subsequent 48 hours effectively deletes that experience from your life. You had time but you didn't have attention, so the time had no practical value.

The choice-minimal lifestyle becomes an attractive tool when we consider two truths.

1. **Considering options costs attention that then can't be spent on action or present-state awareness.**
2. **Attention is necessary for not only productivity but appreciation.**

Therefore:

Too many choices = less or no productivity
Too many choices = less or no appreciation
Too many choices = sense of overwhelm

What to do? There are six basic rules or formulas that can be used:

1. Set rules for yourself so you can automate as much decision making as possible [see the rules I use to outsource my e-mail to Canada, included at the end of this section, as an example of this].

2. Don't provoke deliberation before you can take action.

One simple example: Don't scan the inbox on Friday evening or over the weekend if you might encounter work problems that can't be addressed until Monday.

3. Don't postpone decisions just to avoid uncomfortable conversations.

If an acquaintance asks you if you want to come to their house for dinner next week, and you know you won't, don't say, "I'm not sure. I'll let you know next week." Instead, use something soft but conclusive like, "Next week? I'm pretty sure I have another commitment on Thursday, but thank you for the invite. Just so I don't leave you hanging, let's assume I can't make it, but can I let you know if that changes?" Decision made. Move on.

4. Learn to make nonfatal or reversible decisions as quickly as possible.

Set time limits (I won't consider options for more than 20 minutes), option limits (I'll consider no more than three options), or finance thresholds (Example: If it costs less than $100 [or the potential damage is less than $100], I'll let a virtual assistant make the judgment call).

I wrote most of this post after landing at the monster that is ATL airport in Atlanta. I could have considered half a dozen types of ground transportation in 15 minutes and saved 30–40%, but I grabbed a taxi instead. To use illustrative numbers: I didn't want to sacrifice 10 attention units of my remaining 50 of 100 total potential units, since those 10 units couldn't then be spent on this article. I had about eight hours before bedtime due to time zone differences—plenty of time—but scarce usable attention after an all-nighter of fun and the cross-country flight. **Fast decisions preserve usable attention for what matters.**

5. Don't strive for variation—and thus increase option consideration—when it's not needed. Routine enables innovation where it's most valuable.

In working with athletes, for example, it's clear that those who maintain the lowest bodyfat percentage eat the same foods over and over with little variation. I've eaten the same "slow-carb" breakfast and lunch for nearly two years,[88] putting variation only into meals that I focus on for enjoyment: dinner and all meals on Saturdays. This same routine-variation distinction can be found in exercise vs. recreation. For fat loss and muscle gain (even as much as 34 pounds in four weeks), I've followed the same time—minimal exercise protocol with occasional experiments since 1996. For recreation, however, where the focus is enjoyment and not efficacy, I tend to try something new each weekend, whether climbing at Mission Cliffs in San Francisco or mountain biking from tasting to tasting in Napa.

Don't confuse what should be results-driven with routine (e.g., exercise) with something enjoyment-driven that benefits from variation (e.g., recreation).

6. Regret is past-tense decision making. Eliminate complaining to minimize regret.

Condition yourself to notice complaints and stop making them with a simple program like the "21-day no-complaint experiment" made famous by Will Bowen, where you wear a single bracelet and move it from one wrist to the other each time you complain. The goal is 21 days without complaining and you reset to 0 each time you slip up. This increased awareness helps prevent useless past-tense deliberation and negative emotions that improve nothing but deplete your attention.

---

88. For the exact breakfast, just serach "slow-carb" on www.fourhourblog.com or both "slow-carb" and "Ferriss" on Google.

. . .

DECISION-MAKING ISN'T to be avoided—that's not the problem. Look at a good CEO or top corporate performer and you'll see a high volume of decisions.

It's deliberation—the time we vacillate over and consider each decision—that's the attention consumer. Total deliberation time, not the number of decisions, determines your attention bank account balance (or debt).

Let's assume you pay 10% over time by following the above rules but cut your average "decision cycle" time by an average of 40% (10 minutes reduced to 6 minutes, for example). Not only will you have much more time and attention to spend on revenue-generating activities, but you'll get greater enjoyment from what you have and experience. Consider that 10% additional cost as an investment and part of your "ideal lifestyle tax," but not as a loss.

Embrace the choice-minimal lifestyle. It's a subtle and underexploited philosophical tool that produces dramatic increases in both output and satisfaction, all with less overwhelm.

Make testing a few of the principles the first of many fast and reversible decisions.   —*FEBRUARY 6, 2008*

The Not-to-Do List:
9 Habits to Stop Now

"Not-to-do" lists are often more effective than to-do lists for upgrading performance.

The reason is simple: What you don't do determines what you can do.

Here are nine stressful and common habits that entrepreneurs and office workers should strive to eliminate. The bullets are followed by more detailed descriptions. Focus on one or two at a time, just as you would with high-priority to-do items.

1. Do not answer calls from unrecognized phone numbers.

Feel free to surprise others, but don't be surprised. It just results in unwanted interruption or poor negotiating positions. Let it go to voicemail, and consider using a service like GrandCentral (you can listen to people leaving voicemail or receive them as text messages) or Phonetag.com (receive voicemails as e-mail).

2. Do not e-mail first thing in the morning or last thing at night.

The former scrambles your priorities and plans for the day, and the latter just gives you insomnia. E-mail can wait until 10 A.M., after you've completed at least one of your critical to-do items.

3. Do not agree to meetings or calls with no clear agenda or end time.

If the desired outcome is defined clearly with a stated objective and agenda listing topics/questions to cover, no meeting or call should last more than 30 minutes. Request them in advance so you "can best prepare and make good use of the time together."

4. Do not let people ramble.

Forget "How's it going?" when someone calls you. Stick with "What's up?" or "I'm in the middle of getting something out, but what's going on?" A big part of GTD (Getting Things Done) is GTP—Getting To the Point.

5. Do not check e-mail constantly—"batch" and check at set times only.

I belabor this point enough. Get off the cocaine pellet dispenser and focus on execution of your top to-do's instead of responding to manufactured emergencies. Set up a strategic autoresponder and check twice or thrice daily.

6. Do not over-communicate with low-profit, high-maintenance customers.

There is no sure path to success, but the surest path to failure is trying to please everyone. Do an 80/20 analysis of your customer base in two ways—which 20% are producing 80%+ of my profit, and which 20% are consuming 80%+ of my time? Then put the loudest and least productive on autopilot by citing a change in company policies. Send them an e-mail with new rules as bullet points: number of permissible phone calls, e-mail response time, minimum orders, etc. Offer to point them to another provider if they aren't able to adopt the new policies.

7. Do not work more to fix overwhelmingness—prioritize.

If you don't prioritize, everything seems urgent and important. If you define the single most important task for each day, almost nothing seems urgent or important. Oftentimes, it's just a matter of letting little bad things happen (return a phone call late and apologize, pay a small late fee, lose an unreasonable customer, etc.) to get the big important things done. The answer to over-whelmingness is not spinning more plates—or doing more—it's defining the few things that can really fundamentally change your business and life.

8. Do not carry a cell phone or Crackberry 24/7.

Take at least one day off of digital leashes per week. Turn them off or, better still, leave them in the garage or in the car. I do this on at least Saturday, and I recommend you leave the phone at home if you go out for dinner. So what if you return a phone call an hour later or the next morning? As one reader put it to a miffed co-worker who worked 24/7 and expected the same: *"I'm not the president of the U.S. No one should need me at 8 P.M. at night. OK, you didn't get a hold of me. But what bad happened?"* The answer? Nothing.

9. Do not expect work to fill a void that non-work relationships and activities should.

Work is not all of life. Your co-workers shouldn't be your only friends. Schedule life and defend it just as you would an important business meeting. Never tell yourself "I'll just get it done this weekend." Review Parkinson's Law (pages 75–78) and force yourself to cram within tight hours so your per-hour productivity doesn't fall through the floor. Focus, get the critical few done, and get out. E-mailing all weekend is no way to spend the little time you have on this planet.

It's hip to focus on getting things done, but it's only possible once we remove the constant static and distraction. If you have trouble deciding what to do, just focus on not doing. Different means, same end.   —AUGUST 16, 2007

The Margin Manifesto: 11 Tenets for Reaching (or Doubling) Profitability in 3 Months

Profitability often requires better rules and speed, not more time. The financial goal of a start-up should be simple: profit in the least time with the least effort. Not more customers, not more revenue, not more offices or more employees. More profit.

Based on my interviews with high-performing (using profit-per-employee metrics) CEOs in more than a dozen countries, here are the 11 basic tenets of the "Margin Manifesto" . . . a return-to-basics call that gives permission to do the uncommon to achieve the uncommon: consistent profitability, or doubling of it, in three months or less.

I review the following principles whenever facing operational overwhelmingness or declining/stagnating profits. Hope you find them useful.

1. Niche Is the New Big—The Lavish Dwarf Entertainment Rule
Several years ago, an investment banker was jailed for trade violations. He was caught partly due to his lavish parties on yachts,

often featuring hired dwarves. The owner of the dwarf rental company, Danny Black, was quoted in the *Wall Street Journal* as saying "Some people are just into lavish dwarf entertainment." Niche is the new big. But here's the secret: It's possible to niche market and mass sell. iPod commercials don't feature dancing 50-year-olds, they feature hip and fit 20- and 30-somethings, but everyone and his grandmother wants to feel youthful and hip, so they strap on Nanos and call themselves Apple converts. Who you portray in your marketing isn't necessarily the only demographic who buys your product—it's often the demographic that most people want to identify with or belong to. The target isn't the market. No one aspires to be the bland average, so don't water down messaging to appeal to everyone—it will end up appealing to no one.

2. Revisit Drucker—What Gets Measured Gets Managed

Measure compulsively, for as Peter Drucker stated, What gets measured gets managed. Useful metrics to track, besides the usual operational stats, include CPO ("Cost-Per-Order," which includes advertising, fulfillment and expected returns, chargebacks, and bad debt), ad allowable (the maximum you can spend on an advertisement and expect to break even), MER (media efficiency ratio), and projected lifetime value (LV) given return rates and reorder percent. Consider applying direct response advertising metrics to your business.

3. Pricing Before Product—Plan Distribution First

Is your pricing scalable? Many companies will sell direct-to-consumer by necessity in early stages, only to realize that their margins can't accommodate resellers and distributors when they come knocking. If you have a 40% profit margin and a distributor needs a 70% discount to sell into wholesale accounts, you're forever limited to direct-to-consumer . . . unless you increase your pricing and margins. It's best to do this beforehand if possible—otherwise, you'll need to launch new or "premium" products—so plan distribution before setting pricing. Test assumptions and find hidden costs by interviewing those who have done it: Will you need to pay for co-op advertising, offer rebates for bulk purchases, or pay for shelf space or featured placement? I know one former CEO of a national brand who had to sell his company to one of the world's largest soft drink manufacturers before he could access front-of-store shelving in top retailers. Test your assumptions and do your homework before setting pricing.

4. Less Is More—Limiting Distribution to Increase Profit

Is more distribution automatically better? No. Uncontrolled distribution leads to all manner of headache and profit-bleeding, most often related to rogue discounters. Reseller A lowers pricing to compete with online discounter B, and the price cutting continues until neither is making sufficient profit on the product and both stop reordering. This requires you to launch a new product, as price erosion is almost always irreversible. Avoid this scenario and consider partnering with one or two key distributors instead, using that exclusivity to negotiate better terms: less discounting, prepayment, preferred placement and marketing support, etc. From iPods to Rolex and Estée Lauder, sustainable high-profit brands usually begin with controlled distribution. Remember, more customers isn't the goal; more profit is.

5. Net-Zero—Create Demand vs. Offering Terms

Focus on creating end-user demand so you can dictate terms. Often one trade publication advertisment, bought at discount remnant rates, will be enough to provide this leverage. Outside of science and law, most "rules" are just common practice. Just because everyone in your industry offers terms doesn't mean you have to, and offering terms is the most consistent ingredient in start-up failure. Cite start-up economics and the ever-so-useful "company policy" as reasons for prepayment and apologize, but don't make exceptions. Net-30 becomes net-60, which becomes net-120. Time is the most expensive asset a start-up has, and chasing delinquent accounts will prevent you from generating more sales. If customers are asking for your product, resellers and distributors will need to buy it. It's that simple. Put funds and time into strategic marketing and PR to tip the scales in your favor.

6. Repetition Is Usually Redundant—Good Advertising Works the First Time

Use direct response advertising (call-to-action to a phone number or website) that is uniquely trackable—fully accountable advertising—instead of image advertising, unless others are prepurchasing to offset the cost (e.g., "If you prepurchase 288 units, we'll feature your store/URL/phone exclusively in a full-page ad in . . ."). Don't listen to advertising salespeople who tell you that 3, 7, or 27 exposures are needed before someone will act on an advertisement. Well-designed and well-targeted advertising works the first time. If something works partially well (e.g., high response with low percentage conversion to sales, low response with high conversion, etc.), indicating that a strong ROI might be possible with small changes, tweak one controlled variable and microtest once more. Cancel anything that cannot be justified with a trackable ROI.

7. Limit Downside to Ensure Upside—Sacrifice Margin for Safety

Don't manufacture product in large quantities to increase margin unless your product and marketing are tested and ready for rollout without changes. If a limited number of prototypes cost $10 per piece to manufacture and sell for $11 each, that's fine for the initial testing period, and essential for limiting downside. Sacrifice margin temporarily for the testing phase, if need be, and avoid potentially fatal upfront overcommitments.

8. Negotiate Late—Make Others Negotiate Against Themselves

Never make a first offer when purchasing. Flinch after the first offer ("$3,000!" followed by pure silence, which uncomfortable salespeople fill by dropping the price once), let people negotiate against themselves ("Is that really the best you can offer?" elicits at least one additional drop in price), then "bracket." If they end up at $2,000 and you want to pay $1,500, offer $1,250. They'll counter with approximately $1,750, to which you respond: "I'll tell you what—let's just split the difference. I'll overnight FedEx you a check, and we can call it a day." The end result? Exactly what you wanted: $1,500.

9. Hyperactivity vs. Productivity—80/20 and Pareto's Law

Being busy is not the same as being productive. Forget about the start-up overwork ethic that people wear as a badge of honor—get analytical. The 80/20 principle, also known as Pareto's Law, dictates that 80% of your desired outcomes are the result of 20% of your activities or inputs. Once per week, stop putting out fires for an afternoon and run the numbers to ensure you're placing effort in high-yield areas: What 20% of customers/products/regions are producing 80% of the profit? What are the factors that could account for this? Invest in duplicating your few strong areas instead of fixing all of your weaknesses.

10. The Customer Is Not Always Right—"Fire" High-Maintenance Customers

Not all customers are created equal. Apply the 80/20 principle to time consumption: What 20% of people are consuming 80%

of your time? Put high-maintenance, low-profit customers on autopilot—process orders but don't pursue them or check up on them—and "fire" high-maintenance, high-profit customers by sending a memo detailing how a change in business model requires a few new policies: how often and how to communicate, standardized pricing and order process, etc. Indicate that, for those clients whose needs are incompatible with these new policies, you are happy to introduce other providers. "But what if my largest customer consumes all of my time?" Recognize that (1) without time, you cannot scale your company (and, oftentimes, life) beyond that customer, and (2) people, even good people, will unknowingly abuse your time to the extent that you let them. Set good rules for all involved to minimize back-and-forth and meaningless communication.

11. Deadlines Over Details—Test Reliability Before Capability
Skills are overrated. Perfect products delivered past deadline kill companies faster than decent products delivered on time. Test someone's ability to deliver on a specific and tight deadline before hiring them based on a dazzling portfolio. Products can be fixed as long as you have cash flow, and bugs are forgiven, but missing deadlines is often fatal. Calvin Coolidge once said that nothing is more common than unsuccessful men with talent; I would add that the second most common is smart people who think their IQ or resume justifies delivering late.   *—JUNE 24, 2008*

The Holy Grail: How to Outsource the Inbox and Never Check E-mail Again

What if you never had to check e-mail again?
　　If you could hire someone else to spend countless hours in your inbox instead of you?

This isn't pure fantasy. For the last 12 months, I've experimented with removing myself from the inbox entirely by training other people to behave like me. Not to imitate me, but to think like me.

Here's the upshot: I get more than 1,000 e-mails a day from various accounts.[89] Rather than spending 6–8 hours per day checking e-mail, which I used to do, I can skip reading e-mail altogether for days or even weeks at a time . . . all within 4–10 minutes a night.

Let me explain the basics, followed by tips and exact templates for outsourcing your own inbox.

1. I have multiple e-mail addresses for specific types of e-mail (blog readers vs. media vs. friends/family, etc.). tim@ . . . is the default I give to new acquaintances, which goes to my assistant.
2. 99% of e-mail falls into predetermined categories of inquiries with set questions or responses (my "rules" document is at the bottom of this post—feel free to steal, adapt, and use). My assistant(s) checks and clears the inbox at 11 A.M. and 3 P.M. PST.
3. For the 1% of e-mail that might require my input for next actions, I have a once-daily phone call of 4–10 minutes at 4 P.M. PST with my assistant.
4. If I'm busy or traveling abroad, my assistant leaves the action items in numerical order on my voicemail, which I can respond to in a bullet-point e-mail. These days, I actually prefer the voicemail option and find that it forces my assistant to be more prepared and more concise.

Each night (or early the next morning), I'll listen to my assistant's voicemail via Skype and simultaneously write out the next actions (1. Bob: Tell him that . . . 2. Jose in Peru: Ask him for . . . 3. Speaking in NC: Confirm . . . , etc.) in a Skype chat or quick e-mail. How long does the new system take? 4–10 minutes instead of 6–8 hours of filtering and repetitive responses.

---

89. This has thankfully decreased to 2,000–3,000 per week as of this writing.

If you only have one e-mail account, I recommend using a desktop program like Outlook or Mail instead of a web-based program like Gmail for a simple reason: If you see new items in your inbox, you'll check them. Like they say in AA: If you don't want to slip, don't go where it's slippery. This is why I have a private personal account that I use for sending e-mail to my assistant and communicating with friends. It's almost always empty.

E-mail is the last thing people let go of. Fortune 500 CEOs, best-selling authors, celebrities—I know dozens of top performers who delegate everything but e-mail, which they latch onto as something only they can do. "No one can check my e-mail for me" is the unquestioned assumption, or "I answer every e-mail I receive" is the unquestioned bragging right that keeps them in front of a computer for 8–12 hours at a stretch. It's not fun, and it keeps them from higher-impact or more rewarding activities.

Get over yourself. I had to. Checking e-mail isn't some amazing skill that you alone possess.

In fact, checking e-mail is like everything else: a process. How you evaluate and handle (delete vs. archive vs. forward vs. respond) e-mail is just a series of questions you ask yourself, whether consciously or subconsciously. I have a document called "Tim Ferriss Processing Rules," to which my assistants add rules when I send them a note via e-mail with "ADD TO RULES" in the subject. Over the course of a week or two with a virtual assistant (VA), you will end up with an externalized set of rules that reflect how your brain processes e-mail. It often shows you how haphazard your processing is. I've included my "rules" here to save you some time.

A few tips:

1.   Setting appointments and meetings takes a lot of time. Have your assistant set things up for you in Google Calendar. I input my own items via my Palm Z22 or iCal, then use Spanning Sync

and Missing Sync for Palm OS to sync everything. On my überlight Sony VAIO, which I still use for travel, I use CompanionLink for Google Calendar. I suggest batching meetings or calls in one or two set days, with 15 minutes between appointments. Scattering them throughout the week at odd times just interrupts everything else. (Update 2009: The Palm Z22 has been discarded, and I now use a 13-inch MacBook and BusySync to synchronize iCal with Google Calendar.)

2. If you jump in your assistant's inbox and answer anything, BCC them so they are aware that you handled it.

3. Expect small problems. Life is full of compromises, and it's necessary to let small bad things happen if you want to get huge good things done. There is no escape. Prevent all problems and get nothing done, or accept an allowable level of small problems and focus on the big things.

Ready to jump in and test the holy grail? Here are the steps.

1. Determine exactly which accounts you will use and how you want them to respond to (or just categorize or purge) e-mail for you.

2. Find a virtual assistant.

3. Test for reliability before skill set. Have the top three candidates do something on tight deadline (24 hours) before hiring them and letting them in your inbox.

4. Use a probationary period of 2–4 weeks to test the waters and work out the problems. Again: There will be problems. It will take a good 3–8 weeks to get to real smooth sailing.

5. Design your ideal lifestyle and find something to do other than let your brain fester in the inbox. Fill the void.

· · ·

TIM FERRISS PROCESSING RULES[90]

[Note the Q&A format—some of the questions are my standard points for VAs, some have been added by my assistant, who put together this document.]

Passwords

Calendar	www.SpamArrest.com
http://calendar.google.com	Username: XXXX
Login: XXXX	Password: XXXX
PW: XXXX	
Google G-mail Account	www.Amazon.com
http://mail.google.com	Username: XXXX
Username: XXXX	Password: XXXX
PW: XXXX	
www.NoCostConference.com	www.PayPal.com
Username: XXXX	Username: XXXX
Password: XXXX	Password: XXXX

Reader-Only Resources
http://fourhourworkweek.com/wms/members/members.php >>
PASSWORD FOR READERS ONLY IS: **XXXX**

Team Requirements

[I often have exec-level assistants manage 4–5 other "sub VAs" who handle certain repetitive tasks, often at half the exec VA's hourly rate. The exec VA takes on an office manager or, in some cases, COO-level function.]

---

90. This post is, of course, available on the blog for those who would like to copy and paste the rules for their own use.

- ►Download: www.alexa.com—Toolbar
- ►Learn Statistics, Rank for Business Prospect and Joint-Venture Opportunities
- ►Deadlines are extremely important. Be Aware of them, and Be Punctual!
- ►If Tim says "Call me back," CALL HIM BACK, do not send an e-mail. This is an important point, as Tim does not always have e-mail access because he is traveling a lot.
- ►Even if it is late in the evening, he is up late, if he does not want to answer his phone, he will not. But PLEASE call him back when he asks you to. He much prefers a phone call to an e-mail.
- ►Purchase and read *The Elements of Style* regarding proper grammar and punctuation. We are dealing with high-profile clients on Tim's behalf and the proper writing techniques and message says a lot about his team.
- ►Become as familiar as you can with his book and his website as to answer questions accordingly.

Contact Information

Tim Ferriss
[mailing address]

Tim Cell (your use only): [private cell]
Number to give others: [GrandCentral number]
Skype: XXXXX
Billing Address (Private):
[billing address]

Purchases

ASK [head VA], for his AMEX NUMBER. SHE WILL ADVISE WHETHER PURCHASES CAN BE APPROVED.

Question and Answer (Preferences)

1.   How do you feel about joint ventures?
     I'm open to them, but my brand and respectability is #1. I will
     not do anything with anyone who comes off as deceptive or
     amateur. "Make millions while you sleep in our super-insane
     foreclosure program!" on the website disqualifies someone. I
     cannot be associated with anyone who might be seen as a liar
     or snake-oil salesman. Just ask yourself: If the CEO of a well-
     known company saw this, would he lose interest in speaking
     with me? If so, it won't work.

        For those who pass that criteria, what have they done al-
     ready? I'm not looking for first-timers, generally, unless they
     have an excellent track record and reputation elsewhere.

2.   Do you focus solely on profit-generating tasks?
     No. I also look for prestige (Harvard, government, etc.), wide
     exposure, as well as building networks with people who have
     world-class skills in some area.

3.   How do you handle spam?
     SpamArrest and Gmail. I have no problem with spam at this
     point.

4.   What is your optimal response rate (i.e., respond to all e-mails no
     later than 48–72 hours after received)?
     Same day. I'm bringing you on to respond quickly.

5.   Do you respond to any e-mails?
     Yes, but I'll want you to filter them first, respond to all you can,
     then mark the ones I should look at with the label "TIM" in
     Gmail. [Note earlier in this article how I am now asking VAs to
     leave to-do's via voicemail.]

6.   Do you put in any events in your calendar?
     Yes, but I expect I will move more and more to having you do it.

7. Do we "manage" your items, or do you delegate? We are cool with both, but prefer to manage. :-)

    I'll try to give the list to you to take care of. I NEED confirmations that you received the task ("on it—will be done at X P.M." is enough) and like status updates on larger projects with milestones.

8. Who is on your team?

    Me, the publishing team, and some PR folk at this point. I might have you get involved with my other businesses later, but that's it for now.

9. Who do we have to collaborate with on a regular basis?

    See above. 90% me, then possibly my publicist(s), tech support and web staff, and my book agent. More will come, I'm sure, but that's it for now.

10. Who calls the shots for you?

    You can decide anything under $100. Use your judgment and report the decisions.

11. Do you have "days" off (as in no business appts.)?

    Let's shoot for no appointments on Fridays, but let's play it by ear. [Update: I now only have appointments on Mondays and Fridays.]

12. Who has been handling your appts. up until now?

    Me. I haven't had any in-person meetings for close to four years. Things have changed with the book :)

13. Explain to us your "optimal" work week (i.e., how long between phone calls, how many meetings per week, travel preferences, etc.)?

    ►I go to bed late, so try and avoid calls before 10 A.M. PST when possible.

    ►Try and "cluster" phone calls and meetings so that I can bang them out at the same time, as opposed to having one at 10 A.M., another at 1 P.M., and another at 4 P.M. Have them all in a row with 15–20 minutes in between whenever possible. I'd like to do phone calls before 1 P.M. PST when possible (so 10 A.M.–1 P.M.). Calls should be kept to 15–30 minutes, always with a defined end time. If someone asks to "jump on the phone" with me, send them something like: "To make the best use of everyone's time, Tim likes to have a well-defined agenda with objectives for a call before jumping on the phone. Can you please send over some bullet points with what you'd like to cover and decide on the call?" Something like that.

14. Do you like us to schedule personal items in with your business calendar (i.e., order your mother flowers for Mother's Day, etc.)?
Absolutely.

15. What are "all" the e-mail addresses we respond to for you?
See earlier text.

16. Do you like us to respond as "you" or something like "client support for Timothy Ferriss."
The latter, probably something like "Executive Assistant to Tim Ferriss" below your name—I'm open to suggestions.

17. How many times a day do you want e-mail checked?
Twice should be fine to start. Let's aim for a minimum of at 11 A.M. and 3 P.M. in your time zone.

18. What are your working hours?
10 A.M.–6 P.M. PST, then often 11 P.M.–2 A.M. PST. [Before you cry, "What happened to the four-hour workweek?!" realize that "work hours" here could be replaced with "active and available-by-phone hours." I have lots of projects and do not preach idleness. I am VERY active. See the sixth comment on this post on www.fourhourblog.com for more elaboration or reread the "Filling the Void" chapter in this book.]

19. Do you like using IM?

Not really, unless it's a scheduled discussion. Just leave yourself logged in, and I'll log in if I need something. [I tend to use Skype chat these days, as it's encrypted and I can avoid a separate IM program.]

20. Do you prefer a phone call or an e-mail to answer a quick question?
PHONE CALL, absolutely. DO NOT e-mail me for anything urgent. I really follow my own advice and don't check e-mail that often.

21. What is your favorite color?
Green like cedar leaves in July.

22. Call at the end of every day (if) there is something that Tim needs to respond to in his e-mail.

23. E-books: Tell them they can download the e-book from www.powells.com.

24. Label all e-mails from "Expert Click" for Tim. No need to respond or forward.

25. All Linked-In e-mails can be archived or deleted as Tim receives notification of invites as soon as he logs into his Linked-In account.

26. For start-up inquiries in the health and wellness industry (or BrainQUICKEN start-up inquiries) please see the templates in Gmail titled: Congratulations and General Business Questions—BrainQUICKEN Templates.

27. For language inquiries, please see the templates in Gmail titled: Reader Question on Language Resources—Language Templates.

28. When Tim types "dictate" in the e-mail response, this means that we can say to the recipient: As Tim is traveling at the moment and not able to personally respond to your e-mail, I

mentioned your message while on the phone to him, and he asked me to dictate. This makes the process easier as we do not have to change the context of the person responding.

[This is to avoid having an assistant convert my first-person "Please tell him that I . . ." to third-person "Tim says that he . . ."—providing shorthand for "cut and paste" saves hours of assistant time.]

29. If someone e-mail blasts a bunch of people and I am one of them, usually safe to ignore or delete. Read them carefully, of course, but if it says for example "a few influential people I know" or something like that then if someone can't take the time to personalize for me, forget them. If Tim is copied, of course, that's a different story.

30. Tim's address is XXXX. THIS E-MAIL IS NOT TO BE DIS-TRIBUTED OR GIVEN TO ANYONE. If you want to copy Tim on an e-mail, please use the BCC field, so that it remains private.

31. Mark anyone from Princeton for me to look at (TIM label). [Note: I've since had to modify this due to volume.]

32. If I decline someone and they persist, give them one more reply—"Tim appreciates the persistence, but he really can't . . ." etc.—and then archive future requests. Use your judgment, of course, but that's the general rule. Some people don't know when persistent turns into plain irritating.

33. Please also create a rule to respond with "scheduled" for all items I send to be put in the calendar (when they're put in the calendar). Missing calendar items can cause big problems, so this is a check and balance to confirm.

34. No need to follow up with someone after a call has taken place unless Tim instructs otherwise, or they request something from us.

35. Send all speaking requests to XXXX and ensure that he confirms receipt. (However, also see items 38 and 39).

36. Foreign language requests (i.e., purchasing rights, if the book is available in a particular language, etc.) send to [the appropriate person at my publisher].

37. XXXX's replacement at Random House is XXXX.

38. Inquire with Tim first before booking any speaking gigs on a specific date, as he may be traveling.

39. When booking appointments in the calendar, be sure to also ask which topics they would like to discuss, and put them in the calendar description for Tim so he can prepare. Also be sure to ask for a backup phone number in case they are not able to reach Tim. [I almost always have people call me unless I am abroad, as this is another safeguard against missing appointments.]

40. Put initials in the subject line of calendar events so we know who (which virtual assistant) put the item in the calendar.

41. Prepare inquiries for Tim before sending to him for his review, i.e., get their Alexa ranking, possible dates of the event, a link to past events they have held, their budget, other confirmed speakers, etc. Then send this info to Tim for his review.

42. Respond to PX Method inquiries with the following response:

> Hi [name],
> Thanks for your inquiry about the PX Method, however the PX Method page is designed as just a template others can look at as a reference for testing their own product ideas.
> We are not sure if or when Tim will offer the PX Method for sale, but there are no plans at this time. We appreciate your inquiry nonetheless. Thanks!

[I get quite a few e-mails from readers who do not see the disclaimer on the PX Method mock-up page and thus attempt to order a product that isn't ready to ship.]

43. Download eFAX viewer to view Tim's faxes. His fax number is: XXXX.

44. Event or speaking inquiries can be responded to as such:

> Thanks for your e-mail and for your invitation to Tim. In looking at the event online, I see that the event is April X and X, 20XX in Portland, Oregon [for example]. Before I present this to Tim, could you answer a few questions for me, so we can make a more informed decision?
>
> > ►Would you like Tim to be at the entire event?
> > ►How long would the keynote presentation be? Or would it be a Q&A panel?
> > ►Do you cover travel and accommodation along with a speaker's fee?
> > ►What is your budget for keynote presentations?
> > ►Have any other speakers confirmed to present?
>
> As soon as I hear back, I can speak with Tim about the possibilities of making this happen. Thanks again!
> Warmly,
> [Name]

this e-mail is: [ ] blogable [x] ask first [ ] private

[name]
Executive Assistant to Timothy Ferriss
Author: *The 4-Hour Workweek*
(http://www.fourhourworkweek.com)
(Random House/Crown Publishing)
Bio and Fun: http://www.fourhourworkweek.com/blog

—JANUARY 21, 2008

Proposal to Work Remotely on a Contract Basis

This is the actual remote-work proposal reader Autumn Brookmire used successfully to move to Argentina while retaining her job and cutting back to 5–10 hours per week of work.

AUTUMN BROOKMIRE   July 2008

Background

After working for the [company name] for more than two years, I have a great loyalty to the people and mission of this organization. I believe I have added a great deal of value to the organization in my position as marketing coordinator. With my creative problem solving and my cost effective solutions I have changed the way we produce and distribute our holiday cards and I've developed a contest to bring in more usable photos for our marketing and publications. I would like to propose continuing to perform the following tasks for [company name], but on a contract basis, remotely. I plan to live in Argentina for 6–12 months starting in September of 2008. My goals are to develop my fluency in the Spanish language and immerse myself in another culture and completely foreign environment so that I develop my skills in adaptation to new ways of thinking.

I am more than happy to discuss different ways to make this possible and I have some suggestions if [company name] would be willing to consider them. We can test this arrangement for a few months to see if it works for both of us, since that would make the most sense.

Role #1: Graphic Design and Print Advertising Coordinator

Responsibility:
Create timelines for print materials and coordinate with respective program teams.

Expectations:
- Print materials will be completed on time.

Responsibility:
Coordinate design projects with program directors and outside graphic artists/designers.

Expectations:
- Print materials designs are suitable for the audience, accurate, and appealing.
- Print materials are professional quality and produced within set timelines.

Responsibility:
Maintain relationships with print vendors to minimize cost relative to time and quality in producing program print materials.

Expectations:
- Print materials are printed within the established budget, unless budget overages are specifically approved by the Director of Marketing.

Contract Solution:
By using e-mail and web-based programs such as *ConceptShare, I can continue to coordinate these design projects from a distance. I currently maintain relationships with print vendors and designers at a distance so physical presence is not necessary for this to continue. For meetings with program directors and the marketing team, I would use a free video and phone conferencing service called *Skype. We usually meet once or twice to discuss changes to their marketing materials and the rest of the process is continued through e-mail and ConceptShare.

Role #2: Special Marketing Project Manager

Responsibility:
Maintain a collection of updated, appropriate marketing images.

Expectations:
- Images needed for marketing materials and websites are anticipated and acquired.

Contract Solution:
I am still able to complete this task remotely by doing images searches on web databases such as *iStockphoto.com. If the experiment with the *Seminar Photo Contest fares well, I could also manage that process via the web using Aptify, e-mail, and Skype.

Responsibility:
Identify and implement new opportunities to leverage marketing materials.

Expectations:
- Ideas are researched for feasibility and effectiveness.
- Chosen projects are designed and sent out within the budget and timeline.

Contract Solution:
I would utilize e-mail and Skype to communicate any new ideas and opportunities to leverage marketing materials. I have recently proposed creating a one-page calendar of our program deadlines to distribute to our recent seminar alumni in a fall mailing. This way students will have an easy way to remember all of our deadlines for our programs and may potentially boost our number of applicants.

Role #3: Web-based Marketing Coordinator

Responsibility:
Contribute to online advertising efforts and track results.

Expectations:
- Online efforts are increasingly cost effective.
- Marketing Director is informed of web-based marketing results as requested.

Contract Solution:
I am familiar with our online advertising efforts and can continue to help with this process from a distance. I will be able to access Facebook Ads, Google Ads, Blog Ads and aid Keri in gathering and entering data. I have experience working with our Facebook and Google Ads and have created images for Blog Ads in the past. Launching new Ads will be easily managed abroad.

Responsibility:
Compile collection of updated, appropriate web photos.

Expectations:
• Attractive, updated photos will be available for program and marketing uses.

Contract Solution:
As stated above with the stock photo inventory, I am still able to complete this task remotely by conducting image searches on web databases such as iStockphoto.com. The Seminar Photo Contest will also be used as a tool to aid in this compilation of images while I am abroad.

In order to more effectively track the cost of production of our print materials, I think [company name] would find value in transitioning to a contract basis for this position. I have really enjoyed working at [company name] thus far and would like to continue working for this organization from a remote location. Thank you for your consideration of this proposal.

Explanation of Software and Programs Mentioned:

*ConceptShare—www.conceptshare.com, ConceptShare allows you to set up secure online workspaces for sharing designs, documents, and video and invite others to review, comment, and give contextual feedback anytime and anywhere without a meeting. [Company name] has used this site for a few months to test its usability and has also been tested on multiple computers in Argentina (thanks to my sister testing it out for me while she was in Argentina).

*Skype—www.skype.com, Skype is a free software that allows you to talk for free via the Internet. You can also use Skype with regular phones to make calls internationally for a low rate of about .04 cents a minute. Skype also has video chatting capabilities and conference call capabilities for meetings. The setup requires downloading the Skype software (free) and buying a headset with microphone ($10) and webcam ($ ranges) for each computer. I have tested this software with my sister and it works well for her in Argentina and for me here.

*iStockphoto—www.istockphoto.com, iStockphoto is an Internet royalty-free image and design stock photography website. This is one of the many sites I use to find photos for [company name]. We have already used a few photos from this site for our marketing materials.

*Seminar Photo Contest—This contest was created by me and developed with Keri as an experiment to collect more relevant and usable photos for our marketing and publication efforts. Since we have found it to be a bit invasive to try and take the photos ourselves, we wanted to try a new approach to capture photos for our needs. All participants of our Summer Seminars 2008 are able to submit photos they have taken at their seminar with a chance to be rewarded with a $5 Amazon Gift Certificate for each image we choose.

Living the 4-Hour Workweek

►CASE STUDIES, TIPS, AND HACKS

- ►Zen and the Art of Rock Star Living
- ►Art Lovers Wanted
- ►Photo Finish
- ►Virtual Law
- ►Taking Flight with Ornithreads
- ►Off-the-Job Training
- ►The 4-Hour Family and Global Education
- ►Doctor's Orders
- ►Financial Musing
- ►Who Says Kids Hold You Back?
- ►Working Remotely
- ►Killing Your BlackBerry
- ►*Star Wars*, Anyone?

ZEN AND THE ART OF ROCK STAR LIVING
Hi Tim,

Here's the story. I'm a musician based in Munich, Germany. I'm running my own label and it has been difficult to get it off the ground. While working on that, my creativity slowly decreased until I hit rock bottom (a couple of times).

While it is still difficult to survive in the music industry I find it not hard at all now to do what I want to do. And that's all I do. I do what I want to do. It includes being a father, making music, composing, taking care of business, traveling, learning languages (mostly Italian), riding my bike, etc. . . . It's all in the following paragraphs.

1. I read the book step by step for about two months from September/October 2008 (plus surfing your blog) and just made tabula rosa with my life. (Lots of brainvomiting on paper.)

2. I started outsourcing things that bothered me most (and therefore kept hanging out in my to-do list the longest). I outsourced:
   - research, most of which is music-industry related (research outsourced saves about 2–3 hours/day)
   - website maintenance (social websites like Facebook, Myspace, etc). I'm planning on doing most of my marketing through these sites in 2009 and I'm on about 25+ sites as an artist.

     My VA (getfriday.com, as recommended in your book) does all the updates and checks the sites once a week to gather e-mail messages, comments, etc., filters them and sends me a report once a week including all the details for me to respond to. (Saves about one to two hours/day.)
   - photo retouching for my press pics is done by elance (saved five hours of work time and about $500).
   - management of my mailing list for gig dates, album updates, etc. (Saves about one hour for each mailing.)
   - I started testing muses (learning languages with music to sell online). I'm still testing!
   - I decided to open a publishing operation online for film companies to license music for film with just a mouse click, without having to negotiate deals for months. It will happen in 2009 (I start testing soon).

People are generally surprised and amazed that a person who doesn't seem to be very corporate (I look like a retired punk rocker, haha) outsources parts of his life and lives like a millionaire (I guess we do although we're far from it!).

I realized that I could do it after I got the first positive feedback from my outsource VA. I got the results of my project posted on elance and a day later I got the results. I went, yeah baby, this is MINE!

The biggest change is, that I now have my life under control. I take care of my little daughter (20 months) half the day (second half, my wife takes care of her), I take care of business, and I take time to do things I always wanted to do. Revenue-wise I'm pretty much the same I was before but I have a lot more spare time and a clear head (so I guess I've gotten a lot richer!).

I work whenever I want (no boss) about 24–30 hours/week (including office hours and music-studio hours) and what I do now is only what I really love to do. I'm still step-by-step optimizing efficiency to reduce office hours (currently about 10 hours/week). My dream is to dissolve my office altogether, go paperless, and basically only have my laptop as an office.

I eliminated all work that has gotten me down or was wearing me out (eliminated an extra workload of about 10 hours/week). I do not take on jobs (writing/producing music) unless I really love the project. I eliminated all complainers and haters (saves my stomach).

I just started my blog juergenreiter.com, "zen and the art of rockstarliving," where I want to share the changes I made to my life (mostly for musicians to see the light at the end of the tunnel).

And I recorded an album of my music and for the first time in my life did all the lyrics myself! It's going to be out in spring on my label ORkAaN Music+Art Productions.

I'll be on mini-retirement in New York this year for six weeks. I'll be in Sicily to learn Italian for about two weeks in May. I'll be back in Sicily to travel the island by bike for another 2–3 weeks in September. And am planning on going to either Mexico, Central America, or Australia in the winter.

I learned to shave with a straight razor within about 30 minutes, which I wanted to do for years. Shaving is a real exciting ritual now and a lot of fun! I will do a master course for coffee experts in April (I'm a coffee junky!) and become a "maestro del café." I helped my wife quit her teaching job and fulfill her dream to run a cafe in Munich, Germany. It's called Frau Viola and opened its doors in October 2008. It is running great! (www.frauviola.wordpress.com)

Can you measure all of that? I think it speaks for itself!

The general mindset of 4HWW has given me the calmness of being able to take time to play with my daughter and enjoying my "free time" without getting the fear of missing out on something or wasting my life. I'd say overall (with all the above-mentioned changes) my productivity increased at least 70% and doubt decreased by 80%.

For those just getting started:

1. start small think big.
2. identify what excites you vs. what bores you
3. eliminate and focus on what excites you
4. stick to what excites you no matter what people say. It's your life, live it the way you know is right for you.
5. read *4-Hour Workweek,* obviously!   —*J. REITER*

ART LOVERS WANTED

I saw my father work himself to the bone for 20 years as a garbage-man when we immigrated from Mexico. As I looked at my life in April 2007 in a lonely hotel room after another endless week of travel for my employer far from my family and those I love, I realized that at 33 I was on the same path to work myself into the ground and give up on my lifelong dream of pursuing my love of music and theater.

In life there are no accidents and that night as I was checking an e-mail from an old friend he suggested the 4HWW. I devoured the book in a few hours and began immediately to apply the key principles. When I told people about the book and about what I intended to do everyone said I was crazy. I focused most of my efforts on Dream-lining, Elimination, and Liberation. As an employee I wanted to first achieve liberation with a remote work arrangement. Despite several failed attempts I persevered (great lesson in negotiating) and was granted the opportunity to work remotely. This changed everything. I went from 9+ hours of work a day with weekly work-related travel to four hours a week, one week of travel per month, and I managed to get a $10,000 raise and deliver 2× the productivity in my job from the previous unproductive year.

As a result I now live with my once long-distance girlfriend in Seattle (my hometown). I spend my newly found time pursuing my passion for music (I sing in a choir and write my own folk-rock music), theater (I am performing in my first fully improvised 60-minute play this weekend), and fitness. I am training for my second marathon now.

Most of my friends cannot believe that I can actually spend most of my time pursuing my love for the arts and still make a full-time income on only four hours a week. The best part of this is that I have found mentally the meaning of freedom. Reality is truly negotiable and now my reality is that I can spend endless hours enjoying the company of my father, who waited twenty years till he retired to enjoy the freedom that I have found less than 24 months after reading *The 4-Hour Workweek*.

As an immigrant I want to spread the message that to succeed in America in the 21st century we must NOT work hard, instead we must follow the principles of the 4HWW and work smarter so that we can truly achieve the New American Dream: Freedom to enjoy the most precious resource we have in life . . . our time on this earth.

—*I. BARRON*

PHOTO FINISH

Hey Tim,

I wanted to tell you that your book, *The 4-Hour Workweek,* has been a true inspiration and life-changing resource for me this year!

I bought your book in November. Before then, I didn't know what "workflow automation" was. I had a part-time employee, but her work was actually *creating* more work for me. I would work until sometimes 3 A.M., and get up at 7. I'd tell you I wanted to travel, but the truth is that it seemed impossible to me. I didn't have time or money.

I was listening to your audio book one day. I had been listening to each of the chapters, sometimes over and over again. I was jogging. I stopped in my tracks. I believe I was listening about a case study about someone who sold music files over the Internet.

I'm a photographer. Weddings mostly. I wondered how I could sell digital images over the Internet. Then I came up with a fantastic idea for a family photography company. I stopped right there, and reserved a website on my iPhone.

Two months later, I had a website, access to thousands of photographers across the country, and our first sale. Even better, I am now in the family photography business, and I never have to shoot myself. Even better +1, we are the first family photography business that doesn't sell prints. Only digital files. It worked! I have now adopted this for my wedding photography as well. Other photographers are so offended, but I am making WAY more $, my costs are almost eliminated, and my time is free!

I know the above is vague, but it's not the point. The point is that now I work better, faster, I have two more employees, I turned off my

e-mail notifications on my computer and my iPhone, despite all of
what it's capable of, it doesn't even ring. E-mail has been disabled.
I just check it every so often to see what calls I missed.

Today, my fiance loves me because I come home in time for dinner
and I leave my laptop at work. It's a life I never thought I'd be able
to live. In the meantime, systems are working in my place and this
year looks to be a lot better, financially, than last.

Then I decided it was time to try my first mini-retirement. The
goal: ski the Swiss Alps and spend five days in Switzerland and spend
less than $1,000 total. I got a roundtrip ticket for about 500 bucks.
My ski pass for one day at Engelberg was $80. Lodging was free,
thanks to your suggestion www.couchsurfing.com, and I ate roasted
chestnuts, brats, fish and chips and drank great beer all week long.
I did it!

I am forever grateful, and am excited for more mini-retirements.
Here's to living during the best years of my life.

P.S. I leave May 11 for a month-long work vacation to Italy
(I have been hired to photograph two weddings in Siena). I plan
on vacationing a LOT more than I will be working.

—*MARK CAFIERO, Photographer*

VIRTUAL LAW

I used to work at a large Silicon Valley law firm, but one day I
woke up and decided that I wanted to travel for a year and learn a
foreign language. Six weeks later I was living in Cali, Colombia—
I'd never visited Cali before and hardly spoke a word of Spanish, but
that's what made it exciting to me. Well, almost two years later, I
still spend 95%+ of my time living and working from Cali, Colombia
(I recently bought a gorgeous apartment here that I could never
afford if I lived in California). I also have a full-time maid/cook (well,
five hours per day, five days per week), which costs me less than
US $40 per week!

I started my own virtual law practice and then joined forces with
my old boss. My U.S. number rings through to me wherever I am in
the world (originally I'm from New Zealand so I travel back there a
lot, too), and all my U.S. mail is delivered to Market Street, San Francisco, and scanned so I can view it online. If I need to mail letters, I
have another service which prints the letter and sends it within the
U.S. so there are no international shipping delays.

Definitely use www.fourhourblog.com/earthclass for mail receipt/ scanning. They have different packages but it's around $20–$30/month. You can also choose one or more P.O. boxes or physical addresses. My Market Street address is actually an earthclassmail address.

For printing small letters and mailing within the U.S. I use www .postalmethods.com. It's a little clunky at first but it's fine when you get used to it. It's very cheap since you only pay when you send (a four-page letter works out to just over $1 including the postage).

Come visit me sometime. Colombia is nothing like what you hear about—I feel a lot safer walking around late at night here than a lot of places in San Francisco. But don't tell anyone, those of us living here want to keep it a secret!   **—GERRY M.**

TAKING FLIGHT WITH ORNITHREADS

Tim—

My mentor gave me your book this past July and it had a tremendous impact on my life, its arrival could not have had better timing. About the time I read it, I was a few weeks away from competing in my first Olympic distance triathlon. I had trained for five months, felt and looked strong, but even more important the discipline and working toward a physical goal resulted in a creativity I hadn't felt in years. I posted a competitive time in the event and felt so optimistic about my abilities that I signed up for a half ironman competition.

Riding that high and following the principles of your book, I thought of dozens of ideas for products/businesses and am on the verge of launching the first of those ideas. It is a line of apparel called OrniThreads which will provide modern, scientific designs of birds to Gen-X and Gen-Y birders.

The reasons for focusing on this demographic are twofold:

1. For my "day job," I work at [company name]. I have learned a lot about their audience/membership, e.g., like the fact that there are 70 million Americans who actively bird (a staggering statistic from the U.S. Fish & Wildlife svc). Birders are a passionate lot and their interest only seems to grow over time—it never dies! They also tend to skew from the middle to upper class and are educated.
2. I took an ornithology class this summer at Columbia University (where I am enrolled in a conservation biology program)

and fell in love with the illustrations in my textbooks and wanted to surround myself with these images.

I am launching www.ornithreads.com in the next week or so and the first of my three designs are being printed as we speak.

I have big aspirations for the company, but am just trying to get the first collection to customers and learn as much as I can. Your book has been incredibly helpful in outlining the necessary steps I need to take to succeed and hope that my idea has some legs (or wings) which translates into an automated income.

If you are in NYC anytime soon—promoting your book or otherwise—I would love to meet you. Sincerely,   —*BRENDA TIMM*

OFF-THE-JOB TRAINING

I used concepts from the 4HWW to work remotely from August of '08 until January of '09. I went to Portugal, Europe, Spain, Sweden, and Norway surfing and snowboarding my brains out. Best part about it? I came home with three times as much money in the bank than I would have had if I continued the normal 9 to 5. I work for [world-famous design company] as a software developer, and was able to put the concepts to use and really change my life. I paired my iPhone + Fring (Fring is voice over IP on the iPhone, it allows you to use one device for everything, and have a local number abroad).

I spent four months prior to departure being sure to never be at my cube, but always be just around the corner. I made a point to ALWAYS be available on Instant Messenger, so when people would walk over to my cube and look for me in person they would see I was somewhere else, then hop online and ask, "Where are you?" My response was always similar, just down the hall in the cafeteria . . . just down the block at the coffee shop, or at co-worker X's desk. After two months of this a magical thing happened: People always looked to get me via Instant Messenger and stopped dropping by my desk altogether. That allowed me to be 6,000 miles away without anyone noticing.

Something else to consider . . . how **time zone** affects remote work environments. I noticed, while in Norway (nine hours away), that it was the perfect amount of time. I was, in a sense, living in the future. My day was almost over by the time my boss woke up . . . this allowed me to explore Norway's fjords, mountains, and undiscovered frigid surf spots in complete peace and without ever having to worry about getting a call from overseas. It was perfect . . . If I wanted, I could explore all day, come home and have some dinner, then ichat with my boss for 20–30 minutes and check in. The few times he needed something urgently, he was able to give me work when he went to bed, and have it completed in the morning when he woke up.   —*B. WILLIAMSON*

DOCTOR'S ORDERS

Hi Tim:

Here's my story . . .

My dream started about four years ago. I was in the process of taking my psychology licensing exam, and after speaking to a friend, decided that I would reward myself with a trip to South America. We were both exhausted from our 9-to-5 (and sometimes 6, 7, or 8 P.M.) hospital and clinic jobs.

I had traveled extensively throughout the United States and some parts of Europe, but I had never experienced South American culture.

My trip there was absolutely fantastic and really opened my eyes to other ways of living and culture. During my trip, I spent a lot of time speaking to expatriates about how they used their retirement funds and pensions to live the lives of kings there. One thing was evident: Most of the expatriates who attempted to "set up a business" to help fund their lifestyle had failed miserably. I hypothesized that there just wasn't enough currency (pesos) in the marketplace to really sustain a "gringo"-oriented business.

After my trip, I told my friend that I needed to dedicate all my energies to developing a method of receiving income from U.S. citizens while living elsewhere. VOIP had recently been introduced to the marketplace and Internet service was improving in South America and other parts of the third world.

The business had to be based upon absolute mobility. I boiled the whole business down to two basic functions: reliable telephone via VOIP and high-speed Internet.

At the time I had a small research consultation practice where I was helping doctoral students on the phone and via e-mail to complete their dissertations, theses, and statistical analyses. I had a small website that was getting traffic but I was relying on others for web and marketing services. I subsequently learned more about search engine optimization and web marketing and eventually took control of all web marketing and promotion of my website, http://www.ResearchConsultation.com, allowing me to expand my business substantially.

During the next three years I conducted numerous "mobile tests" . . . traveling to Costa Rica, the Dominican Republic, Venezuela, and Colombia in order to fine-tune my system of conducting business from abroad.

I finally left my job last November, the day before Thanksgiving, vowing to never return to the mundane 9-to-5 structure. My job had even recently instituted a "bio-metric fingerprint" identification system where you had to "punch in and out" at the beginning and end of your hospital shift with your fingerprint to ensure that you were working your eight hours. This was just another sign that I had to leave.

I now live in NYC and Colombia and travel to other parts of the world throughout the year: speaking to customers, managing my contractors (U.S. and Colombian) in order to acquire U.S. dollars while living for a fraction of the cost abroad. I'm also developing other websites and businesses (community forums) that will hopefully be more automated, requiring less day-to-day interaction and monitoring.

Well, that's my story for now . . . today South America, tomorrow anywhere I can get a high-speed connection (banda ancha)! My stress level has dropped significantly since leaving my old job and my quality of life has improved enormously.

My family and friends in NYC still think I'm out of my mind, and I continue to fully agree with them. . . .   —*JEFF B.*

THE 4-HOUR FAMILY AND GLOBAL EDUCATION

Tim,

We moved to a totally digital nomadic life traveling the world as a family in 2006, so we discovered your book and ideas after we had begun and loved it! Our life has changed totally and is more fulfilling and much more simple. We are greener, leaner, healthier, happier, more connected.

Other people thought we were absolutely nuts when we decided to do this in 2004/5, but now many of those same people think we are smart and psychic.

Problems finding a good school fit (despite having many award-winning excellent ones at our disposal) was probably the most specific moment (John Taylor Gatto says it best on why schools do not educate) that helped us to change as well as wanting more time together and forecasting the house/economy crash coming.

I think more families will be taking mini-retirements and living slower, traveling digital nomadic lives. If you are away for months as a family, you need to be informed about all the wonderful educational opportunities which are actually richer than staying home (which few realize)!

There are a TON of fantastic resources like Classroom 2.0 and many innovative educators online. My daughter just turned eight and is having a blast with her online course with John Hopkins University/CTY and it is also a nice resource for friends. Today one can immerse deeply in one culture and still maintain one's home culture. This is important information for families who still fear the outdated negatives on Third Culture Kids (TCK) based on studies from the fifties.

Maya Frost[91] has excellent information about older kids and even a new paradigm when it comes to going to university. I think education is one of the things going through a total transition due to the Internet, and parents need this info to make important decisions.

We have had a fantastic experience in going to a local school in Spain that has allowed my child to immerse very deeply in her second language, culture, and literature. More info (in the book) on local schools is needed and how to experience it as a family for months at a time.

We have used local people like a wonderful flamenco teacher for our child and we have also used online sources like our piano teacher in Chicago who teaches our child in Spain via Skype.

E-libraries are very important (especially with a child who is a voracious reader). Http://learninfreedom.org/languagebooks.html is an excellent resource on language education with great books on raising a bilingual child, even if you are a monolingual!

—*SOULTRAVELERS3*,
a family living abroad and loving it

---

91. Maya Frost, *The New Global Student* (Crown, 2009).

FINANCIAL MUSING

I graduated from Stanford University and started working in investment banking in July 2006, and, in a sick way, almost enjoyed it at first. Yes, it was a terrible lifestyle and all, but I was learning a lot and moving up very quickly. I have (had) a type-A personality, so it appealed to me on some level.

As the year progressed, though, I realized it wasn't sustainable and that I wanted out . . . but like so many other people, I failed to take action immediately.

In May 2007, I was driving home at 3 A.M. one night after having pulled 4–5 all-nighters previously, and crashed into a tree on the side of the road. If you've never crashed into an inanimate object while asleep at the wheel, just imagine waking up five feet from the ground while bungee jumping as the cord is about to snap to get an idea of what it feels like.

"At the ER"

That was the subject line of the e-mail I sent out the next day to my entire office. Luckily, everyone understood and told me to take a rare three-day weekend. Luckily I survived with no major injuries, but at that point I decided it was time for a change.

I met up with some friends for dinner a week or two later and relayed my story. One friend there (who recently quit her job to pursue professional acting—her dream—while selling information products online) told me about this book she recently read called *The 4-Hour Workweek.*

I thought it was a scam, of course, but I really hated my life and decided I needed to check it out at the very least. I read it in one sitting. And then I read it again, just to make sure I wasn't hallucinating. Before ever getting into finance, I had done some work online with graphics and web design and I had a technical background, so nothing in the book seemed outrageous to me—I just didn't realize how easy and accessible it all was. Also, I had lived in Japan for half a year in college and loved it—and long-term world travel had always been one of my goals.

I sat on the ideas in your book for a while, took a quick vacation to return to Japan in October 2007, and when I came back decided that I had to get started. My muse: sell an investment banking interview guide. It's a niche, high-demand subject and I knew I could make a better guide than anything else out there. One problem: I had to stay anonymous since I was still working, and advertising with Pay-Per-Click would be way too expensive given the high CPCs for related keywords.

In November 2007 I decided to start a blog, Mergers & Inquisitions (http://www.mergersandinquisitions.com), about the investment banking industry and how to break in, aimed at a mix of college students, MBAs, and working professionals. While I built my audience, I never had the time to finish my muse—the interview guide. But I was getting tons of requests to do consulting from my readers, so I started with resume editing and expanded into mock interviews—yes, not very "muse-like" but I charged high rates and could make my old salary in a fraction of the time. I did this ALL while staying completely anonymous out of necessity—because I didn't want to get fired without an alternative income stream. Amazingly, my services took off even though I couldn't tell anyone who I was.

At the same time, I decided I would not get another job in finance, and would instead leave in June 2008. So I had a very short amount of time to make everything work. Almost every single one of my friends, roommates, and family doubted me and said it would never work. I decided they were all wrong and I would just do it anyway—worst-case scenario, I could always reduce my expenses and move to Thailand to teach English.

To boost my income, I completely revamped my site to sell more of my offerings, which took me from pocket change to full-time income from part-time consulting over July–August 2008. This allowed me to travel to Hawaii and Aruba to go snorkeling, surfing, and shark-cage-diving and visit friends in other parts of the U.S. all while making an investment banker's income from part-time work.

As the recession and economy worsened, my business picked up because it was counter-cyclical—anything that helps people find jobs is in huge demand in a poor economy. I've since helped scores of laid-off bankers and other financiers find work elsewhere. However, I was also starting to work a lot more because I was effectively trading time for money . . . so over the fall I started to work on my original product idea—my interview guide—and released it to great success later in 2008.

It has gone on to free up a ton of time, double my revenues, and put the majority of my income on autopilot. If I didn't do any further work from this point onward, I could make 2–3× my previous monthly income simply by writing once or twice a week for my site (4–5 hours) and doing limited consulting on the side (10 hours). So you could say I've increased my income almost 3× while reducing my hours 6×–9× and making myself completely mobile.

I admit that often I do "work" more than this, but it's all on related educational projects that I want to work on, not anything that I have to work on. And if I don't feel like working one week, I can reduce my hours to the 5–15 hour range and spend my time on learning languages, sports, or traveling to exotic destinations.

This setup allowed me to take an amazing trip to China, Singapore, Thailand, and Korea in December–January and get in some ridiculous adventures. I'll be moving to Asia in a few months and after that, traveling the world indefinitely while running my business from coffee shops.

Incidentally, I met up with a lot of customers in Asia who thought this was the coolest thing ever!

Your book has changed my life and infinitely improved my lifestyle, and I just wanted to thank you for everything.

—*B. DECHESARE*

WHO SAYS KIDS HOLD YOU BACK?

My first action was to think "what is the worst that can happen on a scale of 1–10" if I quit my well-paid, very secure government job? The power of this thought process is incredible.

I quit my job, sold my house, and went camping for three months with two kids under two and a half and a pregnant wife (mini-retirement). We (very slowly) drove the SE coast of Australia from Sydney to Adelaide.

With the complete clarity of mind that comes from being in a field with your family with no immediate worries, I put into action a plan that I had been tinkering with for 12 months. I bought a wireless Internet dongle and created an info product for electrical engineers, and wrote some software to go with it.

Managed this by (a) going on info diet, (b) working 9 P.M.–midnight in a campsite with no other distractions, (c) outsourcing everything that I would find difficult or time consuming (like the tricky programming stuff and the illustrations for my book).

After about four weeks I had an automated informational website that had replaced ½ of my full-time income—requiring < four hours per week to maintain.

The original plan was to arrive in Adelaide and get a J.O.B. But with my passive income, I decided to simply grow my new business and am currently very close to replacing 100% of my previous income. It feels f&*#ing brilliant.

Now we plan to travel the world slowly until the kids are ready for primary school . . .

Who says kids hold you back?!   *—FINN*

WORKING REMOTELY

One month and one year ago, I read 4HWW on the recommendation of my sister's boyfriend after I had been talking for months about changing my life drastically and moving to Argentina to learn Castellano. After reading the book I stopped talking about my dreams and immediately started setting short-term and long-term goals. I bought a notebook to track my monthly goals and tasks. I did lots of research on potential remote working situations and I started telling my close friends and family about my new plans. Everyone that I told thought it was just an idea and I wasn't actually going to go through with it. They thought it was a "some day I'd like to do this" idea and that I wasn't actually setting daily goals to get me there. They knew that I loved my job so why would I leave it for a life of uncertainty? I didn't think of it that way. I wasn't scared, I was excited at the prospect of a new way of life, a fresh start, and even though I loved my job I also had other things I wanted to accomplish in my life. At first I thought about teaching English to make a living down there, but deep down inside all I really wanted to do was continue working for my current company, just doing it remotely. The book gave me the confidence to think this was actually possible, when everyone around me thought it was impossible.

I decided to write up a proposal[92] and present it to my boss even at the advice not to do it from everyone I knew. If my boss rejected my proposal, I had enough money saved up to live in Argentina for at least six months to get me by until I could figure out how I wanted to make money there. I was not giving up on my dream of living a freer, happier life with less work and more time for myself. All odds were against me but I took a calculated risk and had faith in myself. After I handed in my proposal, I was ready to expect the worst. Everyone

---

92. A simple, actual proposal is provided on pages 345–349.

around me was waiting with baited breath and words of encouragement after I got rejected. When I left the meeting with my boss I couldn't believe it. She accepted and was eager to talk to me about the details. She even had a smile on her face and told me how awesome my proposal was. No one else could believe it when I told them. After the shock wore off, I realized that I could actually do this, and a huge weight was lifted from my shoulders. The hardest part was over and now I could start thinking of more possibilities for my new life.

I set my goal to move to Argentina for September 2008. I arrived here on September 3 and have been here for about six months now. I live in the capital city of Jujuy, Argentina, a small province in the northwest of Argentina. I work about 5–10 hours a week and I find that I am much more focused now that I am out of the office and working alone. I have a private Spanish tutor that I meet with for two hours, five days a week. I have a handful of friends that I spend time with, practicing my Spanish. I go to the gym three times a week and go to yoga two times a week—something I didn't do in the States because I didn't have enough time. I eat healthier because I have more time to focus on what to eat. I have more time to dream up bigger things that I want to do with my new free time. I have dreams of owning a bar or cafe, so maybe a few years from now that will be my next endeavor.

My advice to 4HWW readers is to take from my experience. I rely heavily on the advice of my friends and family, but sometimes you have to ignore the advice of your loved ones to really make something happen. If you believe the impossible can be made possible, it will happen.   **—A.K. BROOKMIRE**

KILLING YOUR BLACKBERRY

I'm a 37-year-old Subway franchisee owning and operating 13 stores. Been doing this for seven years. Prior to reading 4HWW I was KING at W4W (translate: work for work's sake)! I'd never given myself "permission" to behave differently than I did as an employee in the past. 4HWW was absolutely liberating for me. I literally "caught myself" and began the process of curing my addiction to W4W. I used to always be "on" and I was never really "present" anywhere—too busy doing the "blackberry prayer" at the dinner table instead of spending quality time with those who were present. Holidays were just a remote office for battling the e-mail tsunami. 4HWW gave me a new paradigm and I began to look at my business as a "product," the (original) purpose of which was to provide me with a disproportionate amount of income vs. time invested personally by me—to what end? To ENJOY MYSELF and to have complete autonomy over my schedule and activities. So I got off my own back, told myself it was OK to pursue the original purpose and here's what I did:

Crunched my "always open" workweek into four days and 20 hours. I immediately began taking Mondays OFF, giving me a nice three-day weekend. (Fridays are in the "CROSSHAIRS" next!) Tuesday to Friday I work 11 A.M.–4 P.M. (20 hours per week). With the "unluxury" of time in this crunched workweek I was forced to appraise everything through the 80/20 filter and found that 50% of the 80% was pure crap and the other 50% of the 80% could be done by someone on my payroll. Great!

Everything I do now has to somehow either increase sales or decrease costs otherwise "it's someone else's job." You can't be "half-pregnant," so when I'm "on" I'm really on and when I'm "off" I'm off—good luck trying to contact me. I still carry portable e-mail but I've killed "auto-sync" (the bane of modern mankind in terms of interruption) now it's on a Tues–Fri, 11 A.M.–4 P.M. schedule. Outside of that window it waits.

My e-mail autoresponder eliminated 50% of my e-mail within two weeks as people sending me meaningless crap got fed up looking at my autoresponder and stopped including me—love it! I keep a short, compact "to-do" list and anything time-bound is in my calendar. These get my attention before any other "inbox" does because I've previously decided what's important for me to get done—the rest can wait.

I could go on, but all in all I think this is a message that the self-employed need to hear so badly. With no "boss" and no "clean edges" to work-life/home-life it's so easy to fall into a W4W grind and your business becomes a tractor beam that trails you inexorably down that path. 4HWW is the antidote!" **—ANDREW, self-employed in the UK**

STAR WARS, ANYONE?

I knew my quest for the 4-Hour Workweek was working when my daughter's kindergarten teacher asked her the question: "What kind of work does your father do?" As the teacher re-told the story back to me, it was my daughter's answer that really struck a chord. "Your daughter turned and looked up at me with the most serious look on her face and said, 'My dad just sits around and watches *Star Wars* all day.' "

It's funny how this one simple question, and not to mention my daughter's answer, would be the moment of true 4HWW self-awareness for me. You see the answer my daughter gave her teacher has a deeper meaning. I believe what she meant to say, if she could articulate it, was "My dad sort of does whatever he wants to do."

I read the 4HWW almost two years ago when I was on vacation at the beach with my family. I remember it well, because I kept reading parts of the book to my wife, bothering her to no end. I am a developer and enterprise administrator for a large financial institution in Atlanta, Georgia. Part of my job is supporting the large complex document captures systems that I help build. Due to the importance of these systems I am expected to be reachable 24/7/365. That is good for job security, but can be bad for my family life. I have four beautiful children and I strive to be a true "hands-on" dad who is present in my family's daily lives. So armed with your book and a fresh (ocean air) perspective, I set out to put many of the 4HWW principles into practice.

First, I worked on changing my e-mail habits. I took a hard look at my inbox and used several of the techniques outlined in the 4HWW to eliminate all the waste and noise. I formed new habits around batching my e-mail sessions and it didn't take long to achieve a zero inbox using the "trusted trio" folder method. I also applied the less is more philosophy to composing my e-mails. I went to great lengths to ensure I am as clear and concise as possible. Only communicating exactly what is needed to the right audience and not to the world. By eliminating all the noise and fat from my e-mail diet it became much more clear what "actions" or "to-do's" were important.

Meetings and conference calls were the next area of attack. I scrutinized each meeting invite and began declining requests left and right. Most of the time I would claim I had too much going on to attend. I started asking for the minutes of the meeting or for someone to IM me if they had a specific question I needed to answer. When I do attend a meeting it is almost always via a conference call. Due to conference room restrictions and geographic challenges in our company most of our meetings are done virtually anyway.

Less wasted time meant more time to focus on work and tasks that really mattered. I felt like I was doing less but getting more things done and with better results. The right people were starting to notice and the perception of my ability to get the job done had never been better. I was making my management look good, and when that happens they stop asking questions or micromanaging daily activities. I kept proving to them I can do it without interference. Now was the time to make the push for what I really wanted and that was to go virtual!

Going virtual was actually very easy. I had a solid foundation with my manager and others in the chain of command. Almost all of my daily work was already remote-ready. At home, I have a great dedicated office in our finished basement. It is situated well away from the rest of the house and is mostly free of distractions. I have my own bathroom with shower and I even have a mini-fridge and microwave. I dare say that my home office rivals the amenities of the top executives at my company. Most of all, I have a wife and family that totally understand and respect the rules I set for myself to continue this success.

At first, I worked one or two days a week from home, but it didn't take long before I found myself working four out of five days a week from home. When the Southeast was hit by the gas shortage and the price of gas nationwide was cresting $4 a gallon, the company made working from home even more accepted and official. I became an overnight model for others to follow. As people around me were in a panic as to how to get to work when no gas could be found, I was happily working away at home just business as usual.

At this point, things were working better than I ever expected. Using my 4HWW skills I now had more time to be that hands-on dad I wanted to be. I became a regular up at the elementary school. I eat lunch in the cafeteria with my girls, especially on fried chicken day! I participate in a program called D.E.A.R. which stands for Drop Everything and Read, where a few times a month I come in and read to each class. I drive my kids to school and I get to see them when they come home. For my entire family, I am present in their everyday lives, and can't put a price on that. I felt like I had achieved my goal. That was that. So I thought . . .

Other things started to happen. Without conscientiously knowing it, people around me at the school or church had a weird respect for me. I say weird because people literally mistook me as a doctor or just some sort of self-made millionaire. I am not kidding. There is this one guy who still calls me "Doc." I guess the reason for this is because most people still cling to the old stereotypes of what they think it is to be "rich." I always seem to show up for the school functions or just special days at the school, usually in casual attire and never obsessing over time or my Blackberry. Now I have people nominating me for things like committee chair on the PTA, and just recently I was elected to the board of directors at our local swim/ tennis club. The cool thing is, I actually have the time to do those things and still be effective at work and at home. It goes without saying that new doors are open to me now. More than ever before.

With all of this going on around me I still come back to what my daughter said to her teacher. In truth, I am at a point where if I wanted to "sit around and watch *Star Wars* all day," I certainly could. But, I find myself filling the extra time now doing things that really mean something. Being present in the everyday lives of my family, helping my community, or volunteering at my church. Now I have a plan to take it to the next level and write my own book. The project I am working on is called *The Virtual Employee Handbook.* It is a collection of tips and how-to's on all the tools that are essential to the modern virtual employee, like me. We will see how that goes.
One thing I do know is that I wouldn't even dream of what I am doing now if it wasn't for *The 4-Hour Workweek*! 　　　—*W. HIGGINS*

►RESTRICTED READING
The Few That Matter

A hypocrite is a person who—but who isn't?
—DON MARQUIS

I know, I know. I said not to read too much. Hence, the recommendations here are restricted to the best of the best this book's interviewees and I have used and named when asked, "What is the one book that changed your life the most?"

None of them are required to do what we've talked about in this book. That said, consider them if you get stuck on a particular point. The page counts are listed, and if you practice the exercises in "How to Read 200% Faster in 10 Minutes" in Chapter 6, you should be able to read at least 2.5 pages per minute (100 pages thus equals 40 minutes).

For additional categories, including practical philosophy, licensing, and language learning, be sure to visit our comprehensive companion site.

The Fundamental Four: Let Me Explain

The Fundamental Four are so named because they are the four books I recommended to aspiring lifestyle designers prior to writing *The 4-Hour Workweek*. Still well worth reading, here is the sequence I suggest:

The Magic of Thinking Big (192 pages)

BY DAVID SCHWARTZ

This book was first recommended to me by Stephen Key, an ultrasuccessful inventor who has made millions licensing products to companies, including Disney, Nestlé, and Coca-Cola. It is the favorite book of many superperformers worldwide, ranging from legendary football coaches to famous CEOs, and has more than 100 5-star ratings on Amazon. The main message is don't overestimate others and underestimate yourself. I still read the first two chapters of this book whenever doubt creeps in.

How to Make Millions with Your Ideas: An Entrepreneur's Guide (272 pages)

BY DAN S. KENNEDY

This is a menu of options for converting ideas into millions. I read this when I was in high school and have read it five times since. It is like steroids for your entrepreneurship cortex. The case studies, from Domino's Pizza to casinos and mail-order products, are outstanding, even if outdated in a few instances.

The E-Myth Revisited: Why Most Small Businesses Don't Work and What to Do About It (288 pages)

BY MICHAEL E. GERBER

Gerber is a masterful storyteller and his classic of automation discusses how to use a franchise mind-set to create scalable businesses that are based on rules and not outstanding employees. It is an excellent road map—told in parable—for becoming an owner instead of constant micromanager. If you're stuck in your own business, this book will get you unstuck in no time.

Vagabonding: An Uncommon Guide to the Art of Long-Term World Travel (224 pages)

BY ROLF POTTS

Rolf is the man. This is the book that got me to stop making excuses and pack for an extended hiatus. It covers bits of everything but is particularly helpful for determining your destination, adjusting to life on the road, and re-assimilating back into ordinary life. It includes great little excerpts from famous vagabonds, philosophers, and explorers, as well as anecdotes from ordinary travelers. This is the first of two books (the other was *Walden*, below) that I took with me on my first 15-month mini-retirement.

Reducing Emotional and Material Baggage

Walden (384 pages)

BY HENRY DAVID THOREAU

This is considered by many to be *the* masterpiece of reflective simple living. Thoreau lived on the edge of a small lake in rural Massachusetts for two years, building his own shelter and living alone, as an experiment in self-reliance and minimalism. It was both a huge success and a failure, which is what makes this book such a compelling read.

Less Is More: The Art of Voluntary Poverty—
An Anthology of Ancient and Modern Voices in
Praise of Simplicity (336 pages)

EDITED BY GOLDIAN VANDENBROECK

This is a collection of bite-sized philosophies on simple living. I read it to learn how to do the most with the least and eliminate artificial needs, not live like a monk—big difference. It incorporates actionable principles and short stories ranging from Socrates to Benjamin Franklin and the Bhagavad Gita to modern economists.

The Monk and the Riddle: The Education of a
Silicon Valley Entrepreneur (192 pages)

BY RANDY KOMISAR

This great book was given to me by Professor Zschau as a graduation gift and introduced me to the phrase "deferred-life plan." Randy, a virtual CEO and partner at the legendary Kleiner Perkins, has been described as a "combined professional mentor, minister without portfolio, in-your-face investor, trouble-shooter and door opener." Let a true Silicon Valley wizard show you how he created his ideal life using razor-sharp thinking and Buddhist-like philosophies. I've met him—he's the real deal.

The 80/20 Principle: The Secret to Success by
Achieving More with Less (288 pages)
BY RICHARD KOCH

This book explores the "nonlinear" world, discusses the mathematical and
historical support for the 80/20 Principle, and offers practical applications
of the same.

Muse Creation and Related Skills

Harvard Business School Case Studies
www.hbsp.harvard.edu (click on "school cases")
One of the secrets behind Harvard Business School's teaching success is
the case method—using real-life case studies for discussion. These cases
take you inside the marketing and operational plans of 24-Hour Fitness,
Southwest Airlines, Timberland, and hundreds of other companies. Few
people realize that you can purchase these case studies for less than $10
apiece instead of spending more than $100,000 to go to Harvard (not that
the latter isn't worth it). There is a case study for every situation, problem,
and business model.

"This business has legs": How I Used Infomercial Marketing
to Create the $100,000,000 Thighmaster Craze:
An Entrepreneurial Adventure Story (206 pages)
BY PETER BIELER

This is the story of how a naïve (in the best sense of the word) Peter Bieler
started from scratch—no product, no experience, no cash—and created
a $100-million merchandising empire in less than two years. It is a mind-
expanding and often hysterical case study that uses real numbers to discuss
the fine points of everything from dealing with celebrities to marketing,
production, legal, and retail. Peter can now finance the media purchases
for your product: www.mediafunding.com.

Secrets of Power Negotiating: Inside Secrets from
a Master Negotiator (256 pages)
BY ROGER DAWSON

This is the one negotiating book that really opened my eyes and gave me practical tools I could use immediately. I used the audio adaptation. If you're hungry for more, William Ury's *Getting Past No* and G. Richard Shell's *Bargaining for Advantage: Negotiation Strategies for Reasonable People* are outstanding. These are the only negotiating books you'll ever need.

Response Magazine
(www.fourhourblog.com/response)

This magazine is dedicated to the multibillion-dollar direct response (DR) industry, with a focus on television, radio, and Internet marketing. How-to articles (increasing sales per call, lowering media costs, improving fulfill-ment, etc.) are interspersed with case studies of successful campaigns (George Foreman Grill, *Girls Gone Wild,* etc.). The best outsourcers in the business also advertise in this magazine. This is an excellent resource at an excellent price—free.

Jordan Whitney Greensheet
(www.jwgreensheet.com)

This is an insider secret of the DR world. Jordan Whitney's weekly and monthly reports dissect the most successful product campaigns, including offers, pricing, guarantees, and ad frequencies (indicative of spending and, thus, profitability). The publication also maintains an up-to-date tape li-brary from which infomercials and spot commercials can be purchased for competitive research. Highly recommended.

Small Giants: Companies That Choose to Be Great Instead of Big (256 pages)
BY BO BURLINGHAM

Longtime *Inc.* magazine editor-at-large Bo Burlingham crafts a beautiful collage and analysis of companies that focus on being the best instead of growing like cancer into huge corporations. Companies include Clif Bar Inc., Anchor Stream Microbrewery, rock star Ani DiFranco's Righteous Babe Records, and a dozen more from different industries. Bigger is not better, and this book proves it.

Negotiating World Travel and Preparing for Escape

Six Months Off: How to Plan, Negotiate, and
Take the Break You Need Without Burning Bridges
or Going Broke (252 pages)
BY HOPE DLUGOZIMA, JAMES SCOTT, AND DAVID SHARP

This was the first book to make me step back and say, "Holy sh*t. I can actually do this!" It steamrolls over most fear factors related to long-term travel and offers a step-by-step guide to taking time off to travel or pursue other goals without giving up your career. Full of case studies and useful checklists.

Verge Magazine
(www.fourhourblog.com/verge)

This magazine, formerly known as *Transitions Abroad,* is *the* central hub of alternative travel and offers dozens of incredible options for the non-tourist. Both the print and online versions are great starting points for brainstorming how you will spend your time overseas. How about excavating in Jordan or eco-volunteering in the Caribbean? It's all here.

From the website: "Each issue takes you around the world with people who are doing something different and making a difference doing it. This is the magazine resource for those wanting to volunteer, work, study, or adventure overseas."

This book is not just what you hold in your hands. There was much more I wanted to include but couldn't due to space constraints. Use passwords hidden in this book to access some of the best I have to offer. Here are just a few examples that took me years to assemble:

How to Get $250,000 of Advertising for $10,000
(includes real scripts)
How to Learn Any Language in 3 Months
Muse Math: Predicting the Revenue of Any Product
(includes case studies)
Licensing: From Tae Bo to Teddy Ruxpin
Real Licensing Agreement with Real Dollars
(this alone is worth $5,000)
Online Round-the-World (RTW) Trip Planner

For this and much more reader-only content, visit our companion site and free how-to message boards at www.fourhourblog.com. How would you like a free trip around the world? Join us and see how simple it is.

►ACKNOWLEDGMENTS

First, I must thank the students whose feedback and questions birthed this book, and Ed Zschau, übermentor and entrepreneurial superhero, for giving me the chance to speak with them. Ed, in a world where deferred dreams are the norm, you have been a shining light for those who dare to do it their way. I bow down to your skills (and Karen Cindrich, the best right-hand woman ever) and look forward to cleaning your erasers whenever the call comes—I'll make a 220-pound bodybuilder of you yet!

Jack Canfield, you are an inspiration and have shown me that it is possible to make it huge and still be a wonderful, kind human being. This book was just an idea until you breathed life into it. I cannot thank you enough for your wisdom, support, and incredible friendship.

To Stephen Hanselman, prince among men and the best agent in the world, I thank you for "getting" the book at first glance and taking me from writer to author. I cannot imagine a better partner or cooler cat, and I look forward to many more adventures together. From negotiation to nonstop jazz, you amaze me. LevelFiveMedia is the new breed of agenting, where first-time authors are developed into bestselling authors with the precision of a Swiss watch.

Heather Jackson, your insightful editing and incredible cheerleading has made this book a pleasure to write. Thank you for believing in me! I am honored to be your writer. To the rest of the Crown team, especially those whom I bother (because I love them) more than four hours a week—Donna Passannante and Tara Gilbride in particular—you are the best in the publishing world. Doesn't it hurt when your brains are so big?

This book couldn't have been written without the New Rich who agreed to share their stories. Special thanks to Douglas "Demon Doc" Price, Steve Sims, John "DJ Vanya" Dial, Stephen Key, Hans Keeling, Mitchell Levy, Ed Murray, Jean-Marc Hachey, Tina Forsyth, Josh Steinitz, Julie Szekely, Mike Kerlin, Jen Errico, Robin Malinosky-Rummell, Ritika Sundaresan, T. T. Venkatesh, Ron Ruiz, Doreen Orion, Tracy Hintz, and the dozens who preferred to remain anonymous within corporate walls. Thanks also to the elite team and great friends at MEC Labs, including, but not limited to, Dr. Flint McGlaughlin, Aaron Rosenthal, Eric Stockton, Jeremiah Brookins, Jalali Hartman, and Bob Kemper.

Refining the content of this book from pulp to print has been torturous, especially for my proofreaders! Deep bows and sincere thanks to Jason Burroughs, Chris Ashenden, Mike Norman, Albert Pope, Jillian Manus, Jess Portner, Mike Maples, Juan Manuel "Micho" Cambeforte, my brainiac brother Tom Ferriss, and the countless others who honed the end product. I owe particular gratitude to Carol Kline—whose keen mind and awareness of self transformed this book—and Sherwood Forlee, a great friend and relentless devil's advocate.

Thanks to my brilliant interns, Ilena George, Lindsay Mecca, Kate Perkins Youngman, and Laura Hurlbut, for meeting deadlines and keeping me from imminent meltdown. I encourage all publishers to hire you before their competition does!

To the authors who have guided and inspired me throughout this process, I am forever a fan and indebted: John McPhee, Michael

Gerber, Rolf Potts, Phil Town, Po Bronson, AJ Jacobs, Randy Komisar, and Joy Bauer.

For helping to build schools around the world and for funding projects for more than 15,000 U.S. public school students, I wish to thank—among countless others—the following readers and friends: Matt Mullenweg, Gina Trapani, Joe Polish, David Bellis, John Morgan, Thomas Johnson, Dean Jackson, Peter Weck and SimplyHired.com, Yanik Silver, Metroblogging, Michael Port, Jay Peters, Aaron Daniel Bennett, Andrew Rosca, Birth & Beyond, Inc., Doula Services, Noreen Roman, Joseph Hunkins, Joe Duck, Mario Milanovic, Chris Daigle, Jose Castro, Tina M. Pruitt Campbell, Dane Low, and all of you who believe karmic capitalism is possible. It is.

To all of the readers and lifestyle designers who shared their experiences and helped create this expanded edition—thank you! It wouldn't have been possible without you, and I am humbled beyond words by your generosity. I hope you never stop thinking big and doing the uncommon.

To Sifu Steve Goericke and Coach John Buxton, who taught me how to act in spite of fear and fight like hell for what I believe, this book—and my life—is a product of your influence. Bless you both. The world's problems would be far fewer if young men had more mentors like the two of you.

Last but not least, this book is dedicated to my parents, Donald and Frances Ferriss, who have guided me, encouraged me, loved me, and consoled me through it all. I love you more than words can express.

►INDEX

►About the Author

TIMOTHY FERRISS, nominated as one of *Fast Company*'s "Most Innovative Business People of 2007," is an angel investor and author of the #1 *New York Times, Wall Street Journal,* and *BusinessWeek* bestseller *The 4-Hour Workweek,* which has been sold into 35 languages.

He has been featured by more than 100 media outlets, including the *New York Times, The Economist, TIME, Forbes, Fortune,* CNN, and CBS. He speaks six languages, runs a multinational firm from wireless locations worldwide, and has been a popular guest lecturer at Princeton University since 2003, where he presents entrepreneurship as a tool for ideal lifestyle design and world change.